OUT FROM THE
SHADOW

The Story of Charles L. Gittens
Who Broke the Color Barrier in the
United States Secret Service

Maurice A. Butler

Library of Congress Control Number: 2012915910
ISBN: Hardcover   978-1-4797-0832-1
                   Softcover   978-1-4797-0831-4
                   Ebook   978-1-4797-0833-8

This book was printed in the United States of America.

To order additional copies of this book, contact:
Xlibris Corporation
1-888-795-4274
www.Xlibris.com
Orders@Xlibris.com
120203

To my loving wife, Patricia J. Butler, who has been my life, my inspiration, my soul mate and my best friend. You have always encouraged me to reach beyond my grasp and to have the strength and fortitude to see it through. I am, because we are.

To my parents, Ernest Butler Sr. and Pearl M. Butler, who gave me precious life and the wisdom to live it well. I miss you both.

To Mr. Charles "Charlie" Gittens, who opened my eyes to a whole new world and allowed me to come in and share a moment. I sincerely hope that my effort has brought honor and pride to your memory. Rest in peace. I'll see you when I get there.

Very few people knew what we did. The only time anyone knew about the Secret Service was when we messed up. We lived in the shadows and accepted that. As long as nothing went wrong we were happy because we knew we had done the job right.

—Clinton Hill

CONTENTS

ACKNOWLEDGMENTS

The completion of this book is a result of the support, both inspirational and academic, from many sources. That support is greatly appreciated.

To Dr. Marilyn Tyler Brown, many thanks for the confidence, trust, and support that you have given me as I traveled on this wonderful journey into the life of Mr. Charles Gittens. I don't think I have ever met anyone as industrious, motivational, supportive, and committed as you. Your drive drove me to the completion of this endeavor, and I am forever in your debt. You are a shining example of the "Jewels of Oxford, North Carolina."

To Mrs. Yvonne Gittens, many thanks for your guidance, support, and candor, which I found extremely refreshing. You opened your home to my wife and me at the very beginning of my search for answers. You answered every question I posed, helped me to locate numerous sources from the past, and pointed me in directions that provided exciting twist to Charlie's story. I trust that I have found a true friend in you.

To my friend and colleague Ms. Sharon Gittens Quick, without you none of this would have been possible. Your faith, openness, willingness to trust me with valuable family documents and remarkable recall of minute details helped to bring this story to life. Your enthusiasm and undying support was like a ray of sunlight, and I am truly grateful.

To my readers/editors, Pat Butler, Judith Kelly, and Jackie Shuler thanks so much for your diligence, candor, questions, suggestions, and corrections. I love to write, but I never realized that writing could be this difficult. You helped to make this endeavor an enjoyable one.

To the DC Area Writing Project, you have been the source of my literary birth and the inspiration that helped to unleash the passion in me to write and, more importantly, to publish.

To all of the individuals who so willingly allowed me to pick your memories and share them with the world. I tried very hard to be accurate, and I hope I got it right:

- Toshiko Akiyoshi, professional jazz musician, Japanese citizen, 1940s and '50s
- Alexandria Berry, US Naval Academy, family member, Cambridge
- Hugh Brown, IRS Investigator (retired), close friend, Washington, DC
- Dr. Marilyn Tyler Brown, associate superintendent of DC Public Schools (retired), extended family member, Oxford
- Major Ernest Butler Jr., US Air Force (retired)
- Cassandra Cauls, Office of Special Investigations, Department of Justice (coworker)
- Edwin Donovan, special agent in charge, Office of Public Relations, US Secret Service
- Charles "Kit" Eccles, contractor, family member, Cambridge
- Edward "Ned" Eccles, computer engineer, NASA, family member, Cambridge
- David Gittens, retired police officer, family member, Cambridge
- Nicole Gittens, high school principal, family member, Cambridge
- Yvonne Gittens, assistant director of financial aid, MIT (retired), family member, Cambridge
- Victor Gonzalez, US Secret Service (special agent, retired)
- Dr. Lawrence Hamme, clinical psychologist, extended family member, Oxford
- Thomas Hamme Jr., chemist, extended family member, Oxford
- Ike Hendershot, US Secret Service (special agent, retired)
- Clinton Hill, US Secret Service (special agent, retired)
- Charl Jones, network engineer, DEA, friend, Maryland
- Andre Jordan, assistant chief, US Park Police (retired), friend, NOBLE member
- Patricia Tyler Knight, extended family member, Oxford
- Art Lewis, Federal Bureau of Narcotics (special agent, retired)
- Ken Lewis, childhood friend from Cambridge
- Edward Mascall, family member, Cambridge
- Al Matney, Office of Special Investigations, Department of Justice (coworker)
- Mark Pappas, family member, Cambridge
- Providencia "Provi" Paredes, Jacqueline Kennedy's special assistant (retired)
- Keith Pruitt, deputy director, US Secret Service (retired)
- Sharon Gittens Quick, Charles Gittens's daughter
- Josie Quinones, friend, New York and Puerto Rico
- Eli Rosenbaum, Office of Special Investigations, Department of Justice (director)

- Stuart Rudolph, president and CEO, Virtual Agility, grandson of Hyman Rudolph, Cambridge
- Neal Sher, Office of Special Investigations, Department of Justice (former director)
- Edward Small, family member, Cambridge
- Paul Snelgrove, childhood friend from Cambridge
- Spurgeon Stanard, Korean War Veteran, US Navy (retired)
- Irma Sullivan, family member, Cambridge
- Lois Terman, real estate agent, granddaughter of Hyman Rudolph, Cambridge
- Donald Tucker, US Secret Service, Federal Bureau of Narcotics (special agent, retired)
- Barry Wilkerson, president and CEO, Carolina Energy Heating and Air, extended family member, Oxford
- Charles Leroy Gittens (RIP)

INTRODUCTION
A Thousand Questions

In 1965, NBC aired a popular and historic television program entitled *I-Spy*, which was about a white and black secret agent team who traveled around the world clandestinely battling evil powers in the name of democracy. The show was thoroughly entertaining, but was historic because during the 1960s there were very few black male actors portrayed on television in the United States and those that were, were usually portrayed in a negative light or in a subservient role, such as a servant or chauffeur. In this show, however, the black agent, Alexander Scott, played by actor Bill Cosby, was intelligent, a Rhodes scholar, a witty language expert, and quickly became the star of the show. Little did we know that there was a real Alexander Scott in our government who was highly intelligent, respected, ahead of his time, and who rose to positions of power in the United States Secret Service and the Department of Justice. His name is Charles L. Gittens and in 1956 became the first black Secret Service agent in America.

I had the fortune to meet Mr. Gittens when his daughter, Sharon Gittens Quick, a communications instructor at Theodore Roosevelt High School, located in Washington, DC suggested that I invite him to talk to my students. The students in my journalism class were preparing stories for the annual Black History Month section of the school newspaper, *The Rider Times*, and this year they wanted to write about someone of note who, for some reason, had not received much, if any, attention in their normal history textbooks. When Ms. Quick told us that her father was the first black Secret Service agent in the United States and that he was willing to come in to speak, I was excited. Several students, as was our custom, began a Google search about Mr. Gittens in order to prepare a litany of questions for the press conference. Their search turned up very little about him other than the fact that a law enforcement scholarship was being offered in his name.

On December 19, 2009, the students sat in quiet anticipation, armed with tape recorders, notepads, video cameras, and thousands of questions waiting for Mr.

Gittens to arrive. At precisely the appointed time, in walked this elderly gentleman, who was immaculately dressed, had a closely cropped haircut, and a broad smile etched across his face. He marched to the front of the class, used his melodic voice that was tinted with a New England accent with a touch of southern dialect intertwined and lots of humor to share his fantastic story.

Everyone sat mesmerized as he bellowed out the history of twentieth century America using his experiences and perceptions, from his front row seat, as a guide. He talked about becoming a lieutenant in a segregated army at nineteen years old serving in occupied Japan following WWII. He talked about becoming the first black agent for the Secret Service in the 1950s in the South (Charlotte, North Carolina) of all places. He talked about protecting former presidents from Dwight Eisenhower to Jimmy Carter. He talked about his hunt for criminals on the streets of America and Nazi war criminals around the world. He talked about his international excursions and the people he had the opportunity to meet. He talked about his love for America and his love for the Secret Service.

He freely discussed quite a few historical events and issues initially; however, there were some issues and points of interests that he seemed to avoid. At the conclusion of the presentation, the students and teachers in the audience, most of whom were African American and Hispanic, pummeled Mr. Gittens with questions most of which concerned how he dealt with racism, segregation, and other obstacles that he faced being a black man in America. More importantly, the students wanted to know how he was able to rise to such positions of prominence during a time when it was difficult for people of color to get ahead. Mr. Gittens was a little more evasive and vague when it came to discussing his feelings on subjects of race. He used phrases like "that was the way it was back then," or "it was the law of the land and as a law enforcement officer it was my job to uphold the law." He chose to relay the message of the importance of getting a good education and arming yourself with the necessary skills so that you can overcome any obstacle in your path and to never allow anyone to tell you that you can't do something.

At the conclusion of the ninety-minute session, I was even more excited about what I had just heard and learned, but was left clamoring for more information. I had a thousand more questions, and my thirst for information had been barely quenched. I wanted to know what it was like working with John F. Kennedy and what Mr. Gittens really thought about Richard Nixon. I wanted to know why he thought he was the first African American to become a Secret Service agent, especially in the 1950s and especially in the South! I wanted to know how he internalized and dealt with the hatred and discrimination that I felt he had to endure during his journey. I wanted to know how a black man was able to reach the seat of power and become the special agent in charge of the field office in Washington, DC during the 1970s, a city in which I grew up. I wanted to know the variables that impacted him, enabling him to become an outstanding leader at the various stages of his life. I wanted to know why him, why then, and more importantly why nobody knows about it! I wanted more.

Though an experienced and eloquent speaker, Mr. Gittens reluctantly accepted the invitation to visit our class, I later found out, because he didn't like to speak publically about himself. There have been several requests from organizations, as well as the Secret Service itself, to get Mr. Gittens to tell his story in print, on tape, and in film, but he fiercely and stubbornly fended them off. Part of that reluctance may have stemmed from the fact that he felt that as a Secret Service agent, he took a pledge not to talk about the presidents he was assigned to protect, or that several other former agents and authors had written books casting his beloved Secret Service in a negative light. Part of that reluctance also could have stemmed from the fact that he was reluctant to reopen old wounds, created by the treatment he received from colleagues and constituents alike because of his race, that had been hidden away lying dormant in a slumber that he chose not to awaken. And part of that reluctance could have stemmed from the fact that he felt that he hadn't done anything special, but was "just doing his job" as he so frequently reminded me.

Whatever the reason, I refused to give up until I got the answers I was looking for. I hounded Mr. Gittens for over two years before he reluctantly decided to sit down and share his story with me. One evening I got a call from his daughter Sharon who told me that if I wanted to get the story, I had better do it quick. She was relocating him to an assisted-living community with nursing services because she feared he was beginning to show the early signs of dementia and didn't want him living in his private home by himself. It turned out that her fears were accurate, and seven months later, his exhilarating journey came to a peaceful end.

In March of 2011, I met with Mr. Gittens at the Collington Episcopal Life Care Community located in Mitchellville, Maryland. We walked around the beautiful gated community surrounded by picturesque trees and ponds filled with geese, ducks, and other wildlife and talked for hours. Even at age eighty-two, I found his mind was clear as a bell and filled with details, especially when relaying events from the past. He would get locked into a particular time frame, and it seemed as if he was relaying events that happened yesterday. And he was a great storyteller. I can still see that grandiose smile on his face and hear the laughter in his voice as he told stories of danger, intrigue, and personal disrespect. I often found myself wondering how he dealt with the trauma, the indignity, the trials and the tribulations and still have a positive outlook. It appeared that he looked for the good in every situation and submerged the bad deep into his subconscious. I fought hard to try and get him to unlock that subconscious and reveal the treasures that lay hidden, both good and bad.

We met every Tuesday for five months while he belted out episodes of his past. Throughout the whole process, however, I could tell he was not happy. As beautiful as his surroundings were, it seemed like he felt he was trapped and wanted nothing more than to be free to go and do as he pleased. And who could blame him? After all, here you had a man who at one time held a passport that gave him permission to travel anywhere in the world! He had shared space with presidents, their families, and other heads of state and was responsible for their well-being. He had been raised in Cambridge, Massachusetts, developed his skills in the heart of Oxford, North Carolina, traveled around the world while in the military, served in various field offices of the United States Secret Service in this country and abroad, traveled with presidents wherever they went, went head-to-head with the Italian mob as well as other criminals on the streets of New York City, hunted Nazi War criminals around the world, and was courted by African nations to come and set up secret service agencies in their countries. Not only was he a foot soldier in many of these situations, but was in charge and responsible for the success of many of the operation. He often spoke of returning to Oxford and living out the rest of his days at Aunt Ollie's house where he could go hunting and fishing, or going back to Ponce, a little fishing village in Puerto Rico.

Mr. Gittens was called by many names or colorful adjectives were attached to his description, depending on who you talked to, in which decade you were in, or which prism you were looking through. At times he was considered uppity, militant, called an Uncle Tom, a nigger, the Nigger Nazi chaser, colored, the Negro agent, or just boss, to name a few. I chose to call him an American hero!

Most of us like to read about people who claim to be the first to do something or go somewhere because we are enamored with stories of trailblazers who braved the unknown or overcame insurmountable odds to accomplish a goal. I decided that his story needed to be shared with the world, not just because he was the first African American to become a United States Secret Service agent, but because he was an American hero.

This is an incredible story about a man, who came from humble beginnings, was raised in small town America by immigrant parents, and who rose to positions of power and respect. It is the story of how an ordinary young man of color, from an extraordinary family, was able to transcend the racial and cultural barriers in the North and the South and went on to make significant contributions to the development of this country. The history of twentieth century America is unveiled through the eyes of this young man who had a front-row seat and who took an active role in its development.

This is the story of a high school dropout who grew up in the shadow of MIT and Harvard University and ended up at the crest of power in Washington and Moscow. The story takes us to war-torn Japan following World War II, into the depths of a racially segregated South—at a time when lynching was commonplace—through the Civil Rights era and the turmoil and progress it created, to the desperate streets of New York City where criminals and crime fighters waged war for control, and to an America reeling from the assassination of its political leaders.

It is the story of the growth of America. It is the story of a man who kept scaling seemingly insurmountable walls and beating the odds as he fought for justice. This is the story of Charles LeRoy Gittens.

CHAPTER 1
In the Shadow of MIT

This was a neighborhood of immigrants. I have felt more black or African American in the last six months than I ever did growing up in that situation. There were so many nationalities in that little section of Cambridge that it was called "the Village". There were Polish people, Canadians, Greeks, Italians, Russians, Jews and Blacks and we all got along like we were brothers and sisters.
—Charles Gittens

Mr. Gittens stood in the front of his classroom at Dudley High School, a segregated school located in Greensboro, North Carolina, when all of a sudden an immaculately dressed white man walked into the classroom and sat in the back without saying a word. Mr. Gittens had been teaching Spanish for less than a year when this occurred, so he figured that the strange man in the back of the room was from the board of education or some school official observing his teaching style and techniques. The kids seemed to be in an overly inquisitive mood on this day. Maybe they realized that Mr. Gittens was being observed, and either thought they were helping their teacher out by engaging him in a lively conversation, or maybe they were using this opportunity to get out of doing work. Whatever the case, they started asking Mr. Gittens questions about his experiences in Japan following World War II. He used to tell them make-believe war stories that captivated their attention and ingratiated them. They wanted to know how the Japanese treated American soldiers, especially after we had just defeated them. They wanted to know why a black man joined the army in the first place and how black soldiers were treated. They wanted to know about Cambridge, Massachusetts, and the journey he took that brought him to Greensboro. Mr. Gittens gave in to their demands and diverted from his normal lesson to answer their questions, and the class was engaged in a lively discussion.

During the break, Mr. Gittens went to the back of the room and started talking to the strange man. The man stated that he had permission from the principal's office to come and observe. When asked who he was, the man introduced himself as Special Agent George J. Dipper, reached in his pocket, and showed his credentials, which stated that he was from the United States Secret Service. All Mr. Gittens could think about was that the agent was there to arrest him for something he had done, having no idea what that may be, and he was going to jail. It turned out that the agent was there to observe him because the Secret Service was looking for a minority candidate to join the organization, and the agent had heard that Mr. Gittens was interested in a job as a law enforcement officer with the federal government. Knowing that Mr. Gittens would be the first African American to join the Secret Service meant he had to have not only the physical and mental characteristics needed to be an agent, but the mental and moral strength to be able to handle the emotional obstacles that would certainly come with being the first black man in an organization that may have some issues with his employment during this time in America's history.

The journey Mr. Gittens took which enabled him to become the first African American in the Secret Service did not start, however, on that faithful day in October of 1955 in Greensboro, North Carolina. In fact, it actually started when he was born on August 31, 1928 in Cambridge, Massachusetts.

There has always been a debate surrounding the issue of leadership. The question surrounding this issue is whether great leaders are born or bred. Some say that leaders are born with innate characteristics that make leadership a foregone conclusion and all that is needed is the right set of circumstances to be present in order to demonstrate their leadership potential. Others feel, however, that leaders are nurtured and are a combination of all of their life experiences. The fact that Charles Gittens was born and raised into an extraordinary family, in a unique multicultural community had to have had a major impact on his development as a national leader and lends credence to the latter theory of developmental leadership. Like the five points on the Secret Service star, there were at least five very distinct cultural influences that created a perfect storm that help to mold Mr. Gittens into an American icon. He learned valuable lessons from his parents and their Bajan heritage (term used for people from Barbados), the cultural pluralism he experienced growing up in Cambridge, his military experiences, the Southern influence he received while living in Oxford, North Carolina, and the government experience he received while working with the Secret Service. All of these variables jointly prepared him to handle the numerous obstacles thrown in his path and allowed him to succeed beyond his wildest dreams.

Charles L. Gittens (a.k.a. Charlie) grew up in an environment where accomplishments against the odds were a normal part of life, where he was provided a blueprint for handling the notoriety and obstacles of being the first, and where color had never been an obstacle too great to overcome. He was the last of seven children born to Randolph Aldabert Gittens and Winifred Miriam Moore Gittens. His parents, brothers, and sisters were pillars in the community and provided perfect examples of leadership in the political, social, and religious arena that provided training and the mental tools Charlie would use when it was his turn to lead and succeed.

His parents came to America, from Barbados, when they were in their late teens. According to the 1920 Census Report, Randolph Gittens entered America through Ellis Island in 1910 with Winifred coming in 1913. Both Randolph and Winifred came from middle class backgrounds, where their parents and relatives owned land and held positions of influence while in Barbados, but came to the United States because of the opportunities for advancement were even greater. It was said that Winifred initially did not know how to cook because she grew up with servants who did all of the cooking and cleaning. Many of the Bajans who immigrated to Cambridge already knew Winifred because they had come into contact with her at the King's College where she was a teacher. When new arriving *Bajans* immigrated to Cambridge, they would often seek out Winifred for advice concerning where to find a place to live.

Barbados, according to Dr. Karl Watson (the senior lecturer in the Department of History, University of the West Indies), was one of England's most popular colonies, with a rich economy based on sugar and slavery. It quickly acquired the largest white population of any of the English colonies in the Americas. However, as the cost of labor in England went up, planters turned from European indentured servants and prisoners to West Africa (mainly Ghana and Nigeria) for their source of manpower. By 1684, the island population shifted from having a majority white population to having a majority black population. This shift in population patterns facilitated a process of creolization (the mixing of English, French or Spanish, and West African descent speaking a dialect of English, French or Spanish, and West African mix), which saw West African and West European cultural patterns acting on each other under the influence of a small tropical island environment to produce a new *Bajan* culture. By the beginning of the eighteenth century, the majority of Bajan blacks were born locally. The high percentage of creole-born blacks, as opposed to African, contributed to the early development of a Bajan identity. In addition, there was an excess of women over men in both racial groups making Barbados different from other Caribbean islands, where there was an excess of men over women in both racial groups. This enabled the black population to reproduce itself rather than rely on fresh imports from Africa to maintain population levels. As a result, Barbados was the only one of the British islands which supported the passage of the act abolishing the slave trade.[1]

Randolph, at one point, earned a living in construction working on the Panama Canal while Winifred was a teacher at the King's College in Barbados. While working on the Panama Canal project, Randolph was introduced to the intricacies of

American segregation. As American workers began to flee the destitute conditions that existed in Panama (e.g., unsafe working conditions, the spread of diseases such as malaria and yellow fever, the constant and torrential rainfall combined with the heat, etc.) 70 percent of the remaining workforce was West Indians mainly from Barbados. John Stevens, the then chief engineer who was hired by Pres. Theodore Roosevelt to coordinate the Panama Canal project, was said to be responsible for instituting similar segregation laws and customs that were prevalent in the United States. According to letters that he wrote, Stevens did not want to use Bajans for this project and preferred to use white Americans and Chinese workers. He felt that Bajans, most of who were dark in complexion with Negroid features, were lazy, ignorant, only good for manual labor, and not to be trusted. Stevens had no other choice, however, but to use Bajans as a source of labor when white American workers began leaving in droves. A recruitment program was actually created to inspire more Bajans to come to Panama to work. Stevens set up a system where whites were used as skilled laborers and blacks were used as manual labor. In addition, whites were paid in gold while blacks were paid in silver. Separate facilities like entrance to buildings, water fountains, and other public accommodations were designated by the words *gold* and *silver* instead of white and black, which determined who could enter or use the facilities. Whites were given perks like paid vacations, luxurious living quarters, dance halls and schools, while blacks were crowded into dilapidated shacks with no perks and paid ten cents per day. It was under these conditions that Randolph learned the value of pretending to be white in order to get a skilled laborer's position and therefore more money and perks. He would use this skill later when he immigrated to the United States and found similar attitudes about race.

Randolph Gittens was a very "fair skinned" black man with "mixed" ancestry. In fact, he was so fair skinned it was said that he looked like a white man, a trait that probably increased his ability to purchase a home in a section of Cambridge, where not many black families had the opportunity to live and obtain jobs that was usually denied to black people. According to the family's oral tradition that was passed down, mainly through the women in the Gittens family, Randolph wanted to purchase a single family home on Henry and Brookline streets in Cambridge, while his wife Winifred wanted to purchase the home at 60 Allston Street because it was a triple-decker (three stories with three separate doors for entry) that could be divided into apartments to generate revenue by renting rooms out. Initially, Randolph was given the opportunity to purchase either house, but when he went back to purchase the house on Brookline Street, the owner asked him if he was black. When Randolph replied yes and that he was from Barbados, he was told that he could not purchase the house because he was black. The house on Allston Street, which was the largest house on the block, was then purchased by the Gittens, but at twice the original price. They rented out two floors to other West Indian immigrants in order to help pay the mortgage.

The lesson Randolph Gittens learned was that in America if you were black, you were denied opportunities his white counterparts enjoyed. Therefore, in an attempt to provide for his family and obtain employment, Randolph was forced to lead a double life, one as the West Indian patriarch of a black family and the other as a white employee at Boston University. In the black community this was referred to as passing. Many immigrants used this form of assimilation in order to obtain employment, status, or to fit into the fabric of American society. This was done easily, in most cases, by merely changing one's name, abandoning some of one's social customs, or by moving out of segregated neighborhoods (i.e., ghettos) and living in integrated communities. It was much more difficult for black immigrants because of the skin color. Randolph, who had always been an outstanding organizer and leader in his community, got a job as a supervisor in a janitorial position at Boston University. To keep the ruse going, no one in his family, including his wife, Winifred, who was described as a brown-skinned West Indian woman with Negro features, was allowed to contact him or visit him at his place of employment. Charlie did not spend much time with his father and barely knew him because when Charlie was young, his father was sent to a mental institution after being diagnosed with a mental defect.

Randolph was attracted to the Cambridge area because other family members had already migrated to the area and because it was an area that attracted poor immigrants from all over the world looking for work. Today, Cambridge has a very diverse population and attracts even more diversity because of the location of schools like Harvard University, Massachusetts Institute of Technology (MIT), and Radcliffe College. It is also a popular site for moviemakers who were attracted to this area to make films such as *Good Will Hunting, With Honors, Love Story, and Legally Blonde.* According to Wikipedia, however, "First settled in 1630 by English Puritans, Cambridge developed as an agricultural town and was not really convenient to Boston until bridges were built over the Charles River in 1793 and 1809. The latter of these opened up East Cambridge for industrial development led by furniture and glass factories. A major influx of penniless Irish immigrants fleeing the potato blight in 1845 increased the Irish population to 22 per cent in the next ten years. Toward the end of that century they were followed by immigrants from Italy, Poland, Portugal, and Germany. French Canadians and Russian Jews also came at this time. A small African American population had been growing from colonial times, attracted by the integrated schools.[2]

Cambridge was incorporated as a city in 1846.... The coming of the railroad to North Cambridge and Northwest Cambridge then led to three major changes in the city: the development of massive brickyards and brickworks; the ice-cutting industry launched by Frederic Tudor on Fresh Pond; and the carving up of the last estates into residential subdivisions to provide housing to the thousands of immigrants that arrived to work in the new industries.[2a]

Natural disasters, global war, economic chaos, industrial growth and discrimination as a result of bigotry-motivated thousands to come to the Cambridge area creating a global village where everyone was different, but set in an environment where they lived together and forged a new life . . . together.

> *Not like the brazen giant of Greek fame,*
> *With conquering limbs astride from land to land;*
> *Here at our sea-washed, sunset gates shall stand*
> *A mighty woman with a torch, whose flame*
> *Is the imprisoned lightning, and her name*
> *Mother of Exiles. From her beacon-hand*
> *Glows world-wide welcome; her mild eye command*
> *The air-bridged harbor that twin cities frame.*
> *"Keep, ancient lands, your storied pomp!" cries she*
> *With silent lips. "Give me your tired, your poor,*
> *Your huddled masses yearning to breathe free,*
> *The wretched refuse of your teeming shore.*
> *Send these, the homeless, tempest-tost to me,*
> *I lift my lamp beside the golden door!"*

—Emma Lazarus 1883

"Our neighborhood was really diverse," stated Ken Lewis a childhood friend of Charlie Gittens. "We had a number of Italian families. We had black families, we had people from Canada. My father came in 1926, and my mother joined him in 1927. They came from Lower Island Cove, Newfoundland. There was no work in Newfoundland, and just about all of the people left and came here [an earthquake and following tsunami hit Newfoundland in 1929 causing $1 million in property damage, death, and destruction causing more people to flee.] Many of the immigrants from Newfoundland came as carpenters. Most of them, however, like my father were fishermen. Many of the people who came from Italy did motor-type work, brickwork, and sidewalks. People from various places did other things. Everyone in those days brought something, and this is how we got so many wonderful tradesmen. Everyone in those days came here, worked, had a function, and made a living for themselves. No one came to this country with their hands out. People came to work, and that is how they built America. Charlie's dad, I believe, did some building and construction work."

Hyman "Hymie" Rudolph, a person who became a mentor, father figure, and close friend of Charlie, came to America from Russia around 1916. Stuart Rudolph, the grandson of Hymie Rudolph, stated that his grandfather came to America because he was fleeing the violence and discrimination of the Russian *pogroms* (a Russian word meaning *devastation* or *to wreak havoc*. Jews were viciously attacked by mobs which were either condoned or instigated by the authorities in Russian during the nineteenth century).[3] Stuart's father, Bernard "Bernie" Rudolph, described how his family fled on foot from Russia to Poland to escape pogroms against Jews in an interview following the dedication of Fort Washington in Cambridge in his honor:

> There was no law and order in Russia at the time and they were killing Jewish people. Once, bandits broke into our house and lined us up against the wall. They were going to shoot us and I started to cry, begging them not to kill my mother. Then, more bandits burst in and let us go. My father [Hyman Rudolph] had already gotten out of Russia and had come to Cambridge, where he worked as a painter then a store and luncheonette owner waiting for the day when his family could join him, but World War I broke out and we were trapped in Russia. Bernie's two sisters were killed while in Russia, but he, his mother and other family members walked into Poland, travelling at night so they would not be detected. Once the family got to Poland, they had to wait three or four years before being eligible to enter the United States. 'Before my father left Russia,' Bernie said, 'people used to tell him, *'Go to America Hymie, there's gold in the streets,'* so my father wanted to see the gold, and this country never disappointed him.'[4]

"We all grew up together and we all suffered together," Stuart said when asked to describe the neighborhood in Cambridge. "There was no majority of an ethnic group or race. Everybody was there. In our backyard there were all sorts of industries. There were rendering plants and a trucking company. One of Charlie's brothers (Sonny) worked at the Simplex Wire and Cable Company. We used to see the dead animal carcasses open in the trucks around the corner, and this is where we played. In the rendering plants they would take the dead carcasses and turn them into Jell-O, or soap, or hot dog cases. There were seven slaughter houses where we grew up. Think about what Cambridge is today and what it was back then [1940s]. It was very blue-collar. The slaughterhouses used to send all of the carcasses to this place called Reardon's, and that's where they used to do the rendering [the process that converts waste animal tissue into stable useful material]. We used to play between the trucks that carried the dead animal carcasses. Our neighborhood was on the edge where the homes were and the places where people did their work. "

"It was a very poor neighborhood," Lois Terman reflected. Lois was Stuart's sister and the granddaughter of Hymie Rudolph. "We lived in the house diagonally across the street from Charlie. It was a neighborhood where we enjoyed each other and ate in each other's homes. You were a person and you either liked the person or you didn't like that person. It wasn't because of his ethnic group or race because we were all different. Down the street was a chocolate factory (Nabisco) and depending on which way the wind blew you either got hungry from the sweet smell of chocolate or were repulsed by the horrendous smell of dead animals from the rendering plants. Because of the collection of various ethnic groups and the location of the rendering plants and slaughterhouses, our neighborhood was referred to as the greasy village."

According to Yvonne Gittens, the former director of financial aid at MIT who was born and raised in Cambridge and married into the Gittens family, "there were a lot of Barbadians who migrated to this area [Cambridge]. My grandmother [Violet Viola Gibbs Layne], who was from Bridgetown, St. Michael's Barbados, didn't come through Ellis Island, like so many others did. She came right to Boston. She was fifteen years old and was headed to New York to live with her uncle who was a doctor. According to the story she tells, the ship was supposed to go to New York, but the sea was real rough so they had to reroute it to Boston. The boat docked in Boston because of the weather. She never made it to New York because she was not getting on anything that moved. It was such a rough passage that she was done. She had a cousin here so I am assuming there were a lot of other people from Barbados here already."

"There were a lot of industries in the area when I was growing up," Yvonne stated. "The soap factories had houses referred to as soap cottages, which they built and rented to families that worked at the soap factories. There was the Simplex Wire and Cable Company and down on Main Street there was the Car Fastener. That was where they made door handles for refrigerators and car doors. So there were a lot of industries in the area. Budweiser used to bring their horses in the summer. My mom worked in an ice cream factory not too far from where they had the horses, the Clydesdales. I can remember as a child that there was a man who sold ice and coal and had a horse stable. My father worked next to the stable, and his horse would always chase us."

The abundance of industrial factories and warehouses in such a close proximity to each other created job opportunities for young industrious individuals. Charlie was not afraid of hard work, took advantage of these opportunities at an early age, and thus developed a "Puritan work ethic." After graduating from the Morse Grammar School, he was selected to go to Cambridge High and Latin High School. There were two high schools in the area: Rindge Technical School and Cambridge High and Latin. They were located next to each other, and there was a very clear distinction between the two. Rindge was for the kids who probably would end up working in the factories, and Cambridge High and Latin was for the "smart kids," where romance languages were taught and students were prepared for college. For Charlie to be selected to go to Cambridge High and Latin was a really big thing. Not only was Charlie an intelligent young man but he had developed a sense of duty to help support his family with his father not being around most of his teenage life. When he was not in school, he worked at the Schuler Potato Chip Company unloading the huge trailer trucks that brought the potato chips from New York and then loading them onto smaller trucks that delivered the potato chips to the neighborhood stores and bars. At the age of fourteen, he drove a truck delivering flowers for Traynor Florist. He also took on part-time jobs working for the Watertown Arsenal and the West Side Battery & Lead Company. He and classmate Ken Lewis were selected by their high school chemistry teacher to work on Saturdays at a company that produced solutions used to flush automobile radiators.

Shortly after Winifred arrived in America in 1913, Randolph and Winifred Gittens purchased a home in a predominately white community referred to as the Village. Over time the nickname Greasy Village dropped the greasy part and just became known as the Village. This neighborhood exemplified and put into practice the "melting pot" concept that was supposed to be what America claimed to be about. The Village was comprised of immigrants from all over the world who came to work in the numerous industrial jobs. This was a neighborhood of immigrants that was about eight or ten blocks. "Across the street was a Jewish family, and we might as well have been brothers and sisters," stated Edward "Ned" Eccles, who was the son of Charlie's youngest sister Miriam "Babe" and who also lived at 60 Allston Street. "The Italians lived on the other side across the street. There was an Irish family also. In this section, everybody got along really well. If a child was out playing, you wouldn't think of him out there by himself. He had his aunts and uncles watching, and they were his neighbors who looked out for him."

"There were only three black families in the neighborhood all of them coming from the West Indies, all from Barbados," Charlie reflected. "We got privileges I guess because we were light-skinned. There was no segregation in this section of Cambridge. I went to the Morse Grammar School and graduated in 1942. There were only two black males in that school and one black female named Ruth Spooner. Ruth was a mulatto, and she looked white. After grammar school I went to Cambridge High and Latin. You didn't know you were colored because there weren't many colored students there. Everybody was treated the same, Black, Polish, Irish, and Jewish. Boston was a very segregated city back then, but in Cambridge, I wouldn't know what segregation was even if you gave me $100. We all went to the same schools and lived in the same neighborhood. This was a neighborhood of immigrants. Our parents were dirt-poor, but all of the different races and nationalities worked and got along together. My niece married an Irish man, and my sister married a Puerto Rican man. The parents, all speaking different languages and coming from different parts of the world, came to this foreign land, all welcomed to our shores and they worked hard. Some did better than others, but everybody worked hard to eke out a good living."

On another block in Cambridge, however, things were a little different. People who lived in the neighborhood referred to as the Coast were people who were struggling to make it economically, according to Charlie. "You wouldn't even know you were in the same state if you lived in the Coast," Charlie stated.

Many of the Bajans who immigrated to the Cambridge area were forced to settle in the Coast (which included River Street, Western Avenue, and parts of Putnam). This was a result of economic status and the inability to afford homes in other sections of Cambridge; the refusal of owners to sell their property to blacks, as well as the fact that it was more comfortable to live in a neighborhood where the culture, language, and people were similar. "The city of Cambridge had always been the second home to a large West Indian community, especially those from Barbados," stated Yvonne Gittens. "The Cambridge Community Center, which is the only community center in the city and probably the state, was created and paid for by black ministers over eighty years ago. It was created at the time because black youth, especially young black men were not welcomed at the YMCA. The ministers pooled their money together and bought an old school building and started the community center, which still exist today. The Port was another black neighborhood but was comprised mostly of migrants from the South."

Growing up in the Village probably had a lot to do with Charlie's views on racial and ethnic tolerance in America. He was lucky not to experience the type of racism that was prevalent throughout America. When he decided to join the military, his sister Grace stated, "Charlie is finally going to find out what it means to be a Negro." Even though he left Cambridge at a young age, the Village never left him. Being raised the way he was, probably insulated him from the reality of the real world. He didn't have to worry about being judged because of his skin color, but by the content of his character. He probably learned that if you worked hard and prepared yourself academically, you could achieve almost anything. This belief would be put to the test time and time again later in life.

There is an adage that says we are the products of our past. If that is true, then Charlie's experiences and early childhood acquaintances went a long way in paving the way for him to accomplish great things. He was the last of seven children, all born in Cambridge, in the Gittens household where community and political involvement became a family tradition and a standard for excellence had been established. The Gittens family became well-known and respected in the Cambridge community. They were the black family that transcended the racial barrier. People held them in high esteem. The Gittens family included Ruth Olga (referred to as Ollie), Grace, George (a.k.a. Sonny), John (a.k.a. Pepper), Thelma (a.k.a. Ookie), Miriam (a.k.a. Babe) and Charlie. They lived in a three-story house, the largest house on the block, located down the street from MIT and seven blocks from Harvard University.

Charlie's mother, Winifred, was a housewife, whose major responsibility was to raise the children, but she was so much more. She was the person that newly arriving West Indians would come to see when they were looking for housing. The word was out; if you needed a place to stay, go see Winnie! Being a former teacher, she made sure that all of her children had chores around the house and got trained in some specialty that would help them out later in life. Though poor, she bought a piano and required that all of her children learn music. Charlie, as a result, became an accomplished violinist, a skill that would bear fruit later in life. She was an avid churchgoer and a grandmotherly figure for all of the children in the neighborhood. She would also have political fund-raisers in the house and have many politicians who would stop by to meet and greet people. Representative John Kennedy came by the house, as well as Edward Brooke, before he became the attorney general and senator for Massachusetts.

Winifred's sister Eleanor Katrina Young was a nurse in Staten Island. She rose to the position of head nurse where she was responsible for supervising the entire hospital. In addition, she held a part-time job as the supervisor for the Salvation Army. For a black female during the 1940s and '50s this was a great accomplishment and a beacon that would inspire others in the family to accomplish great things in spite of the odds.

John Gittens (Pepper) was described as a very handsome man who was sharp with the ladies and very articulate. "The way he dressed and the way he spoke would make you say who in the world was this Negro," Charlie once said. "You wouldn't even think he was a Negro by the way he spoke!" It was very interesting that people used to say the same thing about Charlie as he got older. John became a corporal in the army during World War II. Because of his ability to write so eloquently, he was sought out by other soldiers to write letters for them to send home. When he returned from military service, he got a job working at the post office. He became the first self-appointed union leader, ex officio, at the post office. Blacks had the worst jobs there, and he held classes at his house, or wherever they would meet him, to teach Blacks how to prepare for the postal exam. This gave more Blacks the opportunity to become mail carriers, which during the 1950s was a very big job. He recruited Blacks, especially veterans, and he was largely responsible for integrating the post office. He preached education and that with training any black man was just as good as any white man and that black men should not have to accept subservient positions. He was relenting and driven, and his demeanor would become caustic if you disagreed with him or tried to prevent him from accomplishing his goals. He organized and created the Cambridge branch of the National Association for the Advancement of Colored People (NAACP) and became its first president. He was the president and founder of EEOCC Postal Organization. He was the founder of Charles Fulmore Park, which used to be an empty lot where people would just leave their abandoned automobiles.

Charles Gittens graduating from the Morse Grammar School, 1942

Randolph Gitten   George (Sonny) and Millie Gittens   John (Pepper) Gittens

(From L–R) Thelma (Ookie), Grace, Miriam (Babe),
Winifred (Mother), Ruth-Olga (Ollie)

THE GITTENS FAMILY

Randolph Gittens - Winifred Gittens
1894–1941   1897–1962

Gittens Children

1. **Ruth Olga "Ollie"** (1915–1982)
   Married to Samuel Braithwaite
   Children: Robin, Richard, Sam Jr., Raymond, Barbara, Marjorie, Myrl

2. **Grace** (1916–1986)

3. **George "Sonny"** (1917–2004)
   Married to Mildred Muller
   Children: David, Stephen

4. **John "Pepper"** (1919–2002)
   Married to Alyce
   Children: Joan

5. **Thelma "Ookie"** (1921–1983)
   Married to Jorge Munoz
   Children: Irma, Pedro

6. **Miriam "Babe"** (1923–2007)
   Married to Alfred Eccles
   Children: Edward, Charles, Alfred

7. **Charles "Charlie"** (1928–2011)
   First Marriage
   Married to Ruthe Hamme
   Children: Sharon
   Second Marriage
   Married to Maureen Espersen
   Children: Cherri, Carolyn

After a little boy was hit by a car and killed, John spearheaded the drive to get the lot turned into a beautiful renovated park for children to play. It had a basketball court, which is no longer there, but the swings and other structures are still there today. The park was named after the little boy who was killed but was often referred to fondly as Gittens Park. John retired as a postal supervisor and was one of the first Blacks to move into Beacon Hill, which was an upper class predominately white section of Boston. "The only person in my family that got upset about racial things was my older brother John," Charlie said. "He was the one who was angry at white folks. Those who had it in their blood to call you a nigger would not say that to John because he would beat the shit out of you."

Charlie's older sister Grace graduated from the Cambridge City Hospital for Nurses where she worked for many years. "She was the only black professional nurse in the neighborhood to wear the white uniform," according to Charlie and "that was a big thing in those days." When WWII broke out, she joined the army and rose to the position of lieutenant in the Army Nurse Corps. She received the Victory Medal and a Meritorious Service Unit Plaque. She later became the assistant director of the Alpha and Omega Missionary Society at the Evangelical Baptist Church in Newton, Massachusetts.

His sister Thelma, or Ookie as she was so fondly referred to as, became a secretary. Her last job was for the Commonwealth of Massachusetts. In 1943, she married one of the tenants in her mother's house, Jorge P. Munoz, more popularly known in Boston as Chico. Chico became an important and popular activist throughout the city of Boston. He made it his personal goal to provide and advocate for equity to opportunities, resources, and access in city government and within local community–based organizations for Hispanics. He served on the Boston Human Rights Commission and was the cofounder of Boston's first Hispanic Social Service Agency, the Spanish Action Center, later recognized as the Association Promoting the Constitutional Rights of the Spanish Speaking (APCROSS). Through his activity as the first Hispanic trustee of the Department of Health and Hospitals, Chico paved the way for Hispanics to receive services and employment within Boston City Hospital. He was also known as the father of the Puerto Rican community and organized the city's Puerto Rican festival, an annual one-week celebration of the island's culture featuring a road race in his honor.

Charlie's sister Miriam "Babe" became a secretary as well. She had the fortune of working for Noam A. Chomsky at MIT Linguistics Department and for Sen. Benigno S. Aquino Jr. of the Philippines at the Department of International Studies at MIT. Choosing the path of religion to highlight her leadership ability, she became an associate minister of St. Augustine A.O. Church and held Bible classes at Harvard Divinity School and at MIT.

It was probably Charlie's brother George, or Sonny as he was affectionately called, who helped Charlie develop his sense of humor, his quit wit, his smiling gregarious attitude, his level-headed thinking, and his sense of duty to family. Sonny was an average guy but was the life of the party and was well-known in the community. When Charlie's father was committed to a mental institution, it was Sonny who took on the role as father figure. He and his wife Millie would often take Charlie to the circus and other activities. "John was the academic person, but Sonny was the fascinating, interesting guy," Charlie exclaimed. "I would much rather go out with Sonny than with John. Sonny knew how to have fun, and John was a bookworm. Sonny used to fix stuff, and he taught me how to fix things and that became my job. I liked fixing things like bicycles." Sonny was always the voice of reason and tolerance. When his sister Thelma's daughter Irma wanted to marry a white guy, members of the family were dead set against it, but it was Sonny who said, "You guys talk about all of God's children all of the time! Isn't he one of God's children?" Irma married Paul and lived happily ever after.

It was against this backdrop that Charles Leroy Gittens was developed, nurtured, and groomed. He grew up living with many examples of family members forging ahead and being a pioneer in areas that, in this country, were not supposed to be set aside for people of color. He had seen that with hard work, tough skin, and educational training, you could accomplish anything. Imagine sitting around the Gittens dinner table during Thanksgiving and listening to all of the political and community conversations that took place. Imagine sitting on the porch or hanging out in the neighborhood stores and listening to the parents of his many friends tell stories of life in the old country and how they were so grateful to be in America. Imagine a young child yearning to see what that world was really like. Imagine the experience one could get working more jobs between the age of twelve and sixteen than some people had in a lifetime.

Paul Snelgrove, who is currently eighty-three years old and was a childhood friend and schoolmate of Charlie's, shared a story that seemed somewhat prophetic. Charlie and Paul attended the Morse Grammar School together in 1942. One day a friend brought a bunch of fireworks to school, which in those days was legal. Several of their friends got together on the playground and opened the fireworks, spreading the powder on a huge, flat rock. Someone lit the powder and a huge puff of smoke emerged, filling the playground. As everyone jumped back in astonishment, Charlie suddenly leaped forward and jumped through the smoke, declaring, "Shazam, I'm Captain Marvel!" He had a sinister grin on his face that would become his trademark later in life. Everyone rolled on the ground in laughter at this impromptu display.

Captain Marvel was a fictional comic book superhero who was the champion of good and fought injustice and cruelty. He was the most popular comic book superhero in the 1940s outselling Superman by a landslide. Little did anyone know that right there, in the midst of a poor neighborhood where industries flourished and immigrants flocked seeking freedom, jobs, and equality, a real Captain Marvel would emerge. No one could have imagined that this black kid from Cambridge,

Massachusetts, the son of immigrants would rise and jump through the smoke of injustice, hatred, and ignorance in order to fight crime, racism, and cruelty and to keep Americans and the American ideal safe at home and abroad. It was his ability to ignore danger, to see the humor in every situation, and to make those around him feel comfortable, that enabled him to rise to positions beyond his wildest dreams.

CHAPTER 2
We Love You, Chocolate Solider

I desperately wanted to go into the military because guys were getting knocked off and killed so fast that I wasn't going to get a chance to get killed like Billy, or this guy, or that guy. I figured that you got to die sometime. I decided that if I died I wanted to die with one of Hitler's bullets in me!

—Charles Gittens

America woke up on a bright Sunday morning and found itself finally engulfed by the clouds of war. The world of Charlie Gittens and so many other young men and women across the nation changed forever on December 7, 1941, when Japan launched a surprise attack on Pearl Harbor, killing thousands of Americans. Pres. Franklin Delano Roosevelt asked Congress to declare war on Japan, and a new era in American history began. Actually the world had been engaged in this deadly conflict for over two years prior to the United States' official entry. By declaring war on Japan, the United States joined forces with the Allied power (Great Britain, France, and later the Soviet Union, etc.) to battle the countries aligned with the Axis powers (Germany, Japan and Italy).

Americans were outraged by Japan's vicious attack, and young men and women all over the country flocked to recruitment offices to join the war effort. This swell of patriotism swept through the quaint neighborhood in Cambridge where Charlie and so many sons and daughters of immigrants resided. It seemed that many immigrant families wanted to show their patriotism and appreciation for having the opportunity to come to America and earn a living, and they were more than ready to return the favor. In addition, the American war machine romanticized the war through a brilliant propaganda effort that included movies, movie stars, colorful posters, radio shows, and returning war veterans who were paraded around the country motivating citizens to help the war effort in any way possible.

On that faithful morning in 1941, Charlie Gittens was a thirteen-year-old, mischievous schoolboy attending the Morse Grammar School in Cambridge, Massachusetts. He was not a bad kid, his brothers would not allow him to get into any real trouble, but he did have a knack for exploring and wasn't afraid to participate in things that were a little dangerous. He and his friends used to play on the roof of his three-story home, and one day he fell through the skylight, cutting his leg so badly that his sister Ruth Olga had to carry him to the Cambridge City Hospital. Or there was the time he would do things like hop on a moving train and throw coal off onto the road where his friends would gather it up and then take the coal to help heat their homes. Then there was the time when he skipped school and was caught with a friend riding horses through the street (one of the horses got hit and killed by a passing automobile).

His brother Sonny taught him how to fix things, and Charlie became fascinated with inventions and ideas on how to make things better. He kept and raised pigeons and chickens outside of his home. Once he ran an electrical cord outside of his home and hooked up a toaster in the henhouse, thus keeping the warm chickens laying eggs through the winter months. These were small things that young mischievous boys would do when they had spare time, but things began to change drastically when the call for recruits went out in Cambridge and Sonny decided to join the Army Air Corps in 1942. Sonny, who was eight years older, had been Charlie's surrogate father in the absence of his real father, who had died in a mental institution when Charlie was thirteen years old (1941). Later his sister Grace left and became a first lieutenant in the Army Nurse Corps, followed by his brother John, who became a corporal in the army. The departure of his siblings and other neighborhood friends for the war ignited a flame in Charlie that could not be easily extinguished.

Charlie used to hang out in a little store called the Village Spa or the Spa for short. It was a small store which was a combination old corner store, drugstore with a soda fountain, and a Saturday night hangout for the young boys and girls in the neighborhood. It was reminiscent of the old general store which at one time was so typically a part of the American scene. Charlie became friends with the Jewish proprietor who went by the name of Hyman Rudolph or Hymie as he was admirably called. Hymie was the "unofficial mayor, philosopher, and psychologist" of the neighborhood. Hymie, a refugee from Czarist Russia, and Charlie developed a special mentor-mentee relationship. Hymie had developed a similar relationship with most of the kids and adults in the neighborhood, but he played a big role in Charlie's life now that his big brothers were gone to war. During the war, Hymie sent packages to his "boys overseas" and received numerous letters and souvenirs from all of his boys. Hymie would share those letters and war stories with Charlie. Charlie saw the effect that these letters had on his mentor. Hymie always kept check on the progress of his boys and was devastated when he received reports that one of them was missing or killed in action.

When Charlie got into high school at Cambridge High and Latin, it seemed like many of the neighborhood older boys were leaving home and going to fight in the war. "There weren't many kids from Cambridge High and Latin who were scrambling to get into the military," Charlie reminisced. "They'd go because their big brothers went. They would say, 'Yeah, I'd like to go and shoot a rifle and kill those Germans.' We had many war heroes who came back from this part of the country. I thought that was pretty neat because guys came back as heroes. They would march down the street and showed their medals and the stuff that they brought back from Europe. We called the guys who were already in the service "the big guys." When they came back, they were heroes, and their parents were heroes too. If I had to do it all over again, I would have done the same thing. I knew at seventeen years old I was going to be in law enforcement. One of the things that urged me along that path was the fact that the war was almost over, and I said I was going to miss all of the fun. So I dropped out of school when I was sixteen, altered my birth certificate, and made myself seventeen and went to the recruitment office to join the army. The recruitment officer took one look at me and said, 'Get out of here and come back when you are old enough.' And I did one year later. When they accepted me, I was the happiest young black man in Cambridge, Massachusetts."

When Charlie's mother first found out he wanted to drop out of school and join the army, she was upset. Unable to convince him to stay in school, she wrote to Charlie's big brother John and told him that Charlie was adamant about dropping out of high school to join the military. John wrote his little brother and tried to convince him not to join. The letter was dated 1944 somewhere in Iran and stated,

I've been hearing lots about you Charlie,—that you've grown like a weed and become a man overnight,—that you've left school and now your greatest ambition is to join some branch of the service, any branch that'll take a fifteen year-old man. I know how you feel, Charlie. There are thousands of kids your age in the same situation, nervous, restless, and anxious to be off to the wars. The flaming beckoning posters, the stirring martial music, the beat of marching feet, and all the thrilling sights of a war-torn nation tempt and lure you to join and respond like moths to a flame with just as disastrous results. The ear-splitting scream of dive-bombers, the staccato chatter of a machine gun, and the thunderous din of bursting bombs that you see and hear in the movies is music to your ears.

To you kids it would be glorious and even glamorous to fight victoriously on the field of battle and come home idolized heroes covered with shiny medals. Yes, I know how you feel all right; I felt the same way when I was a kid. But war is hell, Charlie, actual living hell. Ask Kel about the glory. Ask Tony about the glamor. Ask Pat about the shiny medals. They know, they've been there. Ask them if they'd go back to hell for a million dollars . . . for ten million. It's not a pretty story, Charlie. It's ugly and sordid and cruel. And there are other things, things that you know nothing about, bitter, heart-rending things like prejudice, discrimination, and segregation. That's not for you, Charlie, not you who've always been looked up to and respected as a leader by all the neighborhood kids. It would age you overnight and cause you to lose faith in humanity.

You were just a little guy when I left, Charlie, only twelve years old, a normal healthy kid, a little fresh at times, but I loved you an awful lot. The little brother that I remember was the smartest kid in the world, always tinkering with machinery, building things, interested in telegraph, radio, and electricity and getting better marks in school. How often have I said to myself, "By the time that guy finishes MIT he'll be famous." I was proud of you then, make me proud of you now. Finish high school and go to MIT. That's the best way to really help your country and your people. We need more skilled technicians, and the way is open in every field for ambitious, intelligent youngsters like you.

Well, Charlie, I've got to close now. Be good and listen to Mom, she's always right. When you write again, I want to hear that you're back where you belong, in school.

Your loving brother,
John

Charlie refused to heed his brother's warning and dismissed his mother's plea and continued to hound the recruitment officer to let him get in. Even after Japan officially surrendered on September 2, 1945, which meant that WWII had come to an end, Charlie persisted on his course of action. He continued his pursuit of enlistment, and finally on April 23, 1946, Charlie became an official member of the United States Army. "If you could find that recruitment sergeant today," Charlie said, "he would probably say, 'Oh, so you are the one who used to come in here all of the time! So you finally got in. Did you win any medals?' I was fascinated with the military and knew that I just had to get in."

After entering the military, the reality of life in America began to set in. Casted outside the comforts of a tranquil, culturally pluralistic environment where everyone was treated as equal human beings, Charlie was now in the real world with all of its imperfections, contradictions, and unfairness. The United States had just struck a blow for freedom and against tyranny and injustice abroad, on the one hand, and was trying to come to grips with its own political and social/racial inequities at home that made their rhetoric to the world seem somewhat hypocritical. black men and women, though eager to enlist in the armed services and fight for their country, found that they were continuously disrespected and discriminated against on all levels. Charlie's brother Sonny found out early that life outside of the Village was quite different. When he joined the Army Air Corps, he wanted to be a gunner only to find out those positions were not for "men of color." It was a shock to him that segregation existed in the service, and black men were forced to sit together in the mess hall and had separate living quarters from the white soldiers. His zeal to fight for his country was tempered by the fact that black soldiers had to "know and keep their place" and were treated as second-class citizens.

"The army was the only branch which accepted blacks routinely. The air force had a few blacks in construction companies. The navy only took blacks as mess men. In all branches, blacks had separate quarters, training facilities, and entertainment."[5] "In response to the Selective Service Act (September 14, 1940), which contained a clause barring racial discrimination, the air corps organized nine aviation training squadrons whose duties were "vaguely defined." What would be done with the black airman was left to the discretion of each base commander, but there was no intent to train blacks as pilots until Yancey Williams (a student at Howard University) and the NAACP filed a lawsuit against the War Department because they refused to consider his application for enlistment in the air corps as a flying cadet. A short time after Williams's suit, the War Department announced the formation of the first black air corps squadron to be located near Tuskegee Institute in Alabama."[6]

Both the air force and the navy developed innovative and more inclusive programs for black servicemen and women by the end of the war, but the army continued to segregate by race throughout the war. Because of the climate and availability of space, many of the army's training facilities were located in the South where segregation was still a way of life and the law. Many of the white officers who were put in charge of black units were from the South and held on to attitudes about what black people were able to do and what positions in the social order they should maintain. Blacks were often put into trucking companies, whose purpose it was to transport troops and supplies, or regulated to servile positions as cooks, cleanup details, and support services. "While touring army camps in 1941, *Pittsburgh Courier* editor P. L. Prattis commented, 'The Negro area, in nine cases out of ten, was in the most inaccessible section of the camp. . . . At Camp Lee, Negro soldiers told the writer that they had started at the center of the camp and had successfully cleaned up areas which were turned over to future incoming white troops while the Negroes were always kept in the woods.'" [7]

Neither segregation nor the end of the war diminished Charlie's enthusiasm for military life or his desire to see the world and start a new life. It seemed to be a mere inconvenience, to be tolerated until he could do something about it. "I did my basic training in a small town in Maryland [Havre De Grace]," Charlie exclaimed. "We'd get on the train and ride down to Maryland. It was my first time with a bunch of guys I didn't know. As I recall, somewhere along the line we got separated. I mean the white guys and the black guys. That was my first time dealing with segregation. I still don't know how they did that because we started together and then we got separated. Segregation was easy for me to handle at basic training because you were in the army! You did what you were told. I was seventeen years old, and they would say, 'This, Negro soldier, is where you are going to sleep, this is where you are going to eat, and this is where you are going to work.' Was it discrimination? It might have been, but I didn't know it because it was the army. They might have been treating me like dog shit, and I wouldn't have known it because it was the army, and I liked the army. They did make us pick up stuff off of the street within the compound, however, and there was a great difference between how they treated people of color versus how they treated people of non-color. But I loved the army."

One thing that Charlie didn't like about the army, however, was one particular duty, and that was kitchen patrol or KP. In a letter he wrote to his mother (May 5, 1946), he gives a glimpse of army life. He wrote,

Hi Mom,
*   Well, well, as the old Romans would say—"Tempus Fugit." It seems like only a day or two ago that I was home. The army isn't so bad after all. At least, that's how I find it. I think this is just what I need—a change. I even feel healthier and more vigorous now. There's only one thing I don't like. In fact, when I hear my name called for it, I feel like going AWOL. That duty or "necessary chore" as they put it is KP. Yesterday at exactly 4:00 a.m., we got out of bed, went down to the mess hall and worked steady without any rest, except to eat, until 6:30 that night. Kinda long hours, huh? But that doesn't happen often. I only had it twice since I joined up.*

There were three very fortunate events that occurred, making Charlie's stay in the military not only tolerable but advantageous to his development and future. One was being stationed in Yokohama, Japan. The second was being assigned to the 289th Army Band and was finally meeting and working under Lieutenant Oscar W. Williams.

When Charlie initially joined the army, his desire was to go to the European theatre and fight Hitler. With the Russian army invading Germany from the east and the Western Allies from the west and the news of Hitler's suicide, Germany surrendered unconditionally on May 7, 1945, bringing WWII to an official end in Europe. Japan, however, continued their fruitless effort to wage war until after the United States dropped atomic bombs on Hiroshima and Nagasaki, causing Japan to surrender unconditionally on September 2, 1945. Charlie had no desire to go to the Pacific theatre and was hoping to somehow get sent to Europe anyway, but a ruse by the army caused him to be sent to Japan anyway. In a letter (June 30, 1946) to his sister Ruth-Olga (Ollie), he expressed his displeasure in how he got duped into volunteering to go to Japan. He wrote,

> *Ollie, I've lost faith in all humanity. This man's army cannot be trusted. Almost every one of the fellows in my company are volunteers like myself and signed for the ETO* [European Theatre of Operation]. *Well, the other day they took us over to classification, and the colonel spoke to us and told us that the ETO is closed, and all other theatres except the Pacific were closed. He also stated that if we didn't sign up to go to the Pacific that our furloughs would be held up and we'd be sent to a holding camp and go to the Pacific anyhow.*
>
> *Well, at the time, the fact that my furlough would be held up if I didn't sign, was enough for me, so like a doggone fool, I went and did it. Now that I had a little time to think it over, I could kill myself for doing such a foolish thing, but what's done is done and I'll just have to make the best of it. Pray, Ollie, for something to come up that'll delay me for a while in the States.*

And making the best of things was something Charlie was good at doing, and he later discovered that going to the Pacific theatre was a blessing in disguise. His battalion was sent to Yokohama, Japan, in October 1946. Yokohama was the second largest city in Japan at that time and was located just south of Tokyo. It had been virtually destroyed by American B-29 bombers during WWII. During one particular air raid, known as the Great Yokohama Air Raid, in just one hour and nine minutes, eight thousand people were killed and 42 percent of the city was in rubble.[8] During the American occupation, Yokohama was a major transshipment base for American supplies and personnel, especially during the Korean War.

"I don't remember anything but enjoying my entire stay in Japan," Charlie recalled. "You didn't have to worry about segregation, and the Japanese people loved us. We were called the chocolate soldiers. I didn't run into any black soldier who objected to that because that was the Japanese way of saying, 'We love you, chocolate soldiers!' I had a Japanese girlfriend nicknamed Kitty. I was really lucky. I still had to get used to being around mostly colored fellows after being raised in Cambridge. I was so proud to be from Boston, and there weren't many colored people from where I was from. I used to lay my Boston accent on the other colored troops and acted so dignified that I had to laugh under my breath. I had all of the fellows believing that I was a wealthy man's son. I used to love to brag and show the fellows, especially the ones from below the Mason-Dixon Line, letters from those little white girls I used to date. I was such a devil."

The worst part about being in Yokohama was the ride there on that raggedy ship. The ship was horrible, and everybody got sick. It was old and rickety and not sail hardy. You got sick and then you got over it. The trip took twenty-seven days, and we had to stop in Honolulu for repairs. But we had fun, especially when we finally made it to Yokohama. Some of the more pleasant times were on Friday and Saturday nights when the big tent went up and you could go dancing and get beer and stuff like that. I was never really much of a party guy, but the other guys were."

Visiting a foreign country and experiencing a foreign culture proved to be very interesting to Charlie. In Cambridge, he had the opportunity to compare the cultural habits of the many different immigrant cultures of the people who resided in the Village, but the Japanese culture was something totally different for him. He was like a sponge, viewing, evaluating, and comparing everything he witnessed. He described his observations to his mother in a letter dated December 1946:

> To see the way these people lived—the way they clung to their old ancient customs, you'd never believe that they had the highest rate of literacy in the world. They were really smart people. Almost every one of them spoke some English, and they certainly knew how to work with figures. The average ten-year-old kid could tell you in a few seconds how much a certain amount of Japanese yen would be in American money, whereas we almost had to use pencil and paper to figure out what our money was worth in theirs. And you can't cheat or pull the wool over the dumbest "Japs" eyes. They were extremely shrewd people.
>
> The suffering that the people had to endure was horrible. They were just about on the verge of starvation. Whenever our ship docked in Yokohama, swarms of kids and old people begged us to throw them food. It was a shame the way they would fight and scramble for the bread, apples, meat, bones, etc., that we got out of the galley. To make matters worse, we had an earthquake over here. It was the worst earthquake in Japan's history (8.1 to 8.4 on the moment magnitude scale). Although no American soldiers or dependents were killed, about one thousand Japanese civilians were killed and something like six thousand homes destroyed.

Many African American servicemen returned to the States singing the praises of their wonderful experience in Yokohama. Spurgeon Stanard, an African American navy war veteran from Spotsylvania, Virginia, who served on the USS *Wisconsin*, was stationed in Yokohama and described his stay there as one of the highlights of his military experience:

> When I got to Yokohama we were in control. They didn't have their own police force. Well, they had a police force, but it was being controlled by US soldiers. When US soldiers would go on patrols in jeeps, they would have two Japanese police officers with

them. The whole country was under the control of Gen. Douglas MacArthur (who was assigned as the supreme commander of the Allied powers [SCAP] following the surrender of Japan). He was the boss of Japan at the time. General MacArthur was smart enough and knew enough about the Japanese culture to maintain their structure. The Japanese people were subservient. They went along with the rules and laws. They obeyed and complied. They were fierce fighters during the war, but just as nice in peace as they were fierce in war. General MacArthur recognized the monarchy, which had a lot to do with winning over the people.

Yokohama was nice, kind of primitive with very few cars. Most of the people used bicycles or rickshaws. If you wanted to get one place to another, you would use the rickshaw. It was like a carriage, but instead of a horse pulling it, you had a man pulling it. The nightclubs we went to were geared for us and played our kind of music. They played jazz or swing music . . . the music of the time. Most of the singers sang in English mostly. They did some songs in Japanese, but most of the songs were ones we recognized. The clubs were not segregated in Japan. That only happened in the States. One time I went to a USO club in San Francisco at Treasure Island. The USO was supposed to be for all of the servicemen. The guy at the door said I could come in and get something to drink, but they didn't have any colored girls for me to dance with. The USO used to be sponsored by church groups or social clubs that supported the military. They would have ladies there just for dancing and entertainment. But that's why I was surprised to face that in San Francisco. Now in Norfolk, the USO clubs were segregated. There was the black USO and the white USO. You didn't go to the white clubs, but in Japan I didn't see any segregation.

I enjoyed Yokohama. The Japanese people treated us real nice. They were honest people; they wouldn't cheat you like in some other countries. You didn't have to worry about getting the right change back when you bought something. In Japan, I didn't have any problems being a black man. You really forgot about segregation when you were there. Some of the guys rejoined the navy when their tour was up because they didn't want to leave. They were supposed to head back to the US, and they would volunteer to transfer to another ship and stay in Japan. We had no problems with the Japanese or any port outside of the United States.

Toshiko Akiyoshi, a renowned pianist, composer, and arranger, was born to a Japanese family in Manchuria, China. According to Toshiko, revealed in an interview with Steven Moore, "She started playing piano when she was seven years old in Manchuria. After the war, all the Japanese who had settled in Manchuria went back to Japan. Her parents lost all of their assets when they went back in 1946. One day, she saw an advertisement that said 'pianist wanted.' The occupation brought with it many American soldiers, and they needed many halls where they could go to dance. So Japan needed a lot of musicians. She was hired. Her father was unhappy about her job because he was very traditional. In the average Japanese home, the daughter did not work. They went to school, and if they didn't go to school, they stayed home until they got married."[9]

Toshiko had the opportunity to go to Yokohama, where she found many opportunities to play jazz music in the numerous American and Japanese clubs. She played with several army bands, including the 289th and the 293rd army bands. It seemed that a lot of musicians were drafted into the American army. The 289th Army Band had Bonnie Wandents who became a wonderful tenor player. She remembers that the relationship between American soldiers and Japanese citizen in Yokohama was very cordial and friendly. She reflected on her experience with American troops:

> I think a lot of Americans liked Japan. They may have been very few who did not like it there. This has a lot to do with, even when the yen got stronger, a lot of Americans felt comfortable here. That was the time of occupation and the dollar was very strong. And the Americans had all of the privileges, and the Japanese people were very gentle then. Today it seems to be changing a little bit. I don't know too many Americans who came back and said that they didn't like it. As far as I could tell, there was no animosity. Some of the American soldiers there did not want to stay in camp, so they had apartments that they would rent. That was the time when we did not have much of anything, and it was a problem trying to get daily needs. I think some of the American soldiers would buy things at the PX and give it to or sell it to the Japanese people who they knew. I think some Americans that I knew were there for some time and married their sweetheart there. He would take his wife back to America, and she would have problems adjusting to American lifestyle. During occupation, the Americans had more privileges. The yen was weak, and the American dollar was very strong, and they had a better time. People were very nice. Americans were there for some time and got used to Japanese society. Relationships were good.

Sergeant Gittens in Yokohama, Japan

Sergeant Gittens with the 289th Army Band

Gittens played with the Esquires of Rhythm band

Sergeant Gittens befriends the locals

Sergeant Gittens (far right)
enjoys a night on the town

Sergeant Gittens and friend Kitty

289th Army Band performs
in parade in Yokohama

At that time I was young and wasn't even aware of the relationship between black American soldiers and white American soldiers. I don't think the Japanese people were thinking about that too much. It didn't make any difference whether they were black or white; it only made a difference if they were nice or not nice. As far as my relationship with Americans, it was with musicians, and it didn't matter whether they were black or white.

In the military, there seemed to be a separation. There was separation between black clubs and white clubs in the military. There was an NCO [noncommissioned officer] club with only black soldiers. I was hired to play at a club where there were mostly black soldiers and maybe one or two whites. But that had nothing to do with the Japanese society. That had something to do with the

American armed forces. Of course there was the officers club and the NCO club. I remember playing in the officers' club, and I did not see one black officer there. They were all white, and they had officers and their wives and some officers had their families there. At that particular time, there was not supposed to be separation, but there was a separation.

Upon arriving in Yokohama, Charlie was assigned to the 289th Army Band. The trucking unit he was assigned to did not have a band and was in the process of starting one. When the officers looked at his record, they discovered he had some musical training, and just like that he was assigned to the band. He was really surprised because the training he had was with the violin, which was not suited for band music. But silently he was thanking his mother for her wisdom to make everyone in the Gittens family study music and play an instrument. Charlie toyed with playing the flute, piccolo, baritone, and tuba. He finally decided to play the trombone. He served in the band with Frank Hinton, who later became a famous jazz musician and started a band called the Frank Hinton Trio. In addition to playing at military functions, members of the 289th Army Band, including Charlie, played at local and military clubs in a popular band called the Esquires of Rhythm.

"Being in the band was one of the best assignments I could have ever had," Charlie exclaimed. "It gave me a chance to learn a little bit more about music and helped propel me up the ladder. At first they had me working in the orderly's office doing office kind of things, but the band leader said that everybody in this unit had to learn how to play an instrument, no matter what other duties you were assigned. I decided on playing the trombone, and they started giving me lessons. I learned from the other players and the band master. I chose the trombone because I was kind of a ham, and I liked that military stuff. In the band the trombones were always up front when we had to march and perform in military functions. I wanted to be up front, so playing trombone put me there. I had a good job being a musician. I don't know anyone who had a better job than I did in the military. I was lucky to be in the service at this time because President Truman passed Executive Order 9981 (July 26, 1948), ending segregation in the US Armed Forces. I used to laugh and tell everyone at home that I helped win the war with my flute and piccolo."

Charlie's advancement up the ladder was rapid as a result of his dedication to his job, his ability to learn quickly and apply his knowledge, his ability to get along well with his peers and superiors, and his zeal and fondness of military life. He entered the service at seventeen, and by nineteen, he was a staff sergeant in charge of men twice his age. He got along really well with the commander of the band, Lt. Oscar W. Williams. "He was so fair that I couldn't believe that he was an officer in the military," Charlie said. "You had some real racist officers from the Deep South who were notorious for not being fair." Lieutenant Williams and Charlie had a good working relationship, and because they got along, Charlie was able to get along better with the other members of his unit and would often say, "It's not what you know, but who you know." Anything the guys wanted or needed, they felt they could go through Charlie because he had the commander's ear. One day Lieutenant Williams asked Charlie if he liked the army because most of the enlisted men seemed not to care for the army and wanted to get out. When Charlie enthusiastically responded yes, Lieutenant Williams asked Charlie if he ever considered becoming an officer and recommended him for Officers Candidate School (OCS).

"I think I advanced so quickly," Charlie reminisced, "because I just liked the army, and a lot of people must have liked me. The commander of the band was a young white lieutenant, and he liked me I guess because I was a good soldier. I say that unhesitatingly. I was a good soldier. I would do things like get involved and quickly learned how to play an instrument. I stayed around the base a lot when the other guys were out partying at the clubs. Once, when my instrument broke and it would have been quite a while before I could get it fixed, I went up to the orderly room and asked the first sergeant if he wanted me to do any typing or anything. I didn't want the band leader to think I was goldbricking or just hanging around the barracks doing nothing. Well, he did want me to do some typing, and after a while, he asked me if I'd like to go to company clerks school. Naturally I said yes and then the first sergeant was shipped home, and the company clerk moved up to his place as acting first sergeant, and I got moved up to company clerk. I was able to handle the job without going to school (i.e., typing, filing, company correspondence, payroll, etc.), but I went to the school anyway.

"I was very fortunate to meet an officer with a lot of clout. I was reading the camp newspaper and came across an article about the chief warrant officer in my company. He had been in the army since 1902, and the article told about his army life. Well, being quite interested, I continued reading and was surprised to see that he lived in Cambridge, Massachusetts. Well, that day when I was coming from chow I saw him, so I walked up, threw him a smart salute, and asked if I may have a few words with him. Being a nice old fellow, he returned the salute and replied, 'Certainly, son, what's on your mind?' I told him I read the article about him in the paper and noticed he was from Cambridge, and being a Cantabrigian myself I just thought I'd like to talk to him. He asked me my name, and when I told him he said, 'Why sure, son, I knew your family well!' He then asked me what church I went to. He knew just where it was. 'Right across from the Morse School, isn't it?' he asked. Well, during the conversation, I told him that I attended Cambridge High and Latin High School. This is how I found out who he was. He asked me if I knew his daughter Betty. Naturally, not being a ladies' man, I didn't know her, but then it dawned on me. Betty, of course I knew her, Betty Goodrum. Babe or Ookie went to school with her. Anyhow, I've heard the name mentioned around the house. His name was Goodrum. I'm sure that his influence got me in good with my superiors.

"I got along well with the guys and with my superiors. Lieutenant Williams said that I was a hell of a soldier and that he was going to recommend me for OCS. They made me take a test to see if I could qualify for OCS training. They saw my test results and the next thing I knew I was off to Fort Riley, Kansas for training to become an officer."

CHAPTER 3
Destined to Lead

What a difference there was between being an officer and being an enlisted man. Part of that difference was that you didn't have to take any crap; at least I didn't because I was military police. I was very young when I became an officer. I got commissioned in the military police from the very beginning so I never knew what it was like to be discriminated against.

—Charles Gittens

Charles Gittens was thrust into positions of leadership at a very young age. He was driving a truck and helping to support his family by age fourteen. After joining the army at seventeen, he was promoted to staff sergeant by the time he was nineteen years old and commissioned as an officer by the time he was twenty-one. The remarkable thing was he rose quickly through the ranks in a segregated army that at this time treated its black servicemen as second-class citizens, whose contribution to the war effort, in many cases, was relegated to support positions (e.g., digging latrines, handling supplies, driving trucks, etc.) or menial jobs (e.g., cooking, cleaning, housekeeping, personal servants for officers, etc.) and perceived as incapable of handling leadership roles. But Gittens was able to rise above the stereotypes and the obstacles and, once given the opportunity, demonstrated that not only was he a good leader but was an example of what African Americans could accomplish when given the opportunity.

What is leadership? Why are some placed into positions of leadership while others are not? Franklin D. Roosevelt, John F. Kennedy, and Martin Luther King Jr. were arguably some of the greatest leaders of twentieth century American history and brought America through some very tough times. They were beloved by the people, had the uncanny ability to communicate, to make people around them feel at ease, and they were not afraid to make very difficult decisions that were necessary to solve critical problems. Adolph Hitler, on the other hand, was a powerful and influential leader as well. He was able to motivate the masses to do horrible things and brought Germany from the debts of financial ruin to the brink of world power and domination. So one may ask, what is leadership, and more importantly, what is good leadership? Depending on how one views history or from which prism one is looking, the results of one's leadership style can determine if one is demonstrating good leadership or not. The truth of the matter is that anyone who has a follower is a leader. Some individuals become leaders without saying a word, that is, they lead by example. People either like their looks/image, or the way they carry themselves, or how they handle situations. Some are thrust into leadership positions by virtue of the rank or position they hold in an organization. These examples in history raise several questions that one may ask about the qualities that make a person a leader and, more importantly, why so many people felt Charles Gittens would make a good leader and put him in positions of leadership at such a young age.

The fact Charles Gittens became an outstanding leader shouldn't be hard to answer. After all, most of his life he had demonstrated that he possessed the characteristics that make a person a leader. He was extremely intelligent, articulate, and a good writer, which made him an effective communicator. Communicating one's ideas and thoughts is a crucial element of effective leadership. He was a quick learner and could easily translate abstract theories into concrete realities. He became an excellent marksman, for example, and when told his position in the military was going to be a musician, he mastered several instruments quickly. He had the uncanny ability to make people around him feel comfortable and at ease and was able to help them understand his point of view. He was a great storyteller and often injected humor into situations that might otherwise have been bleak. He was enthusiastic and passionate about his work and employed a "Puritan work ethic" (the emphasis on the necessity of hard work) with every task he attempted. He was a gifted problem solver and often relied on reason to govern his actions as opposed to his emotions. He was not afraid to try new things and always tried to find the positive in every situation. He was a doer. He was unafraid to roll up his sleeves and jump into a task with his men. According to Lois Terman, the granddaughter of Hyman Rudolph, he was a *mensch* (a Yiddish word meaning a person of great integrity). He grew up color-blind, meaning that he never used race or nationality to measure one's ability or character, and he refused to use color as a reason for accomplishing or failing a task. He was arrogant enough to believe he would and should be treated like everyone else and should be given the opportunity to succeed. He was also willing to accept the fact that changing other people's attitude was a process that sometimes took time and innovative strategies. He was a good judge of determining what battles he could fight and win and which ones should lay dormant until he was in a position of strength. He was persistent and would not stop until he achieved his goal. He was also lucky! Some say luck is when opportunity and ability collide, but he was fortunate enough to join the army at a time when racial attitudes were beginning to change. He was fortunate to come into contact with people in positions of power who were willing to reward his hard work and persistence with advancement in rank. The fact that he was extremely intelligent and articulate may also have had an impact on the views of some of the Southern white officers who may have had a certain perception about the ability of black people and thus made them feel he was extraordinary. When given a task that may have seemed too difficult for a black officer to handle, he would always accomplish the task successfully, which led to more responsibilities and advancements.

Another long boat ride and an equally long train ride brought Charlie to Fort Riley, Kansas, where his journey into formal training as a military officer began. The second he stepped off the train into the heat and into the fort, his rigorous training began. It was highly intense, with officers screaming, candidates saluting, and a tough physical training program that shaped your body into a chiseled piece of stone, difficult academic work that sharpened your intellect, reasoning skills, and decision making ability, and the constant psychological hazing all designed to weed out the weak and prepare the survivors to be the best. The best were the few who made it because the dropout rate was extremely high. He also stepped out of the arena of racial segregation and back into an integrated environment.

"When I went to Fort Riley, Kansas, it was a hard chore, but a pleasant chore, Candidate Gittens recalled. "Out of a class of forty or fifty people, there might have been three or four of us black candidates who made it all the way through. There was a major dropout percentage, especially among blacks, but there was a major dropout anyhow whether you were black or white. Let's say there were one hundred candidates, about 48 percent fail to graduate. That's what we were called, candidates. 'Candidate Gittens, drop and give me twenty [push-ups that is]!' You didn't want to get called out like that too many times, which they considered punishment or extra physical stuff. When you left there, you felt like you had a new body, you were remade, and you knew you weren't the same person. The physical stuff was real tough. You had to march every day. You marched every place. In addition to that, you had your academic subjects; and if you didn't do well, you couldn't graduate from there. I finished pretty high in my class without having gone to college or even finishing high school. I didn't graduate from high school because I dropped out of Cambridge High and Latin to join the army. I took a little heat from the guys when I told them I went to Cambridge High and Latin, but I would give it back to them by saying, 'What, are you stupid or something?' Latin was required at my high school. Cambridge High and Latin did not sound like a public school, but it was; and the courses were tough, including Latin. I think most of the students who went there was proud of it. When people would ask where you went to school, we would respond proudly, 'Oh, I went to Cambridge High and Latin.'"

The US Army's Officer Candidate School (OCS) was first proposed in 1938, as the army began expanding in anticipation of WWII. It was developed to provide training to become commissioned officers (graduates received commissions as a second lieutenant) in the US Army. Officer candidates were drawn from enlisted members of the army who were recommended, warrant officers (a person who is designated an officer by warrant because of their technical expertise or because they are a specialist in a particular field), interservice transfers, or civilian college graduates who participated in an Army ROTC (Reserved Officer Training Corps) program. During WWII, the army's policy of racial segregation continued among enlisted members. Army training policy, however, provided that blacks and whites would train together in officer candidate schools (beginning in 1942). OCS was the army's first formal experiment with integration. Black and white candidates lived separately, but all of the candidates trained together. Despite this integrated training, in most instances, the graduates would go on to join racially segregated units.[10]

The movement to end segregation and discrimination in the armed forces was waged in the black press and spearheaded by A. Phillip Randolph, who was head of the powerful Brotherhood of Sleeping Car Porters Union. In July 1941, he proposed a nonviolent March on Washington, which would include over one hundred thousand black labors and would demand that Pres. Franklin Roosevelt sign an executive order that would ban discrimination in war industries and apprenticeship programs. The president opposed the march, which would bring embarrassing light to the fact that America was fighting for freedom and democracy abroad, but not practicing it at home, and tried to get Randolph to call off the march. When Randolph refused, President Roosevelt issued Executive Order 8802 (July 25, 1941), which banned discrimination in war industries and apprenticeship programs.[11] Randolph called off the march, but the order did little to end discrimination. On March 22, 1948, Randolph, who had now helped to create an organization called the Committee Against Jim Crow in Military Service and Training, and other concerned citizens met with Pres. Harry Truman and requested his support for antisegregation amendments to end segregation in the armed services. Nothing was done, and so in June 1948, Randolph formed the League for Non-Violent Civil Disobedience Against Military Segregation. He threatened to urge blacks to resist induction by civil disobedience unless segregation and discrimination in the armed forces was banned. Responding to Randolph's political strength, President Truman issued Executive Order 9981 in July, barring segregation in the armed services.[12] Even though President Truman passed Executive Order 9981, the military was slow in carrying out the mandate. In fact, the day after President Truman passed the order, Army Chief of Staff General Omar N. Bradley stated that "desegregation will come to the Army only when it becomes a fact in the rest of American society."[13] The desegregation of the military was not completed for several years, and all-black well into the Korean War. All-black units weren't disbanded

n to getting the best leadership training the military had to offer, Candida Gittens was also thrown into a different social bracket that motivated him to seek education at a higher level. He was the only black candidate who had not gone to college. Because he was a high school dropout, to be eligible for OCS, Candidate Gittens had to take courses and pass the United States Armed Forces Institute test of General Educational Development (GED). He passed the GED test with flying colors while he was stationed in Yokohama. All of the other black candidates were college graduates who had entered college ROTC programs. ROTC programs offered college scholarships, which helped many college graduates meet their financial obligations. This was an inducement the military provided to get citizens to join the service. Candidate Gittens formed a very tight bond with the other black candidates who survived the grueling six-month program. It was here where he listened to stories about college life and college experiences that sparked a flame in him. Even though he lived down the street from Harvard and MIT when growing up, going to college was never seriously discussed because most of the people in the neighborhood did not have the money to attend those universities. But he now knew he had to go to college and that a college education was necessary if he planned to have a brighter future.

Candidate Gittens made it through the tough program and, upon graduation, was commissioned as a second lieutenant. "There weren't many of us blacks who made it through, and we used to brag that we were the best of the best," Gittens said. "When I got my commission, I really felt like I had died and gone to heaven. I don't remember when they pinned those wings on me to make me an angel, but they did it!"

The experience at Fort Riley exposed Lieutenant Gittens to many new things, reinforced some things he already knew, and taught him a lot of lessons that strengthened his character, sharpened his intellectual skills, and made him realize that there was no obstacle he could not overcome. Like a piece of coal that had withstood immense pressure and was transformed into a diamond, Lieutenant Gittens had withstood the intense heat and come out as sharp as a newly cut diamond. The army had given him their best shot, and he learned that not only could he take it but he could excel where so many others had failed. He trained with white soldiers and black soldiers on an equal playing field and realized that he was better than most and equal to others. He realized that in a true meritocracy, where opportunity is afforded to everyone and you are judged on your performance, his skills and ability could help him rise to a level beyond his imagination. His character and self-esteem had already been developed as a result of his strong family upbringing and his experience growing up in Cambridge, but he realized that challenging educational training and preparedness would be necessary for him to accept the position as a leader in the military and to be able to carry out his responsibilities at the highest level. He realized that the keys to overcoming any obstacle, no matter how difficult, were hard work, persistence, and education.

Lieutenant Gittens (far right) leads his troops

Lieutenant Gittens's first assignment as an officer was with the military police unit at Fort Bragg, North Carolina. He knew he was returning to a segregated situation, and this time it would be in the Deep South, but he was ready for the challenge. Before going to Fort Bragg, however, he was sent to Camp Gordon, Georgia, where he received special training in military police procedures. He took a course that gave him training in the basic duties of a military police officer, such as general investigation, administration, managing traffic problems, operating confinement facilities, and preparation and presentation of evidence. He also received training with the Criminal Investigative Division (CID). Members of CID got respect from other military police officers. The CID officers were plainclothes officers and didn't have to wear the uniform.

While at Camp Gordon, a twist of fate would send him on a different path and ultimately lead him to the Secret Service. He came into contact with agents from the Federal Bureau of Narcotics (FBN) while training for his position with the military police. The Bureau of Narcotics also used Camp Gordon for training their agents. "We were all there together, narcotics agents and military police," Lieutenant Gittens recalled. "They used to tease me about wearing that uniform and being tied down to the military, and they often asked me about joining them. I didn't initially think about being a narcotics agent, but I began to give it some thought."

In February 1950, Lieutenant Gittens got his first assignment with the military police at Fort Bragg. This assignment would prove to be a challenge for him by virtue of the fact he would be confronted with racial attitudes about the ability and social status of black Americans that were ingrained in custom and law in the South.

There was a very rigid caste system that implied that regardless of how intelligent or resourceful a black person was, he still could not rise above the level of his white counterparts in society. Many blacks owned land and prospered economically in the South, but that was allowed as long as they remained in separate black communities and as long as blacks understood that their place in American society was subservient to white Americans. These customs were reinforced by segregation laws, as well as terrorism practiced by groups like the Ku Klux Klan. Following WWI and WWII, black Americans had become more vocal about this inconsistency in a *democratic society*. Black soldiers had fought and died in two world wars to make the world "safe for democracy" and yet when they returned home could not enjoy the fruits of their sacrifice because of racial bigotry and discrimination that seemed to be supported by their own government. The black press led the charge of pointing out these inconsistencies and gave voice to political and social leaders who were adamant about making changes in the government. Black lawyers, political and religious leaders began speaking out and demanding that the government put an end to segregation and the racial practices that made blacks second-class citizens. Their actions spawned the modern civil rights movement.

Lieutenant Gittens realized that not many men of color were given the opportunity to become officers in the military, and he carried the weight of a nation on his shoulders. His success or failure would be a measuring stick by which other officers of color would be measured. Against this backdrop, he dove into his assignments with his normal zeal and demonstrated to his superiors that he was more than capable of handling any task given to him. His first assignment was being second in command of the prison jail. Because of the segregation that existed, there were two separate jails, one for the white prisoners and one for the black prisoners. He was selected to run the black prison, and a white officer ran the white prison. The prisoners, most of whom were barren of any formal education, were given hard labor while they were incarcerated. It was tough working in that hot North Carolina sun.

Another assignment included working with the local sheriff and state police with traffic control. There was a major state road that went through Fort Bragg that was patrolled by the state police, the sheriff's department, and the military police. Lieutenant Gittens was given the responsibility of coordinating that joint effort. Initially the alliance was awkward because not only was he black but he was also from the North, a "Yankee who talked funny!" Remarkably, Lieutenant Gittens's gregarious demeanor and patience, along with the support of the commanding officer, helped him to develop a good working relationship with the local and state police, a relationship that would later pay dividends when he became a Secret Service agent.

Upon seeing the miraculous success Lieutenant Gittens was able to cultivate with the local police force, in spite of the racial difference, the commanding officers gave him a more influential assignment, which in turn gave Lieutenant Gittens more credibility with the local community. This time he was being assigned as the game warden for Fort Bragg. The provost marshal (Col. Joseph C. Grubb) for the military police gave Lieutenant Gittens this assignment. Fort Bragg contained a lot of land where the townspeople would come to hunt and fish. Everyone had to have a license, and it was the responsibility of the game warden to issue those licenses. As a child in Cambridge, Lieutenant Gittens used to love fishing on the Charles River and developed a passion for hunting and fishing, and now he was in charge of the hunting and fishing reserve at Fort Bragg.

"The game warden position was very significant down there, and it was a great assignment for me," Lieutenant Gittens exclaimed. "Here you had a black man in the midst of all of this segregation in charge and running things. It was a great job because the local people had to get their hunting license from me! The game warden was a position that was greatly respected down there. The game warden got respect because if you didn't get along with the warden or you had some problems, you could never get your hunting license. This gave me the opportunity to come into contact with the local people, and they knew who I was. I loved it!"

Lieutenant Gittens was a young officer but had proven he was a competent and hardworking officer. He was frequently called on to conduct pretrial investigations, line-of-duty investigations, and criminal investigations which necessitated the collection, evaluation, preparation, and presentation of evidence, both material and oral in military courts. As a result, the sitting commanding officer put him in charge of military police unit (3420th ASU) detachment 2, which for a new young officer was something very special. Detachment 2 was the code word for the racial makeup of the troops. Detachment 1, which was commanded by Capt. Raymond Carpenter, was the all-white unit, and Detachment 2 was the all-black unit. Even though President Truman had desegregated the military in 1948, the reality was segregation was alive and well and practiced out in the open, especially in the South. Captain Carpenter was "a real honest-to-goodness white Southerner," but for some reason he took a liking to Lieutenant Gittens. When the powers in control of Fort Bragg finally adhered to President Truman's order to desegregate, Lieutenant Gittens became the executive officer of the entire Fort Bragg military police unit. Being executive officer meant he was now the second in command of the entire military police unit, both black and white together.

"I don't know why the sitting commanding officer made me the executive officer on the base," Lieutenant Gittens said. "Maybe it was so the white soldiers wouldn't give me any flack, but I worked extra hard. Maybe it was because I could tell a good story or that I liked to hunt and fish, or that I just worked hard; but whatever the reason, his decision gave me a little more clout and helped me a great deal. I got along well with my commanding officers and the enlisted men as well. I became second in command of that whole detachment that covered all of Fort Bragg. It was quite an experience because during those days, America was not like what young people know America to be now. It was really segregated, and we all had to work together, and that was quite a learning experience. I got through it fine, and everything worked out well. The military police was great background for me. I never had a bad day in the time I was there."

Life in North Carolina was new and different to Lieutenant Gittens, and the rush of new experiences just kept coming. There was a black teacher's college called Fayetteville State Teachers College near Fort Bragg, and Lieutenant Gittens started taking classes there. His experience meeting black college graduates while in OCS had created a desire in him to continue his education. He knew education was a key component in him staying qualified to lead and would also open future doors for him. College life would also introduce him to a new group of people with which to socialize. His military experience had been positive so far, and he enjoyed going to school, so he decided that a career in the military was what he wanted and applied to West Point Military Academy. He began going to social functions at the USO in Fayetteville to meet people, and then she walked in . . .

CHAPTER 4
And Then She Walked In

He and my mother were called the star couple because my mother was pretty and he was handsome. My father wanted to stay in the military. He got accepted at West Point. I saw the acceptance letter, but he couldn't go to West Point if he was married. He decided to marry my mother anyway and gave up his commission. He could have been another Collin Powell, but he chose love instead.

—Sharon Gittens Quick

Lieutenant Gittens walked through the front door, and the joint was jumping. The music of Duke Ellington and Lionel Hampton was serenading the room, and the ladies were lined up on the wall just waiting for a young man to ask them to dance. The NCCS (National Catholic Community Service) Club, which used to be the all-black USO (United Services Organization) club until the USO was disbanded, was located in downtown Fayetteville, North Carolina. The soldiers and townspeople continued to refer to it as the USO Club. It was created so soldiers could relax, listen to some good music, meet some lovely young ladies, who were well chaperoned of course, and engage in conversation. It seemed as if all of the pretty colored girls in Fayetteville were gathered together and herded into the community center for these occasions. Most of the servicemen were enlisted men or NCOs (noncommissioned officers), so when Lieutenant Gittens walked in, he stood out from the rest. He was tall, handsome, and his uniform was immaculately pressed and clean. As he strutted across the dance floor, he caught the eye of many young ladies, but one particular young lady caught his eye, and this would turn out to be a very special Valentine's Day. Her name was Ruthe Loraine Hamme.

Ruthe was not just one of the ordinary young ladies brought in to dance with the servicemen. She was stunningly beautiful with caramel brown skin, a small waist, a shapely body, pretty hair, and piercing eyes. She was a college graduate working as the secretary and assistant director of the NCCS Club to make sure that the black servicemen were entertained and had a home away from home. In addition to her secretarial duties for the NCCS Club, her responsibilities included going to black businesses and fraternal organizations in order to find sponsorship and serving as hostess for the social gatherings. But there was something more regal in the way she sat, the way she spoke, the way she smiled, and the way she carried herself. She was no ordinary Southern girl. She was a member of a very elite black family that owned land, ran businesses, and held power and influence. When they met and she flashed a smile at him, Lieutenant Gittens knew he was hooked and he had to have her.

"I was a young black military police officer, and one day I met this very attractive young black woman at the USO Club," Lieutenant Gittens recalled. "She introduced me to her boss, who was the director of the USO Club. Her name was Mrs. Watkins. Mrs. Watkins used to say, 'Now I think it would be nice for you and Ruthe to get together. She is a lovely, lovely young lady.' From that point on, I continued to go to the USO Club. I guess I made an impression on Ruthe because pretty soon she started inviting me to her home, which was in a little small town called Oxford, North Carolina. That is where I met and got accepted by her family. Ruthe was their star, everybody loved her. It seemed as if she's related to just about everybody in Oxford; and every one of her friends and relatives were teachers, doctors, dentists, lawyers, politicians, and landowners. Oxford itself was one of those typical little college towns, and it is beautiful.

Once Ruthe opened the door for me, there were a lot of parties, and I got a chance to meet the local people. I began meeting a lot of other black officers. Most of them were from college ROTC programs. I was the only officer who rose up through the ranks and was not a part of an ROTC program, so I was different. The fact that I was a northerner and talked differently also made me stand out, which worked to my advantage. The other black officers tried desperately to get Ruthe's attention, and she loved all of the attention she was getting. Ultimately our friendship turned into a courtship, which turned into a marriage proposal, which turned into a marriage."

The Hamme family was considered to be very influential members of the black elite in Oxford and was well-known in the community. Ruthe's grandparents were Ottawai and Kizziah "Kizzie" Hamme. Ottawai was born on November 12, 1862, in the Township of Granville County, Oxford, North Carolina. Both of his parents (Nathan and Lucy) were slaves. Ottawai's mother was given ten acres of land at the time of the Emancipation Proclamation. She willed this land to Ottawai. Kizzie was born in Vance County, Henderson, North Carolina, on January 2, 1865. Both of her parents (William and Catherine) were also slaves. Ottawai and Kizzie married and had seventeen children, eleven of whom lived very long and prosperous lives. Of the eleven children, seven of them earned bachelor's degrees and six earned master's degrees. Together Ottawai and Kizzie were able to purchase approximately 260 acres of land in Oxford and passed this land down to their offspring, who still owns the land to this very day.

"I always knew that we had land, and I always knew that we came up through slavery," Charlie's daughter Sharon reminisced while talking about her family's history. "We always knew that the white people who owned us lived right down the road. Their last name is Hamme also, and we have relatives who are still buried on their land. We had some of the same names, which would often cause some confusion. We had a Richard Hamme, and they had a Richard Hamme. They had an Annie, and we had an Annie. Sometimes the mail would get mixed up, so they were referred to as the white Hammes, and we were the black Hammes. The whispered talk in the town was that we were all the same Hammes because the rumor was that Ottawai's mother Lucy was given her freedom and that ten acres of land because she was the offspring of the slave master. So the color line in Oxford was sometimes a very thin line."

The offspring of Ottawai and Kizzie used those 260 acres of land to establish a landed aristocracy that was independent and financially stable. They used education to further improve their lot in life. They established a standard of living that mandated that their children, regardless of the cost, received a college education to obtain jobs and positions in society that would enable them to live comfortably. After completing their degrees, many of the offspring became educators, school administrators, married college professors, created their own businesses, or earned a decent living off of the land they owned. Most of the male children (Richard, Ashton, Robert, and Cornell) except Thomas Hamme Sr., who became the superintendent of the Colored Orphanage in Oxford, (note – in 1927 the Colored Orphanage Asylum of North Carolina was renamed the Colored Orphanage of North Carolina) stayed on the farm and raised crops and children while the women (Mary, Catherine, Emma, Ollie, Minnie, and Annie Willa) went to college and became teachers. Richard left the farm to become a Pullman porter. During the heyday of railroad travel, the Pullman porters were the workers aboard the trains. They provided service to and attended to the needs of the passengers. In the beginning, the Pullman Company only hired African American men for the job as porters.[14] Richard became very active in the union and was a leader in the AFL-CIO.

Ruthe's parents (Ashton and Arcy) divorced when Ruthe was very young. Ruthe was the only child of this union. In order to earn a better living, Arcy left Oxford and went to New York City to find work when Ruthe was only five years old. Arcy decided to go to New York because she felt she could make more money. She would say, "Why stay down here and get seven dollars a week when I can get ten dollars a day in New York?" She never came back. Ashton continued to farm his land until he decided to seek his fortune in the Big Apple as well. He later remarried to Irene Newman. Ruthe lived on the farm, but when school was in session, she decided to

THE HAMME FAMILY TREE

Ottowai Richard Hamme - Kizziah "Kizzi" Mills
1862–1940   1865–1943

1. Mary Elizabeth Hamme – Married to Claude Parham
   Children: Irene, Julia, Claudia Esther

2. Thomas Arthur Hamme – Married to Lillian Quarles
   Children: Thomas Jr., Gwendolyn

3. Catherine Isabelle Hamme – Married to Andrew McGhee
   Children: Andrew Jr.

4. Robert Marshall Hamme – Married to Martha Cousins
   Children: James Arthur, Thelma

5. Richard Sylvester Hamme – First marriage: Nan Kee
   Second marriage: Jeanette

6. Emma Alice Hamme – Married to Robert Rice
   Children: Robert Jr., Wilda

7. Ashton Alexander Hamme – First marriage: Arcy Gregory
   Second marriage: Irene
   Child: Ruthe Loraine –

8. Ollie Evergreen Hamme – Married to Samuel Johnson
   Child: Ollie Hawley (adopted)

9. Minnie Marie Hamme – Married to Eddie Tyler
   Children: Wilhelmina, Eddie Jr., Marilyn, Joan

10. Annie Willa Hamme – Married to Charles Gregory
11. Oscar Cornell Hamme – Married to Lucy Davis
    Children: Oscar Cornell Jr., Ottowai Richard III, Ashton Theodore,
    Carolyn Veronica, Larry Ellis, Geraldine Lejeune

Children of Ottowai and Kizzi Who Died Young

12. Hessie Hamme
13. Ottowai Hamme Jr.
14. Nathan Hamme
15. Infant died after childbirth
16. Infant died after childbirth
17. Infant died after childbirth

move in with her Aunt Ollie Johnson, who was a master teacher and pillar of the community. Ollie's husband passed away, and they never had any children, so she would help raise the children of her extended family. She owned a house at the edge of town that became the focal point for family gatherings, social events, and a haven for the younger members of the family. When Charlie got older and retired, he would often reminisce about Aunt Ollie's house and would state that he would like to go back down there and live out the rest of his life fishing in the pond in her backyard.

"Aunt Ollie's house was the hangout," said Thomas Hamme Jr., who was one of Ruthe's many cousins and who worked on Ruthe's father's farm during the summer months. "That was the damnedest house you ever saw. It was a converted GI barrack. They dismantled them back then and sold them to people. People would reconstruct the barracks into conventional homes. They were long houses, but not very deep. The back of the house was a kitchen. Next to the kitchen was a bedroom. Next to the bedroom was a bathroom. Next to the bathroom was a set of stairs leading up to the next level. I think there was another room probably a general room with a stove in it. Then there was the dining room, and that was used only for special occasions. All of the kids that she took in slept upstairs while she slept in the bedroom next to the kitchen.

Aunt Ollie created an atmosphere that was very conducive for young people. You could always go to Ollie's house and talk as opposed to other family members who weren't as patient with young people. She created an atmosphere where you knew you could have some fun and you could be open. That was Ollie. She didn't have any children, so she adopted Ruthe. In those days, you didn't have to go down and sign up with social services and ask to adopt a kid. You just took them in. Ollie always kept kids in her house; it made her feel safe, and it made up for the kids that she didn't have. She bought them food and clothes and helped borrow money so they could go on to college. She was something else, she was an icon!"

Ruthe was born on May 30, 1929. She was twenty years old when she met Charlie on Valentine's Day in 1950; he was twenty-one years old. She attended high school at the Mary Potter Academy in Oxford and then went on to North Carolina College for Negroes in Durham, which later was renamed North Carolina College and finally North Carolina Central University, where she earned her bachelor of arts degree. She was very intelligent, and Aunt Ollie made sure that Ruthe came home with good grades at every level she attempted. She was very petite and soft-spoken but had lots of male suitors. After getting her degree, she found a job working as a secretary for the Dean of Students at North Carolina College (Dr. William Brown), which at that time was a very prestigious job. She returned to North Carolina College to get her master of arts degree in business education in 1960.

Meeting Ruthe and coming to Oxford was a life-changing experience for Charlie. Life in Oxford, in the heart of the segregated South, was totally different from his experience growing up in Cambridge. Being introduced to the Hamme family and especially to Aunt Ollie Johnson was an epiphany. He used to attend parties, socialize, and hang out with a lot of people at Aunt Ollie's house. They used to sit in the kitchen and play cards or just talk. He often talked about those Friday- and Saturday-night conversations while sitting in Aunt Ollie's kitchen and how they had such an impact on him. He would often say it was a turning point in his life coming to Oxford and seeing all of those people who were educated.

"Aunt Ollie's house was the party house," Charlie exclaimed. "It was a real country home about a mile out of Oxford. It was a private home, and we kind of turned it into a little bit of a farm. Her husband was Uncle Sam [Samuel Johnson], would you believe that? He didn't live too long, and she never remarried. They were young when they got married. She was a widow for a good number of years. We used to tease her and say, 'We've got to get you a boyfriend!' I used to love to fish, so Aunt Ollie had a fishpond built on her property. It wasn't a little tiny pond either; it was pretty big, maybe an acre or something like that. So when I wanted to go fishing, I didn't have to go far.

Cousins would come over, and we would have a little drink and that kind of stuff. That was the place, the hangout spot. Three or four of the cousins were officers in the military. So they weren't the ordinary black Southern family. They had gone into an ROTC program while in college. The thing that hit me the most, about being with Aunt Ollie and hanging out at her house was before I got there I had never run into so many black officers. All of whom had gone to college and were sold on the idea that this could start a new life and a new career. There were two of them who were brothers and the sons of the undertaker in town. In the South, the black undertaker was a big man in town. He always had a job and became wealthy burying all of those people. Hanging out with those guys got me started in the social circle because they were partying young men.

"Aunt Ollie's house was also the study house. She was a teacher. I don't care what major you were, we all went to Aunt Ollie as the person to go to if you wanted to know about anything. Whether it was horseshit or physics, we went to Aunt Ollie. She talked our language. She was the youngest of all the aunts, and that made a difference too. The respect we showed the other aunts and uncles was a different kind of respect. That was respect for an adult. But for Aunt Ollie, it was a fun respect. We would kid around with her all of the time. She was the one that kept us going to school and made sure we got into good schools and all of that kind of stuff. There was no foolishness about going to school. That was not a toy thing. It was the thing that got you ready for life and you had to do well in school.

When I came to Oxford, Aunt Ollie was teaching, Aunt Catherine was teaching, and Aunt Anna-Willa was teaching. Everybody I would meet while we were playing cards had all been to college. I started meeting her cousins Tom, Randolph, Lee, and everybody had been to college. I almost got a complex because all of those folks had been to college and I hadn't. I said to myself that if I'm going to marry this lady, I've got to get some education!"

After a six-month whirlwind romance and courtship, Charlie and Ruthe got married. The ceremony took place on August 6, 1950, in the living room of Aunt Ollie's house. There was a lot of pressure from the members of Ruthe's family for him to get a college degree because that was the standard for members of the family of which he was now a part. In 1951, while still in the military, he took a course that was conducted by the FBI at the law enforcement officers training school in Fayetteville. He also went back to Camp Gordon, Georgia, in the spring of 1952 where he completed a criminal investigation course for officers. He enjoyed going to school and took courses at Fayetteville State Teachers College. Earlier he had applied and got accepted to West Point but did not go because West Point didn't accept candidates who were married. So he decided to leave the army and use the money from the GI Bill to enroll in North Carolina College, where Ruthe had returned to work on her master's degree. The GI Bill (also known as the Servicemen's Readjustment Act of 1944) was a law that provided college or vocational education for returning WWII veterans as well as one year unemployment compensation. It also provided many different types of loans for returning veterans to buy homes and start businesses.[15] He received an honorable discharge from the army in September 1952.

"I took some courses at Fayetteville State then I met Ruthe, who had gone to North Carolina College, which was a more prestigious university and not just limited to teaching," Charlie said. "So I transferred there. That was the only school for me to go to because Ruthe was there. I decided to go to college because everybody around there was college graduates, and there was a little pressure for me to go. In fact there was a lot of pressure for me to go. I didn't know anybody who went to college in Cambridge, the North, but in the South, all of my friends were college graduates. Every single one of them! And all of the ladies were members of a sorority. I also enjoyed going to school. I finished college in only three years and with high honors. I liked it there. I considered North Carolina College my school, and I could not have been at a better place. Receiving high honors and completing a four-year program in only three years was a major accomplishment especially for someone who dropped out of high school. It was easy for me, especially having come from Cambridge High and Latin where I learned to speak Spanish, French, and Latin."

Charlie and Ruthe had their second child, Sharon, in March of 1953; their first child was premature and died very shortly after birth in October of 1950. He was a college student with a family, but without a steady job. Never the one to be afraid of hard work or duck his responsibilities, he took on several part-time jobs to make ends meet. During the summer of 1953, he worked as a laborer at the American Tobacco Supplier, Inc. During the school year, he worked the night shift at Duke Hospital and Lincoln Hospital as an orderly. During his final year at North Carolina

College, he volunteered as the editor of the school newspaper, *The Campus Echo*, which the school turned into a paid position to help him out. On the weekends, he worked as a waiter at the Saddle Club Restaurant and as a cab driver in the evenings. Ruthe continued to work as a secretary at Lincoln Hospital to help support their growing family. He graduated magna cum laude on May 31, 1955, with a bachelor of arts degree in Spanish and English.

Now that Charlie was out of the army and stripped of his protective officer's uniform, he had to deal with the reality of being a regular black man in the South. Life in the South for a black citizen was often very challenging with the Jim Crow Laws (segregation) and antebellum attitudes. Charlie, true to his nature, however, found the positive in every situation, thrived on the adversity, and was able to overcome the racial barriers to elevate himself and his family. "Everybody else thinks I am crazy, but I loved the South!" Charlie exclaimed. "I got along great down there. There was lots of sun, it was a beautiful place, and it had pretty ladies. This is where I met the future Mrs. Gittens, so I fell in love with North Carolina, literally."

Spending time in Oxford more than likely played a major role in his attitude about the South, for Oxford was like, to coin a phrase from a Charles Dickens novel, a tale of two cities . . . one black and one white.

Ruthe Hamme

The wedding of Lieutenant
Gittens and Ruthe Hamme

CHAPTER 5
Oxford—An Oasis in the South

As far as I know at that time it was fifty-fifty black-white or close to it. The relationship between blacks and whites in Oxford was just like anywhere in the South. Both groups gingerly waltzed around each other and tried to avoid confrontation. I think that was important, not to have controversy on both sides. I don't know much about the white community because we were close but very separate. I know we used to get used schoolbooks. You could see the names of the white kids that had them before. The white kids got the new books, and we got the hand-me-downs.
—Thomas Hamme Jr.

If Charlie Gittens were alive today, one would have to ask him how he could actually say he loved the South. More so, one would have to wonder how he became the first black agent for the United States Secret Service and assigned to the Charlotte office located in the South. Think about it. From the time blacks were enslaved and brought to this country—through the systematic denial of civil and human rights following the Reconstruction era, the turbulent days of terrorism and lynching by state- and county-supported terrorist groups at the turn of the century, the development of Jim Crow laws designed to denigrate, separate, and segregate, and the turbulent, though rewarding, times brought on by the twentieth century civil rights movement—life in the South for black Americans had been a trying experience at best. But Charlie had a special way of seeing things. Maybe it was those superhuman visors he wore as Captain Marvel, the comic book hero, he personified as a child in Cambridge. Maybe it was his ability to look above the misery, find the positives in every situation so he could find strategies to defeat the evil. Maybe he just decided to accept things as they were until he could find ways to change them. Or maybe he had the experience of witnessing a community where people rose above the social and economic barriers and went on to lead professional and productive lives. Such a place existed in a small town in Oxford, North Carolina.

To Charlie there was not that much difference between Cambridge, Massachusetts, where he was born and raised and Oxford, North Carolina, where his wife was born and raised and her family adopted him. According to Charlie, "both were clearly America's representation of small-town USA." Cambridge was a small town in the North, and Oxford was a tiny town in the South. Both were very unique in their own way, and both produced citizens who were active in their community. Both had tight-knit communities where everybody knew everybody else and families looked out for one another. Some of the minor differences were that most of the people in Oxford were born and raised there, whereas in Cambridge many of the residents came from somewhere else. In the South, they were productive on the land, and in the North they were productive in factories. In both areas you had extreme poverty, and the younger generation tried to get an education to overcome that situation. In Cambridge, that meant going to and completing high school, but in Oxford that meant going to college. The major difference, however, was that in Cambridge, blacks and whites lived together in harmony whereas in Oxford there was harmony in segregation.

Oxford is a city in Granville County, North Carolina. Since most of the land in the northern half of North Carolina was part of the proprietary domain of Lord John Carteret (by title known as the Earl of Granville), the county was named Granville in his honor. The town's history dates to 1761, when local legislator Samuel Benton built a plantation home and called it Oxford. By 1860, Granville County plantations and farms had some of the state's best agriculturists, consistently growing large crops of tobacco with the help of a large slave population. Oxford had become a sophisticated town and was famous as a seat of learning by the creation of several academies and colleges. Although Granville was one of five counties with as many as ten thousand slaves, there was also a sizeable community of free blacks claiming dozens of craftsmen, especially masons who helped build the grand homes of the more affluent families.[16]

Charlie was enamored with what he found when Ruthe took him to Oxford. "Their life down there was farming and going to school," he recollected. "It was a small Southern tobacco-growing town. That's what they did there. That's where I learned a lot about tobacco and growing other things like corn and other food products. One of Ruthe's uncles had a vegetable stand where he used to sell his products on the side of the road. He used to brag that he had the best tasting watermelon in town. He had a deep Southern accent, and he used to shout, 'WATERMELON, red to the rind, look so good and taste so fine,' and it sure was!

"You had two classes of black people: the educated people who were not only educated but owned their own businesses and the working class, the farmers. I often wondered how they ever got to be like that. My daughter Sharon had a cousin who earned two PhD's and had two other cousins with PhD's. I used to love to talk about it when I came back home to Cambridge. I'd say, 'You Negroes up here are always talking about college! You don't know what college is. What you need to do is to go down to Oxford, North Carolina, and see what real college people do. None of us, I hate to say it this way, but northern blacks weren't serious about college like blacks in the South. They went to college with a purpose. They went to do well, and they did well. I didn't know any elders in that tiny little town that didn't go, and they made their children go too!

"The neighborhood was a close-knit, all-black community. The preacher lived there, the teachers lived there, and the undertaker lived there. The undertaker was like one of the rich ones. They were farm, churchgoing people. A lot of the kids worked on the family-owned farms during the summer. Their farms were not huge, major producing farms. They grew the tobacco and cotton and picked apples and pears. It was a great life."

As angelic as Oxford may have looked to Charlie, however, it had a dark side. The dark side that was prevalent throughout the South reared its ugly head in the form of racial bigotry, segregation, and racial discrimination.

"When we would visit relatives, we used to ride the train called the Silver Bullet out of New York City," Sharon recalled, when reflecting on her childhood trips to Oxford during the 1960s after her father was transferred to the New York office. "As we got close to Baltimore, we had to eat because when we got close to Richmond we were not allowed in the dining car where the china and linen was located. They still had Pullman porters at this time. My mother made sure we ate in Baltimore so we wouldn't be asked to move out of the car when we got to Richmond. When we got to the stop in Henderson, North Carolina, the racism was very blatant. They had signs saying Colored and White. On the black side of the station, the door was broken, they had floorboards, and the seats were old. The white people had real doors with shiny doorknobs. Their section was closed off to us. You could look out of the window and see the white people going to their side. Our side was run-down and dirty, and that was how it was back then.

"Sometimes we would get in our car and drive to Oxford. The trip would take ten hours. We were told to call our relatives when we got out of New York, when we got to Philadelphia, when we got to Baltimore, and then when we crossed into Virginia. We would always pack three or four shoe box lunches which included fried chicken, hard-boiled eggs, pieces of fruit, and white bread. We would freeze ice water in pickle jars so that when it melted we would have water to drink. We did this because once you got into the Southern regions, you couldn't stop anywhere. We even had a slop jar that we used as a toilet. We had a couple of spreads and pillows because we really didn't want to stop. We did not want to deal with the humiliation that blacks had to suffer being denied access to places to eat or even using restroom facilities.

"I remember once when we were driving South and we were passing into Richmond near Petersburg and were coming toward a small town when my father hit a dog and we were stopped by a state trooper. I remember the panic and the fear. It was raining, which could have added to the poor visibility causing my father to hit the dog. I remember my mom telling me to just sit and don't say anything. At first my mother told me to get my book out and then she said no get your doll out. She told me to put the book under the seat. My father tried to calm her down and said it was going to be okay. The state trooper came over to our car, and my mother touched my father's arm and told him not to use his credentials (the Secret Service credentials) but to use his driver's license ID. I remember being really afraid because we had probably killed a white person's dog and could have been trouble for us. The issue, however, was about the speed we were going. My father had to get out of the car, and my mother made me get close to her. She just had to touch me I guess. When the whole incident was over, we just got a fine for speeding, but the fear remains with me to this day.

"My reaction to white people was probably different from my father's reaction because I was born in the South. For me, I had one great grandmother on my mother's side, which was one generation removed from slavery (Lucy Taylor Gregory, born in 1880). They lived on a working farm in Henderson County and had to live in what was called a plank house. It was made of bark off the wood of a tree. They had an outhouse. The door lock was a piece of wood that slid into a slot, and we had to move the steps away from the house so that the foxes wouldn't come up the steps and get into the house. They always worked in the fields. We had wells, wood-burning stoves, lard soap, chickens, hogs, and roosters. We took baths in tin tubs, heated the water on the wood-burning stove, and would chuck wood for the fireplace.

"They always talked about slavery to me. When I got to my grandmother's house, even when I was a little child maybe two or three years old all the way up until I was eighteen, my grandmother would always tell me stories about slavery and freedom. I would always visit them on the weekends and in the summer. In the summer, I would be there for about two months. My parents were always at work, my father as a Secret Service agent and my mother as an internal revenue agent, so during the week I would stay with the city relatives and on the weekends stay with my country relatives. The conversations I had with my Southern relatives taught me about the problems that Blacks encountered in the South and about racism. I was taught about the Ku Klux Klan.

"My grandmother would comb my hair, and we would have this reoccurring conversation that has been etched into my memory. This is probably one of the ways our history was recorded and passed down from generation to generation. She would say to me, 'How we get free?' I'd say, 'From the union.' She'd say, 'What they do?' I'd say, 'The soldiers, they came and set us free'. She'd say, 'That's right, don't you ever forget it.' She'd then say, 'Who kept us down?' and she made sure I'd say,

'The white people.' She didn't want me to have any other name for them, so I always knew. She'd say, 'How they treated us?' and I had to give her the right response. She'd comb my hair and smacked me upside my head if I didn't say the right thing. It was ingrained in me. She taught me how to watch and get off the sidewalk when the white people came down the street in town. We didn't go into town too often. We went in town on Saturdays to get staples and supplies. There were certain stores we could not go into, certain stores we stayed away from because of the way they treated black people.

I remember once my friend Carolyn and I snuck out of the house and went to the movies and my mother found out. Aunt Ollie said to us, 'Tell me for the life of me, as hard as it is for us to earn this little bit of money, why you would want to go and give it to the white man? Sitting up there in that nasty balcony with broken springs under the seats and the dirty floor . . .'

"And Carolyn said, 'How do you know about the dirty floor and the springs?'

"All I could think about was 'Lord, she is going to get us killed!'

Aunt Ollie said, 'You never mind that! Don't you ever, as long as you live, back talk me, girl! Where did you get your popcorn? You had to go back outside, didn't you? Simple niggers!'

"And we just sat there and listened. That's what I grew up with in the South. Aunt Ollie didn't play that. We only went to the gas station and the one pharmacy where we didn't have to go through the back door. We knew that we could not just run into the local store and get a soda out of the ice chest. You knew that wasn't done. There was a code, and you didn't break the code. So I had a different sense of race relations from my father's experience."

"I grew up when it was segregation today, segregation tomorrow, and we thought it would be segregation forever!" stated Marilyn Tyler Brown, a cousin of Sharon who grew up in Oxford in the 1950s, graduated from Virginia Union University, and who later became the associate superintendent for DC Public Schools. "There was not a lot of hostility between blacks and whites. You knew your place as black folks. We knew we could not go into the drugstore and have a Coca-Cola or ice cream. We did not come up going to the movies because my parents didn't want us going upstairs to sit in the balcony where the blacks were forced to sit. You knew what segregation was, and you accepted it. You just went on. But you knew that if you went to school and got a good education, you wouldn't have to stay there. You could move up if you got something in your head! And they couldn't take that away. There was peaceful coexistence with the whites in town. You did not get in their way, and they did not get in yours."

"Oxford was a segregated town," recalled Dr. Larry Hamme, another one of Sharon's cousins who was born in 1948 and raised in Oxford and graduated from North Carolina Central University with a master's degree in clinical and experimental psychology. "There was a white high school and a white junior high school, a black high school and a black junior high school. Everything was segregated. The black kids had to sit upstairs in the movie theater, which was cool because we could throw popcorn down on the white kids. We didn't do that often though. There wasn't a lot of animosity between blacks and whites because we didn't come into contact with one another that often. I think at that time the so-called Negroes knew their place. There wasn't going to be too many people raising hell. I grew up on a small farm. We didn't get much snow in North Carolina where I lived. Sometimes the white school buses would come by . . . we lived on the same bus route that the white kids who lived on farms used, and we would sometimes get into snowball fights, but that was the worst that would happen between the whites and blacks."

That peaceful coexistence erupted into violent confrontation in 1970 when a Vietnam veteran named Henry Marrow was murdered by three white men. On May 11, Marrow went to join friends after a family gathering. After greeting black women on the street, he gave a friendly nod to a white woman in the area, whose husband was nearby. The husband assumed that it was an inappropriate gesture to his wife, and he, along with two other white men, brutally beat and shot Marrow several times in the street. There were several black witnesses who would unanimously testify in court as to what they saw.

The events sparked a mass riot in the streets of Oxford by black residents that same night. After the three men were arrested, they were tried by an all-white jury and acquitted of all charges, despite the eyewitness accounts and inconsistent testimonies of the suspects. Black Vietnam veterans launched an arson campaign, burning white-owned warehouses. Blacks would conduct a major march spanning fifty miles to see North Carolina's governor. Thousands would join them along the way. In further protest, the blacks would stop using white establishments to do business in the city.[17]

It was riots and numerous rebellions of slaves from the inception of the enslavement of black Africans that gave rise to the development and use of legislation designed to control the growing black population in the South. Over long periods of time the laws transformed into customs influencing racial attitudes that exist to this day. There is documented evidence of numerous slave revolts that occurred wherever slavery existed and not just in the South. As the number of black slaves increased, in some cases outnumbering the white population, there was justifiable paranoia on the part of white plantation owners that violent rebellion could occur. It was this fear that led to the passing of a series of laws restricting slave behaviour. These laws were known as slave codes.

The laws varied from area to area, but there were common threads among them all. Some examples include, legally considered property, slaves were not allowed to own property of their own; they were not allowed to assemble without the presence of a white person; no testimony could be made by a slave against a white person in a court of law; it was illegal to teach a slave how to read or write; the marriage between two slaves was not recognized by law, thus making it easier to justify the breaking up of families by selling one of its members to another owner.[18]

Following the Civil War, white Southerners passed a series of laws designed to regain economic and physical control over newly freed slaves as well as to control the minds of poor whites who were frustrated because they had to compete with blacks for jobs. These legal statutes and constitutional amendments were referred to as the black codes. Again these statutes varied in each state but had some commonalities. For example, Arkansas passed laws prohibiting black children from attending school with white children, while Texas passed laws requiring railroad companies to set aside a passenger car for black passengers. Black codes defined what it meant to be a "person of color" (i.e., black), which also varied from state to state. In some cases you were considered a Negro if you had one-fourth Negro blood in your veins (Virginia), or one-eighth (Georgia) or any amount (Tennessee). Other examples of black codes included blacks had to get off the sidewalk and allow white people to pass by; a black man had to cast his head down and not look a white man directly in the eye; blacks were prevented from voting, holding office, or serving on juries; blacks were prevented from serving in state militias; it was mandated that poor, unemployed persons (usually black) be arrested for vagrancy and then be put to work by the state (convict-lease system); interracial marriages between whites and blacks were prohibited.[19]

The black codes were actually a precursor to the Jim Crow laws and social segregation among blacks and whites that developed in the South and parts of the North. The Radical Republicans passed laws during the Reconstruction period (i.e., Thirteenth Amendment - abolishing slavery, Fourteenth Amendment - providing equal treatment for blacks, Fifteenth Amendment - giving blacks the right to vote) which extinguished the black codes. Political leaders in the South, however, began devising ways to circumvent the laws passed by the Radical Republicans. For example, laws were passed like the poll tax (citizens had to pay a tax in order to vote), literacy test (citizens had to pass a test in order to vote), and the grandfather clause (citizens were eligible to vote only if their grandfather voted before the Civil War) designed to prevent newly freed black citizens from voting. Laws were passed to separate the races (i.e., blacks and whites) in public spaces (public schools, parks, accommodations, and transportation), which theoretically did not violate the constitutional amendments as long as facilities were "equal." When a black man (Homer Plessy) challenged the segregation law on public transportation (in this case the train) in court, the lower court and the Supreme Court ruled (*Plessy v. Ferguson* in 1896) that forced segregation on public accommodations was legal as long as the facilities were equal. Segregation became the law of the land until the Plessy case was overturned by the Supreme Court in the *Brown v. the Board of Education* case in 1954.[20]

The physical separation of blacks and whites was also designed to make the poorest white person feel superior to any black person regardless his economic, political, or social status. As in slavery, the social lives of Southern whites remained absolutely off-limits to blacks, except when blacks acquiesced as servants or in some other way to the superior-inferior relationship that existed in the slavery area. Over a period of time, laws evolved into custom or a way of living. These customs were enforced by a very cruel and harsh system of terrorism sponsored by terrorist groups like the Ku Klux Klan and the Knights of the White Camellia, to name a few, who used violence and intimidation to ensure that the blacks, and those who supported the rights of blacks, adhered to the laws and customs (i.e., the way things were done) and to spread the ideals of the white race being superior. In many cases, the police and legal system turned a blind eye to the violence, thus sanctioning these acts of terrorism.

The sharecropping and tenant farming systems along with the convict-lease system were developed to provide labor on large plantations, replacing the slavery system. In the sharecropping system, poor farmers were allowed to farm a portion of the plantation owner's land in return for a share of the crops he was able to keep as payment. The sharecroppers usually had to rent his seed and supplies from the owner, however, and the owner would rent these materials out usually at a price that kept the sharecropper in debt and thus bonded to the land. The owner kept the financial records, and even if the sharecropper believed that he had cleared his debt, sometimes owner would disagree and thus the sharecropper was forced to raise the crop another year, thus getting himself deeper and deeper in debt. If the sharecropper decided to leave, he would be arrested for failing to pay his debt and was entered into the convict-lease system and sometimes brought right back to the same plantation to work. Tenant farmers were able to rent a portion of the owner's land for a fee and repaid that fee after the crops were harvested and sold.

In spite of these circumstances, black communities all over the South were able to grow and flourish in spite of racial bigotry and segregation and, in some cases, because of segregation. Black families, who were born and raised in this type of environment, developed strategies that not only enabled them to survive but to develop and grow. Blacks knew they were not going to be supported by the state, so they had to avoid confrontation when possible and to rely on themselves and the support of each other, which created a since of community.

"I grew up in my Aunt Ollie's house which was outside the city limits," Sharon reflected. "So we didn't get city services. She had to pay to have a pole brought out in order to get electricity. She had to pay for the wire, pay for the service of the fire truck to come out if there was a fire, pay for the state trooper to come out if there was a problem. The city services stopped at the last white house, and then there was a whole string of black residents who built their homes in a segregated community."

One strategy for dealing with the situation in the South was to leave the South. There was a great migration of blacks who left the South on the "chicken bone express" (nickname given to the train that took blacks to the North) to find their fortune and another form of existence in the North. However, for those who remained, education was a major tool that enabled blacks to improve their situation economically, socially, and professionally. Education did not just mean getting a high school diploma, even though that was better than nothing and in an agrarian society may have been good enough. But for many blacks in the South, getting a college education was critical.

"When we came along it wasn't 'Are you going to college?' but 'Which college are you going to?'" Marilyn Tyler Brown stated. "When I was a little girl growing up in Oxford and saw black nannies pushing those little white babies down the street, my mother used to say to me, 'That's what you are going to be doing if you don't go to school and get an education! You are going to be pushing those little white babies up and down the street, and going in the back door and working on your hands and knees scrubbing that white woman's floor and washing their clothes.' So you knew you had to go to school and do well in order to be able to do something other than being a domestic."

Getting accepted and attending a college was an ideal goal; however, getting the training necessary to be able to get accepted and prosper in a college was an entirely different matter.

There were a plethora of colleges created for blacks following the Civil War. These colleges and universities have been referred to as historically black colleges and universities (HBCUs). There are currently 105 historically black colleges and universities most of which are located in the former slave states. In 1862, Congress passed the Morrill Act, which provided for land-grant colleges to be established in each state. However, seventeen states, mostly in the South, generally excluded blacks from their land-grant colleges. In response, the second Morrill Act of 1890 was passed to require states to establish a separate land-grant college for blacks if blacks were being excluded from the existing land-grant college. Many of the HBCUs were created in response to the second Morrill Act.[21]

There were numerous obstacles, both physical and financial, that made providing an adequate education for blacks in the South an arduous task. The amount of public money provided to black public elementary and high schools was not sufficient, if any at all, in comparison to the racially separate public schools provided for white Southerners. As a result, a series of independently funded private boarding schools were established in small black communities throughout the South to resolve this problem. These private boarding schools were usually funded by northern philanthropist or church groups who understood the importance of education and who felt compelled to do something about the plight of thousands of people who were the victims of overt discrimination. One of the northern philanthropists was Julius Rosenwald, who was the president of Sears and who was responsible for financing over five thousand rural schools for blacks in the South. Some of the schools created by Rosenwald and other philanthropists included the Avery Normal Institute (Charleston, South Carolina, 1867), Bettis Academy (Edgefield County, South Carolina, 1881), Boggs Academy (Keysville, Georgia, 1906), Camden Academy (Camden, Alabama), Fargo Agricultural School (Brinkley, Arkansas, 1920), Gilbert Academy (New Orleans, Louisiana 1865), Gillespie-Selden Institute (Cordele, Georgia, 1902), Palmer Memorial Institute (Sedalia, North Carolina, 1902) and Snow Hill Institute (Snow Hill, Alabama, 1893).[22] These schools provided academically challenging curricular, a nurturing environment, positive support, and a clear mission that was engrained in every student which produced disciplined, voracious, successful leaders. The school that was created in Oxford was the Mary Potter Academy.

Mary Potter Academy was launched in 1889 with George Clayton Shaw as principal. Shaw was born to slave parents in Louisburg, North Carolina in 1863. His mother, Mary Penn Shaw, had been provided with what he described as a "fairly good education," and she instilled the importance of education in her six children, all of whom became educators. George Shaw graduated from Lincoln University in Pennsylvania in 1866. He completed his studies at Auburn Theological Seminary in New York where he met Mary Potter, who was secretary to the Presbyterian Freedmen's Board and benefactor of the educational improvement of freedmen. Potter provided the funding to establish the first school for blacks in Granville County, Oxford. The school was supported by the Board of Missions for Freedmen, New York Syndical Society, and Albany Presbytery and served as a private boarding school until 1950 when it became a public high school. In 1970, it became an integrated middle school.[23]

The school educated many African Americans during its long history. Early in its history, its curriculum was primarily religious in nature. Its talented staff—with instructors from Lincoln, Howard, Shaw, Syracuse, and North Carolina Central Universities—prepared students in normal and preparatory courses with Latin and Greek offered.[24] Granville County did not provide a high school for its black citizens, so the county paid Mary Potter for the county and city kids to go to school there. This was cheaper than providing a separate high school for blacks.

"Mary Potter was a boarding school where people from New York, Tennessee, Virginia, and all up and down the eastern seaboard would send their kids," Dr. Larry Hamme recalled. "Everybody who went there didn't stay on campus, however. It had this history of academic excellence, and that may have something to do with the emphasis on education that was pervasive among blacks in Oxford. The school was very small, and the teachers were very supportive. Teachers were a little different back then. They could spank a kid, and if you got spanked at school and your parents found out about it, you got spanked even worse when you got home."

An ancillary effect of the development of schools like Mary Potter was the creation of small segregated communities where a strong black middle class evolved that served as incubators for developing black leaders—an oasis in the desert so to speak. Students at this academy had the opportunity to interact with blacks from other parts of the country, thus giving them the opportunity to see that life and attitudes everywhere was not the same and people lived differently elsewhere. The education they received encouraged them to think, reason, and challenge conventional antebellum ideology of the so-called place that blacks held in society. This education empowered the students with the knowledge of science, mathematics, and history, which gave them the confidence to seek a better life. It exposed students to examples of great leaders like Gandhi, Shaka, Socrates, and Hannibal who overcame adversity against seemingly insurmountable odds and provided blueprints for accomplishing the same results. Students read about ancient civilizations like Sparta, Mali, Ghana, and how black people had a history other than slavery. There is an old adage that says, 'If I can control what you think then I can control you.' One of the reasons slave owners passed laws prohibiting the teaching of slaves how to read and write was so the owners would have not only physical control but mental control as well. Education, however, enabled blacks to free their minds from those mental shackles, helped them to see themselves in a new light, and created a desire to want more.

Because of segregation, highly qualified black educators could not always find jobs at major universities, so many of them came to Oxford and taught at Mary Potter. They brought with them the message that black students had to work relentlessly to improve and to take no shortcuts. A high standard of academic excellence was therefore established. As a result, Oxford produced a distinguished list of blacks who became pioneers and leaders all of whom received their training at Marry Potter Academy. The list of Mary Potter graduates is long and distinguished and includes,

- Dr. Marilyn Tyler Brown, who became the associate superintendent of the DC Public Schools and director of the Cathedral Scholars Program;
- Dr. Benjamin Chavis, who worked in the civil rights movement as an assistant to Dr. Martin Luther King Jr. and who later became the executive director of the NAACP;
- Joseph Colson Jr., who earned a bachelor's degree in engineering from North Carolina State University in 1968 and a master's degree in electrical engineering from Stanford University in 1969. *Black Enterprise* magazine recently named him one of the twenty-five hottest black managers of corporate America and was selected by *Black Enterprise* magazine as Black Engineer of the Year for Professional Achievement;
- Harold Boyd, who became an associate dean of students at Stanford University;

- Dr. Randolph Johnson, who got his PhD from Notre Dame in the 1950s and became a chemist for the Phillip Morris Company;
- Dr. Larry Hamme, who was one of the first black students to attend the University of Toledo Graduate School.
- John Lucas II, who played basketball for the University of Maryland and later played fourteen years in the National Basketball Association (NBA).

The *Brown v. the Board of Education* Supreme Court decision of 1954 ended de facto segregation, even though it did not become a reality in Oxford until the 1970s. One negative impact that desegregation had on the black community was schools like Mary Potter that nurtured and developed so many talented black students were forced to close down or altered beyond recognition. "When our family left Puerto Rico I wanted to be in New York or North Carolina and go to Mary Potter and North Carolina Central University because I wanted to duplicate what my mother had done," Sharon recalled. "But by 1970, integration was occurring at that time, and I couldn't go to Mary Potter because they had turned it into a middle school and I was ready for high school. During its final year as a high school, they took varsity sports and college preparatory classes out of Mary Potter even though they had one more graduating class (the class of 1971). If you wanted to go to college or continue athletics, you had to take your behind to the all-white Webb High School where they really didn't want black students. That's where I went to high school.

"They took all of the black teachers out of Mary Potter and disbursed them throughout the county, and they lost their seniority. The head counselors at Mary Potter now became regular counselors at the white schools, and they were assigned the noncollege track kids. Mr. Dunn, for example, who had been the dramatics arts teacher for years and had produced all of those plays, was put into a classroom at the back of the stage and was turned into a special education teacher. They denigrated the black teachers and did it in front of the community. We had great respect for these people because they were a part of our community, and to see them smashed like that was horrible. They were really broken by this.

We weren't really welcomed at Webb High School. We had to meet just to see if we could have black cheerleaders for the black football and basketball players because the white cheerleaders wouldn't cheer or congratulate them."

Oxford was a very small town with about eight thousand residents when Ruthe brought Charlie there. The segregated black community was even smaller, so what Charlie was exposed to opened his eyes to what people could do when trained and properly motivated. "I knew lots of carpenters, brick masons, painters, and plumbers who were very prominent in one section of Oxford," Thomas Hamme Jr. said. "There was one street we called PhD road. There were no more than thirty people living on that street, but at least ten or twelve of them had PhD's. That was our community.

However, if you go ten miles down the road to Henderson, you probably had the opposite in that black community. I don't know what in the world happened there, but there was a monstrous difference between Henderson and Oxford academically. You had sharecroppers in both areas, but somewhere there was a difference in the way people felt about education. A lot of the PhD's didn't stay in Oxford, however. Their academic success took them to different places. Ben Chavis was a prime example of what was going on in Oxford. He became a successful civil rights leader, and his two sisters, Helen and June, became professors at North Carolina Central University and St. Augustine College."

"When Charlie came to Oxford, Ruthe brought him to my Aunt Catherine's house," Marilyn Tyler Brown recalled. "Aunt Catherine was a member of the Gardening Club and a member of the AKA Sorority, which was big down there because in Oxford we were all Deltas. She became friends with Dr. Rose Butler Brown, who was an author and well respected in the African American community. Dr. Brown would come to my Aunt Catherine's home to attend the Gardening Club meetings with tea and sandwiches. Everybody would be sitting out there talking proper and acting like they owned a million dollars, which they never did. But Charlie was very impressed with the atmosphere. Then when he went to see my Aunt Mary, he'd say, 'You wouldn't believe those folks lived in the country!' My Aunt Mary was a teacher, and her husband was a farmer. He owned two hundred acres of land, and that was impressive. He had a lot of tenant farmers around the big house.

"They had three daughters. Irene graduated from Bennett College and became the first African American extension agent in Lambert County, which was real big because that was a job black folks usually didn't get. An extension agent is the person that deals with the soil. They go around to other farmers and help them improve their crops. They develop 4-H clubs which helps farmers improve their state of living, the animals and their health. His other daughter Julia graduated from Fayetteville State and became a teacher. Their younger sister Claudia graduated from Tennessee State and ended up marrying one of the deans. All of these people made an impression on Charlie and, I believe, had an impact on him getting out of the army, going to college, and becoming a teacher."

"I think coming to Oxford played a major role in how my father viewed life and what road he decided to take," Sharon said. "The thing about Oxford was that it had a solid black middle class that grew in the heart of a segregated society. But there were other families who established this middle class, not just the Hammes. We did not live in a vacuum. The fact that my father was able to find, I guess what you would call, an incubator that nurtured leadership and social skills and develop a network of people who held positions that were previously denied to black people was an important part in his development. My mother used to say that because we had our own social life and we already knew where not to go, we didn't mix with the whites and segregation didn't bother us as much. We weren't being assaulted daily, and we knew how they [whites] were and how they felt. I think that attitude was very important to my father and helped him get through the conditions he had to face in his career."

Charlie indeed decided to stay in the South and complete his education. He wrote a letter to his sister Grace on October 3, 1954, explaining the reason for his decision. In that letter he wrote,

> Lord, how I'd love to leave here and come back to good old New England to live, but I suppose the "Zeitgeist"—the spirit of the times—has persuaded my mind. The trend now seems to be that most of the better prepared Negroes, both educationally and financially, are staying in the South, and the others are moving to the North. Look around—I dare say you'll find many more Southern Negro families of the lower socioeconomic group now living in Boston than you've ever seen. Probably there are many Southern whites also, because of the war, etc.
>
> Most professional Negroes here feel that if they, the better prepared of the race, leave the South, social conditions will tend to become worse, or at least stand still. The only way to beat the Southern white man, short of an all-out show of physical force, is by education. And believe me, the younger generation here is at last, thank God, beginning to realize that fact. Every Negro college in North Carolina in the past few years has had many more applicants than are possible to handle. Six new building, running into millions, are going up all over campus right now, including one dormitory for graduate women. Several of our friends are at the University of North Carolina (formerly all-white) in the school of law and medicine. At least six of our friends have won fellowships and scholarships for study abroad, and each year since I've been here our graduates win awards for graduate study at just about all of the great universities here in the States. One fellow who finished with Ruthe earned his PhD at Harvard in chemistry and is now on the faculty here at NCC [North Carolina College].
>
> I've already talked much too much about something you're probably not interested in, since never having been South, it's rather hard to comprehend the feeling of Southern Negroes and their problems. But you know, geographical differentiation is on the decline, and the social situation here in the South is of importance to the whole country. These are turbulent times, and the segregation issue in the South is as consequential as "Red-hunting Joe" [McCarthy] and the H-bomb.

Encouraged by what he experienced in Oxford and after a lot of encouragement from members of Ruthe's family, Charlie decided to leave the army and enter college at North Carolina College (NCC). He received an honorable discharge from the army and entered NCC in September of 1952. He graduated with honors on May 31, 1955. He quickly found a job opportunity working at Dudley High School located in Greensboro, North Carolina. Dudley was looking for an English teacher, and after one phone call from Aunt Ollie, he was hired sight unseen.

"I got good guidance and counseling from some of the members of Ruthe's family, most of whom were teachers," Charlie stated. "They told me to take courses in education, and I said, 'Why?' They said, 'So you can become a teacher!' I said, 'But I don't want to be a teacher!' They said, 'Do it!' And so I did, and it was a good thing because soon after I finished college a school in Greensboro, North Carolina—Dudley High School—was looking for an English teacher, and that was my major. So that was my first job."

Charlie enjoyed teaching at Dudley High School, but teaching was never his passion. It was something he did because he needed to support his family at the time. "They certainly find enough things to keep a teacher busy besides teaching classes," he once wrote in a letter to his mother dated October 4, 1955. "In fact I do believe that everything else has priority over teaching. We visit parents, cope with disciplinary problems, sell insurance to the kids, and promote the athletic programs. I could go on forever mentioning the administrative work connected with teaching. Records, records, and more records have to be maintained! Some of the kids are okay, and many are difficult to handle. All told, I have about 160 students each day."

While contemplating other career opportunities he could engage in, Charlie always remembered his early encounter with members of the Bureau of Narcotics while he was being trained for the military police at Camp Gordon. He remembered that the agents were well dressed in tailor-made suits and used to get on him about having to wear a uniform. He remembered the respect they received from other members of law enforcement. Since he was a little kid growing up in Cambridge, he always knew he wanted a career in law enforcement. He decided then that he wanted to be a narcotics agent. The Federal Bureau of Narcotics already had black agents, so this was a position that was obtainable. One day, however, as Charlie arrived in one of his classes, a white man was sitting in the back row of his classroom. That man was from the United States Secret Service.

CHAPTER 6
The Perfect Storm

He applied and got a job as the first African American Secret Service agent in America. He was the perfect person for the job. He fit in. He was humble. He was articulate and fluent in Spanish. He was college educated with a double major (English and Spanish). He could swim very well, and he was a trained marksman—a skill he developed as a military police officer. And it was about time for them to get somebody of color. So I guess they got, what some would consider, the cream of the crop. They got the best!

—Marilyn Tyler Brown

The sun was setting against a brilliant auburn sky on a lazy evening in Aunt Ollie's backyard in Oxford, North Carolina. In the innocence of childhood youth, Sharon swung gleefully on a makeshift swing that was strung between two oak trees that seem to have been there since the beginning of time.

"Daddy, Daddy, look how high I can fly!" screamed Charlie's elated daughter.

As Charlie and Ruthe stood there admiring their daughter's glee, a sudden jolt of terror replaced the joy of parenthood as they saw, with horror, the impending danger slithered onto the scene and took a coiled posture as if ready to attack and devour an unsuspecting prey.

"Stay right there, honey, and keep swinging," Charlie calmly stated as he raced into the house to get a gun. He knew Sharon would act out the normal ritual, which was when he came home he would whistle, announcing his entrance, and his daughter would come running and jump into his arms to say hello. He did not want that ritual to play out on this day.

"Just stay right there, and do what your daddy told you to do!" a very concerned Ruthe demanded.

"All right!" she joyfully screamed and swung even higher to show off her newly discovered ability.

What seemed to Ruthe to be an eternity was only seconds before Charlie returned, gun in hand, and flopped on his belly in a prone position and took deadly aim. Almost instantaneously one shot rang out, and the head of the coiled black cottonmouth snake was gone, startling his daughter but ending the danger. An adult Sharon remembers that day like it was yesterday and shares this story because it was the only time in twenty-three years of his working with the United States Secret Service, she ever saw her father with a gun. But years of military training and hunting made Charlie very familiar with a gun, and he had become quite the marksman.

When asked for some fatherly advice, Charles Gittens once told his daughter Sharon, "One has to have a vision, for where there was no vision, people perish. You have to find your dream, follow your dream, put your best foot forward, and step out on faith!" Becoming a general in the military and leading his troops into combat was one of his dreams. Speeding car chases, jumping out of cars, apprehending suspects, and taking the bad guys to jail was another. Standing in front of a classroom and teaching English and Spanish to a group of children, however, was hardly how he envisioned his adult life. He longed for so much more. Charlie had always dreamed of having a career in law enforcement, but he knew it had to be something more than serving as a local police officer. He was now a world traveler. He was reared in the North, was currently living and learning about the South, had been overseas to the Far East, and yearned to see what else was out there, at the government's expense. He yearned for the night life, he yearned for the excitement, and he yearned to continue to serve his country as he had done as a military officer. He decided to leave the cozy and honorable profession of teaching and "step out on faith," so to speak, for a position in federal law enforcement.

He decided to fill out an application to join the Federal Bureau of Narcotics (FBN), the predecessor to the Drug and Enforcement Administration (DEA). He was told he had to take the civil service examination for treasury enforcement agents in order to qualify for the position. The written portion of the exam was given in Durham, North Carolina, but he had to travel to Atlanta, Georgia, in order to take the oral interview portion of the exam. Many in his wife's family did not understand or support the idea of him leaving a prestigious job like teaching at Dudley High School to become a crime fighter. But Ruthe's Aunt Mary and Aunt Catherine gave him the money to make the trip and gave him the names of people to look up so he would have somewhere to stay—they knew it would be difficult, if not impossible for him, a black man, to find a hotel to stay in while in Atlanta. They supported him because he was family. So he was off to Atlanta to start a journey that would lead him into a world of excitement, travel, and accomplishments.

"I had to take an examination, which was an examination that the US government gives specifically for federal law enforcement aspirants—people who were looking for a career in federal law enforcement," Charlie recalled. "It was a general exam which put you on a list that included a number of different law enforcement agencies. The Secret Service was on that list and so was the internal revenue. The exam made you qualified or enabled you to be chosen for an interview.

"The oral interview was given in Atlanta, Georgia. I didn't have the money to go down there, and one of Sharon's great aunts loaned me the money [$50] to go. She said, 'You're going to take that exam! It is a good thing.' So with a little family help, I made it down there and took the exam. The test was in two parts, written and oral. Well, I had knocked the written part straight out of the park and was informed I possessed the necessary qualifications. But when it came to the verbal part, the comment was made that I spoke "funny." The guy in charge wrote things down, saying I spoke incoherently and I could not be understood. Imagine that! Well, I guess I did speak funny to them because I was from New England. In Atlanta, they weren't used to that broad Bostonian accent, and I guess it sounded a little strange to them as their accent sounded strange to me with words like *y'all* and stuff like that. But I knew the real reason!

"Only eight applicants from the entire fifth civil service region were requested to report for the oral interview—seven white applicants and me. Through talking with the other applicants, I discovered that I possessed more objective qualifications than any of them. I was a veteran of WWII; I served as a military police officer, during which time I was trained for and served as a criminal investigator; I attended two other schools for law enforcement officers, one of which was sponsored by the Federal Bureau of Investigation; I was an active army reservist, first lieutenant, with a military intelligence unit; I graduated with honors from North Carolina College with a double major in English and Spanish; and I was a member of two national honor societies and the National Association of Teachers of English. It was quite apparent from the general atmosphere which prevailed during the interview that the board members were somewhat surprised a Negro interviewee should be in the group. Within a week after the interview, I received an unsigned, handwritten notice from the board simply stating, 'Ineligible oral interview.'

"I wrote a letter to Roy Wilkins, executive secretary of the NAACP, asking for his assistance in registering a letter of complaint to the employment policy officer of the Department of the Treasury stating that I was the victim of racial discrimination. They helped me draft a formal complaint and with the request for a hearing on my complaint. In the complaint, I charged that the oral interview was used as a device to eliminate me because I was colored, and it was the pattern of the revenue service in the region not to employ colored persons in this type of position. I designated the NAACP to represent me in connection with the compliant. I also wrote a letter to the director of the board of the US Civil Service Examiners in Atlanta, Georgia, appealing the decision to declare me ineligible based on the oral interview. I received a reply from the board of examiners, saying they felt the interview was 'conducted in a fair and impartial manner, in accordance with the instructions which were issued for conducting an interview and I did not demonstrate that I possessed the personal qualities essential for successful performance in the position for which I applied.' They also stated I could file to take the examination again.

"I refiled my application and had to retake the civil service exam. I passed again, with flying colors and had to return to Atlanta to take the oral interview again, but this time with auditors from the North. Soon thereafter, I received my statement of eligibility from the Civil Service Commission, and I was the happiest man alive.

"I wanted to get into the Federal Bureau of Narcotics (FBN) because of my military police background, which gave me some experience working with drug trafficking. It was heavy even back then, so I thought that would be a good field to work in. I remembered training with some FBN agents back at Camp Gordon when I was taking courses in investigation. But as I got closer and closer to making a decision about which branch of federal law enforcement I wanted to get into, I began meeting agents from other organizations. There was something about the Secret Service that appealed to me. Maybe it was the way they dressed or the way they carried themselves. I had to make up my mind and was leaning toward the Secret Service. I didn't get into the FBN, but the names of the people who took the test were floated around other government agencies, and that is probably how the Secret Service got my name. That is also probably why that gentleman ended up sitting in the back of my classroom checking me out.

"Sometime after receiving my status of eligibility, I got a call and a letter from the Charlotte office of the Secret Service to go down there for an interview. I went to the interview, and they took me through a process which included one heck of a background investigation. They checked every single facet of my life, practically from the day I was born all the way up to the time I applied to become a member of the Secret Service. Then they said that I failed the eye test requirement, stating that my vision was 20/40. I told them that was impossible, and I intended to see a specialist for a thorough eye exam. I saw the specialists and sent in the results which stated I had 20/20 vision in one eye and 20/30 vision in the other, both acceptable by the Secret Service standards.

"Everything went well, I assumed, because on February 1, 1956, I was hired as the nation's first African American member of the United States Secret Service (USSS). The interesting part about getting started in North Carolina was that this was the Deep South where there was heavy segregation and discrimination and there were no other persons of color in the Secret Service or the Federal Bureau of Investigations (FBI). Here I was a federal law enforcement officer in the Charlotte office, a heavily segregated part of the South."

The interview and subsequent background investigation did go well, in fact better than Charlie could have imagined. It shouldn't have surprised him because he was obviously an outstanding candidate. He was a military officer with an impeccable record and many accomplishments in law enforcement given that he was a man of color in charge of a predominately white military police unit in the South, which in itself was a remarkable feat; he was well educated; he was bilingual; he had been accepted to West Point, even though he chose to give up his commission; he was currently commissioned a first lieutenant in the army reserves serving in a military intelligence unit; he had training in criminal investigative procedures; he had experience in writing criminal investigative reports, and he was articulate, well read, and well liked. His only drawback, however, was he was a black man!

The head of the Charlotte office was so impressed that he wrote a memorandum to the chief of the Secret Service (U. E. Baughman) giving Charlie an enthusiastic endorsement. The memorandum included the following remarks:

Date: August 12, 1955
To: Chief
From: SAIC Spicer – Charlotte
Subject: Recruitment – Charles L. Gittens, Oxford, NC

Reference is made to memorandum report of August 5, 1955 submitted by SAIC Wentz [A.B. Wentz – Special Agent in Charge - Atlanta, GA Office] and having to do with this Service's interest in two colored applicants for the position of Treasury Enforcement Agent. One of these is the above-named and I was requested to interview him.

Mr. Gittens has a command of the English language which is surpassed by few and can express his thoughts fluently. He seems to have an alert mind, is a friendly, pleasant and congenial person. It is apparent that he realizes the position of his race in the South and accepts the situation without the slightest bitterness. After one speaks with him for ten minutes they forget entirely that he is a person from another race and, from his attitude and from the information at hand, I do not believe this Service would ever be embarrassed through having appointed him as a Special Agent.... I feel that if this Service wishes to appoint a Negro as an Agent it will have to look a long time to find a person who appears to be more suitable.

In view of the fact that this applicant is giving up an appointment as a teacher against the possibility of an appointment if you decide that he is to be investigated upon successful completion of the examination, I would like to be able to advise him of the fact so that he will have at least this much encouragement.

Vernon D. Spicer
Special Agent in Charge
Charlotte Office

Later that year (November 1955), Baughman requested that the application and investigation process be expedited and that Mr. Gittens be hired. Special Agent Gittens was to be assigned to the Charlotte office for a period of thirty days for training and then transferred to the New York office for permanent assignment.

Special Agent Gittens took on this challenge like every other challenge in his life, with vigorous enthusiasm, fearless determination, and a philosophical attitude that no matter what others thought of him, he was an equal partner in an elite organization that stood for excellence, professionalism, and service. This was an organization that not only protected the integrity of the United States currency and financial system, but was responsible for protecting the life of the president of the United States. When he walked into the Charlotte office, however, it seemed as if the silence could be cut with a knife. He knew this was not going to be easy. He knew the way some Southern whites felt about black people in general and black men in particular, but he had crossed this bridge before. He abruptly broke the silence by introducing himself and coming up to each agent and, with his huge hands and equally large smile, gripped their hands with a firm handshake and an eye-to-eye stare that said I am good at what I do and I am here to stay! His intelligence, his effervescent personality, his attention to detail, and his work ethic had always enabled him to overcome any obstacle thrown in his path and achieve remarkable results. This well-deserved confidence was bolstered by the fact that he had been in situations all of his life where he was the only black or one of a very few blacks and he was not only able to compete on an equal level, but excel above the rest. His experiences at Cambridge and Latin High School in Cambridge, Massachusetts, his experiences at OSC training at Fort Riley, Kansas, and his experiences at Fort Bragg, North Carolina, where he was put in a leadership position over his white counterparts and subordinates, had not only prepared him to function in a predominately white environment but gave him the confidence he needed to survive in a very delicate situation.

"When I was first hired it didn't take me long to become aware that I was the first black agent. I don't know why it didn't bother me, but it didn't," Agent Gittens reflected. "I was just proud of being an agent in the Secret Service who just happened to be black! I guess my background in the military helped me, and Ruthe and the members of her family also helped me to learn how to understand, to deal and get along down there. It worked out fine. The biggest thing that made it easy for me was the way the members of the federal family treated me down there. When I say the federal family, I'm talking about the staff of the Secret Service from the boss to the lowest clerk, to the seasoned agents to the federal district court judge who swore me in. They were very generous, kind, and understanding and assured me there would be no problems.

"Of course they were very apprehensive about having me as a coworker at first. They seemed to have doubts that I would be accepted by the people in the community which would hinder some investigations. Some of the white guys would tell the boss something like, 'Now how are we going to deal with this? Can you imagine me going around with a black guy who is carrying a gun and introducing him as an agent? What are we going to tell Jim-Bob, the local gas station attendant? We'd love to talk to him in order to help the investigation, but now he might not even speak to us!' My coworkers had their doubts, but they had more doubts than I did.

"The part that made my adjustment easier was the senior agents. There were only about six or seven agents in that office at that time, but each younger agent was assigned to a senior agent for guidance and mentoring. The guy who got to be my mentor had a deep Southern accent, and I could barely understand him, but he helped make my transition more comfortable. When he would take me on an assignment, he would introduce me by saying, 'This is my buddy Charlie, and he's one of our new agents.' We were investigating counterfeiting, check forgery, bond forgery, and all that stuff. They made regular arrests, picking people up from requests from other agencies. We call that collateral investigation. We would get a request to pick up so-and-so in North Carolina, who was wanted in another state. We would go to the groundwork to get the investigation started, which meant we had to check in with the local police, sheriff, or deputy. When going out on assignments, the senior agent would set up the visits, and he would let people know he was bringing a brand-new agent he was mentoring. It was funny to see how I was greeted sometimes, depending on the town or the feeling of whomever the law enforcement officials we would meet. Some would put their hands out to shake and some wouldn't. Sometimes they would look at me funny, and sometimes they were gracious. It would vary. I didn't have many assignments because I was new, and I was only there for six months of training before I was reassigned to the New York office."

First Lieutenant Gittens serves with an Army Military Intelligence Unit in 1954

Charlie gets a job teaching
at Dudley High School

Gittens being sworn in as special agent in
charge of the Washington Field Office

Another thing that made Agent Gittens's transition easier was the fact that he was able to find common ground with many of the agents and other local law enforcement personnel. His knowledge and love for antique automobiles laid the groundwork for discussions outside the realm of office. His love for hunting and fishing played a major role in the social bonding that developed, along with his ability to drink with the best of them and tell a tall tale every now and again.

"I was big into antique automobiles," Charlie fondly recalled. "One of the first things I did with my honest-to-goodness redneck buddies was to go out into the woods hunting and fishing and lighting campfires and stuff like that. Some of them were real honest-to-goodness rednecks like out of the comic books! That was kind of interesting. They were not friendly, especially with blacks, but they loved hunting and fishing and being in the woods. And they cooked whatever they caught, and so did I. For some reason they treated me well, like I was one of the good old boys. Some of them remembered me when I was the game warden at Fort Bragg.

"Now, the one who really had the hardest time with me hanging out with them was Aunt Ollie. She really didn't like me going out there in those woods hunting, shooting, and cooking birds over the fire. Oh no, she didn't like that at all! She was afraid that one of those days I might not come back. She was very serious about it. She would say, 'You don't know what those rednecks will do! They act like they are your buddy, but they may not be your friend. You don't know what they will do!' I understood her concern, but I went anyway and really enjoyed it. I also made some friends, and it made my job easier."

One of Charlie's strategies for dealing with awkward situations was to address it up front and to make light of it using humor to defuse potential tension. He masterfully used this strategy to deal with those coworkers who may have hidden feelings about race or hidden agendas. He would tease them about the KKK or being on an assignment by himself. He would joke around and say things like, "Now what happens when I come to your town and I was out there by myself and had to arrest somebody? Would you help them or help me? Are you going to take them in your car?"

"And they would say, 'Why sure! Why would you say something like that?'

"And I would say, 'You know why I'm saying something like that!' And I would laugh loud and hard."

Whatever strategy he used worked because his tenure in the Charlotte office was successful, though short. Many of his Southern family members (i.e., Ruthe's side of the family) were amazed at his ability to not only fit in but to thrive. "He went about things differently than most folks I knew or observed," Thomas Hamme Jr. responded when asked why he thought Charlie was able to survive in the South. "But he succeeded very well. Everybody admired him. I used to tease him about things, and it didn't bother him. He rolled with the punches. He had that ability. I used to ask him how he was able to get along with those white folks. I would say, 'You know they hate you!' and he relayed a story to me from some law enforcement guy in Georgia that he worked with. The guy wrote a letter to his superiors stating that 'if the Secret Service was serious about integrating itself, they should hire more guys like Charlie Gittens.' I thought that was one hell of a compliment especially at that time. He didn't rant and rave as far as I know. He won them over because he was bright, he could write, and they couldn't say he was dumb. Most of the people couldn't understand what he wrote because it was above them."

"He was a really smart guy," Dr. Larry Hamme stated. "He was a very smooth, low-keyed, articulate, intelligent person who chose his words very carefully. He knew people, he was charismatic, and people liked him. He could mingle with anybody. He could mingle equally with a farmer, a businessman, and obviously could hob-knob with some of the highest citizens in the world. It really didn't seem to matter with him. He knew when to fight and where to fight and which battles he could win at that particular time. He had enough words in his arsenal to outwit his opponents. He was really patient and knew when not to be too black. In the South, being too black could get you killed. In those days, being too black could sometimes mean just speaking up. There is no way he could have been in the 'redneck' world in North Carolina in the 1950s and been too outspoken. I can only imagine how some of those rednecks felt about him being an agent and carrying a gun. For him to not only survive but go up the ladder like he did was truly remarkable!"

The decision to join the Secret Service was easier than Charlie expected. He observed the agents with their closely cropped haircuts, suit jacket, tie and sharply creased trousers, wing-tipped shoes, a plain-colored trench coat and fedora hat and knew this was the organization for him. But why the service wanted him was a question that was very perplexing. Up until the hiring of Agent Gittens in 1956, the Secret Service was an organization made up of impeccably dressed white men who looked more like members of a large corporation than investigators whose job it was to hunt criminal counterfeiters and people engaged in bank fraud. The Secret Service was an elite organization whose illustrious history dated back to a period following the Civil War.

In 1863, the federal government issued a new national currency making the color of the bills green in an attempt to thwart counterfeiters from easily reproducing the bills. By 1864, it was reported that about one-half of all the printed money in the United States was counterfeit. In April 1865, Pres. Abraham Lincoln gave his approval for a new organization to be developed to fight counterfeiting, and by July of that year, the United States Secret Service was born. Unfortunately President Lincoln never saw the organization in action because he was the victim of an assassination shortly after giving the order to start it. The organization started out as a part of the treasury department with twenty-five operatives with only one task—protecting the integrity of our nation's currency and financial system and, by the end of 1866, had arrested over two hundred counterfeiters.[25]

The attorney general added responsibilities to the Secret Service in 1871 when the Radical Republican–controlled Congress condemned the terrorist activities of the Ku Klux Klan. The service began infiltrating and investigating the Klan, and in a three-year period, eight agents arrested over one thousand leaders and members, which slowed down the overt activities of the Klan for a while. The Secret Service was also asked to initiate investigations into nonconforming distillers, smugglers, mail robbers, and a number of other infractions against federal laws. Each year the Secret Service took on new tasks from investigating western land fraud to investigating violations of US neutrality connected with World War I. Many of the tasks that the Secret Service was given were later handed over to a newly developed government organization called the Federal Bureau of Investigations (FBI). Following the assassination of President McKinley in 1901, the Secret Service was given the responsibility of preventing crimes before they occurred by providing protection for the president and his family.

Today, as criminals have become more sophisticated, the responsibilities of the Secret Service have increased in order to keep abreast with new technology. The Secret Service is now responsible for investigating crimes like identity theft, telemarketing fraud, and other forms of fraud—including check, credit card, postage stamp, and food stamps, as well as increasing the protection detail to include political candidates for election to the presidency, family members, foreign dignitaries, and special events of national importance. The Patriot Act (Public Law 107-56) increased the Secret Service's role in investigating fraud and related activity in connections with computers. In addition, it authorized the director of the Secret Service to establish nationwide electronic crimes taskforces to assist the law enforcement, private sector, and academia in detecting and suppressing computer-based crime; increased the statutory penalties for the manufacturing, possession, dealing, and passing of counterfeit US or foreign obligations; and allowed enforcement action to be taken to protect our financial payment systems while combating transnational financial crimes directed by terrorists or other criminals.[26]

It has been often said that luck is when preparation and opportunity collide at a specific period of time. Given that axiom, Special Agent Gittens has been the benefactor of gratuitous timing with regard to being in the right place at the right time. There were several historical variables that may have come together, creating a situation that motivated the individuals in power to seek the services of black Secret Service agents in general and Charles Gittens in particular. Some of those variables include the increasing and documented success of black undercover agents in the Federal Bureau of Narcotics infiltrating criminal organizations in big cities across the nation, the reorganization of the Secret Service under the leadership of U. E. Baughman, the pressure to increase the size and training of the service following the assassination attempt on then President Truman, and the pressure to include blacks in the federal government as a result of the civil rights movement. These variables came together at a specific point in time, creating a "perfect storm" that started breaking down the barriers of institutional racism and discrimination in the federal government.

During the 1950s, the Secret Service had to borrow black agents who worked for the Federal Bureau of Narcotics (FBN) in order to infiltrate organizations that were practicing counterfeiting. Counterfeiting and the selling of illegal drugs often went hand in hand, so the two federal law enforcement agencies would often collaborate on cases. The FBN was also an agency of the Department of the Treasury established in June 1930 to assume the enforcement responsibilities assigned to the Harrison Tax Act 1914. The FBN is credited for criminalizing drugs such as cannabis (marijuana) as well as fighting opium and heroin smuggling.[27]

The Harrison Tax Act was a federal law that regulated and taxed the production, importation, and distribution of opiates and cocaine. In the 1800s, opiates and cocaine were mostly unregulated drugs. In the 1890s, the Sears & Roebuck catalogue offered a syringe and a small amount of cocaine for $1.50. At the beginning of the twentieth century, cocaine began to be linked to crime. By 1914, it was estimated that one US citizen in four hundred (0.25%) was addicted to cocaine. Very inflammatory and racists arguments were used to help pass the Harrison Tax Act. Pres. Theodore Roosevelt appointed Dr. Hamilton Wright as the first opium commissioner in 1908, and Dr. Wright publically stated that "cocaine is often the direct incentive to the crime of rape of white women by Negroes of the South and other sections of the country." He alleged that "drugs made blacks uncontrollable, gave them superhuman powers, improved their pistol marksmanship, and caused them to rebel against white authority." Other arguments in favor of passing the Harrison Act played on the fears of people by claiming drugs created "drug crazed, sex-mad Negroes, and made reference to Negroes under the influence of drugs murdering whites, degenerate Mexicans smoking marijuana and Chinamen seducing white women with drugs." It was also reported that the opium addicts were mostly women who were prescribed and dispensed legal opiates by physicians and pharmacist for "female problems," or white men and Chinese at the opium dens.[28]

According to Arthur Lewis, who was a black special agent for the FBN in 1955 and who later became the first black special agent to rise to the rank of special agent in charge (SAIC) in Philadelphia and the first black deputy administrator of the DEA (successor agency to the FBN), the FBN was the first federal law enforcement agency to hire black agents.

"They [FBN] had black agents going back to the time when they were fighting liquor and alcohol and that kind of stuff," Lewis stated. "The FBI didn't have any, neither did the US Customs Office, the postal office or Secret Service have sworn black agents. But the FBN had several outstanding black agents with stellar backgrounds and service records. We had people like Wade McCree Sr., who was a pharmacist before entering the FBN and became the SAIC of the Hawaii office. His son [Wade McCree Jr.] became the first black solicitor general in the United States. We also had William "Bill" Davis, who spoke seven languages and would study Russian while we were out on surveillances in New York. He later became an ambassador.

"I think that the Secret Service decided to get black agents because the time had come. Certainly we had set the standard in the FBN to show that black men could do the job. It was like the Tuskegee Airmen, who showed that black men could get the job done when given the chance. We were able to infiltrate all types of criminal organizations both white and black. We made a lot of cases against the Italian mobs, especially by agent Bill Davis. We had white informants, and they would take us to East Harlem, and we bought a lot of drugs from them. They did both counterfeiting and sold drugs, but they made most of their money selling drugs. I did some undercover jobs on loan for the Secret Service because they didn't have any black agents. I also worked with the Secret Service detail after the assassination of President Kennedy because there just weren't enough agents to protect everybody. I think it became embarrassing to the other agencies that didn't hire black agents. People are often embarrassed by racism, especially when they think they are fair and generous. So if you had to go to another agency to get someone to work undercover on your case, what did that say about your agency? Think about it—you had to go to another agency to borrow a black agent to do what your agents couldn't do!

"The system was set up so black agents were placed in undercover roles mostly. They were out there alone and by themselves, whereas the white boys would have a partner to do surveillances and make arrests. At that time, the police would not want black sworn agents in undercover roles, and they did not want black agents to make arrest. They definitely didn't want black agents to make arrest of white people.

"Before Mr. Gittens became an agent of the Secret Service, I had been working for the FBN for about a year. I had heard about him but never met him until we worked a case in Cleveland. There were so few black agents that we all knew about each other. I heard about him because the 'grapevine' was powerful! Whenever a black agent was hired, the word went around the world. I was sent to Cleveland where he was working on a money case. We found out about him through the heads of our two offices, the Secret Service and the FBN. We met down there, and he was working one side of the town, and I was working the other. Every black agent had to go through what Mr. Gittens had to go through because there was a higher standard held for black agents than white agents. Charlie Gittens took the test. He passed everything, and then they said that he couldn't speak well so they turned him down the first time. The guy was well educated, a gentleman, and an officer in the military. He wanted to get into the Secret Service, and they said he couldn't speak! Usually when they turned you down that was it, but Charlie hung in there, and they eventually recognized his talent. Eventually things moved ahead because of guys like Charlie, Wade McCree, Bill Davis, and me, but progress was slow."

Urbanus E. Baughman became the chief of the Secret Service in 1948 and has been given credit for reorganizing and improving the organization by improving the training of the agents—the first Secret Service training school was developed under his watch—and improving communication between the field offices and headquarters. Each field office would now have a special agent in charge responsible for managing the office and reporting to the chief. He was a seasoned field agent for twenty-one years before Pres. Harry Truman asked him to become the service director.[29] It was on his watch that agents of color were brought into the Secret Service to expedite the investigative arm of the organization. "When I got to New York, I was the only black agent for five years," Agent Gittens stated. "Then we got a Chinese agent, and then a Puerto Rican agent, and then we got a guy from South America or some place, but it was always one at a time."

Baughman was active in the recruitment of black agents, in part because of the rising number of cases of counterfeiting and check fraud that rose in sections of New York where large number of African Americans and Latinos resided (i.e., Harlem, Spanish Harlem) that necessitated the need for African Americans and Spanish-speaking Puerto Rican-Americans who could infiltrate these criminal groups with ease. He also had an ever-increasing fear of the growth and power of the Nation of Islam that was led by Elijah Mohammed. In his book *Secret Service Chief* published in 1961, Baughman stated that

> the Nation of Islam is a group, whose membership in this country is entirely colored, attempts to arouse violent feelings of racism. It trains its men as soldiers and instructs its young men and women in an odd and distorted form of Mohammedanism. . . . I feel that there is something peculiarly sinister about a rabble which can

be led by such a person [as Elijah Mohammed]. The incredible, blundering, bloody harvest it could reap, in pursuit of its idiot ends! We must keep a vigilant eye on this fanatic group. Many of its members might be capable of attacking our President, even were they not inflamed by such political nonsense. Encouraged to violence, they are potent sources of unthinkable mischief. [30]

It should be noted, however, that Baughman was fired by President Kennedy partially because of Baughman's belief and public comments (cited in an interview in the *Washington Post* published on July 26, 1961) that there was no such thing as the mafia in the United States for over forty years. He further denied the existence of a national crime syndicate.

On November 1, 1950, Griselio Torresola and Oscar Collazo stormed Blair House, the temporary resident of President Truman and his family while the White House was being renovated, and in a blaze of gunfire died trying to assassinate President Truman. The brazen attempt brought to light the need to increase the number of Secret Service agents as well as the training they received. Congress passed a law (Public Law 82-79) that gave permanent authority of protecting the president, his immediate family, the president-elect, and the vice president (upon request) to the Secret Service.[31]

Another factor in the recruitment and hiring of agents of color can be attributed to the changing of the times and the pressure placed on government agencies to change their racial policies as a result of the civil rights movement. Many black soldiers returned to the United States following World War I proud of their many accomplishments and awards, and proud that they played a role in making the world safe for democracy. When they came home, however, they were met with the same form of segregation, discrimination, and indignation that was present before they left. This led to a new enlightenment in the black community across the nation. Black leaders and artists began to speak out against their disenfranchisement and the lack of civil and human rights using various platforms. The black press was instrumental in bringing injustices to national attention and stimulated not only conversation but action from members of the black and white community to rectify this situation. The United States involvement and success in WWII, along with the victorious involvement of black soldiers in all aspects of the war, further heightened the expectation of black Americans that they would finally be accepted as first-class citizens.

When blatant discrimination continued to exist and thrive, the efforts of black and white citizens across the nation were galvanized into a movement for equality and civil rights. This civil rights movement, which was spearheaded by numerous groups like the National Organization for the Advancement of Colored People (NAACP), the Congress of Racial Equality (CORE), and the Southern Christian

Leadership Conference (SCLC), to name a few, provided a catalyst for governmental officials to finally alter the course of race relations in America by enforcing existing laws that banned discrimination, creating new laws that tightened the loopholes in existing laws, and by beginning to include minorities in the mainstream of the social, economic, and political fiber of American society. This movement, created to demand that America equalize treatment of all citizens, started as a trickle, like giving a few blacks the opportunity to participate in mainstream jobs and in positions of political power. The Supreme Court, in the 1954 *Brown v. the Board of Education of Topeka, Kansas* case, theoretically eliminated forced segregation in public venues by reversing the legal precedence established in the *Plessy v. Ferguson* case of 1896, which legalized the "separate but equal" doctrine. That trickle began to turn into a stream as blacks vocalized their displeasure with the status quo using strategies like economic boycotts, literary, and journalistic publications. That stream turned into a river as younger blacks and whites took a different tactic and began to organize and agitate for justice. They began using strategies like sit-ins, marches, and televised civil disobedience to get America to move a little faster in the direction of equality. This movement, however, did not go unopposed by citizens who wished to maintain the status quo, but a residual of the movement was that federal government agencies began to actively recruit "qualified" black candidates for positions that were customarily open only to white men.

Whatever the reasons, Special Agent Charles L. Gittens's dream came true, and after a short training period in Charlotte, he was shipped off to New York City, the Big Apple, where the belief was that if you could make it there you could make it anywhere! "Going to the New York office was indeed a dream come true," Special Agent Gittens stated, with a gleam in his eye and a cryptic smile on his face. "Every agent in the United States Secret Service wanted to go to New York because New York was the place to be if you wanted to make it in the Secret Service! There were a few agents, however, who didn't want to have anything to do with New York City. It was too big for some of the country boys, especially the kinds of crimes that were committed in New York. They had the counterfeit stuff and the mobs, and there was honest-to-God real crime in New York. I loved it! I would do unpaid duty in New York today, if they let me!"

CHAPTER 7
New York Undercover

I worked an undercover case and got an introduction to a member of a counterfeiting ring and bought the usual couple of thousands of fake $20 bills at a 10 percent rate. I arranged to be arrested along with everybody else so that no one knew about the role I had played. One of the counterfeiters came over to me, shook my hand, and begged my pardon, apologizing for getting me into this. Much later, I took the stand—as a prosecution witness—and gave my identity: Special Agent Charles L. Gittens, United States Secret Service. The defendants' jaw must have dropped two or three inches!

—Charles Gittens

Duplicity – the disguising of true intensions by deceptive words or actions (Merriam-Webster)

He walked into the bar, stoic, clean shaven, dressed to the max (wing-tipped shoes, shark-skinned suit, fedora hat, London Fog trench coat), briefcase in hand, soft-spoken with a quaint New England accent, and with a look that indicated he was mad at the world and just didn't give a damn anymore.

"This guy is a cop," cautioned the skeptical mobster.

"Nah, he's Harvard Law," retorted the confidential informant, who was hoping this ruse would not get him killed and would get him off the hook with the Secret Service.

"Harvard Law, what the hell is he doing with you?"

"Cause he's a nigger, and nobody would hire him, so that's why he's out here trying to make this money!"

The buy went off without a hitch, and after Special Agent Gittens gave the signal, the surprised culprits were surrounded by several special agents of the Secret Service, who were lying in wait and arrested them for possessing and selling counterfeit bills. The whole episode left Gittens with a satisfied feeling he had been searching for since he was a little kid playing on the playground in Cambridge, Massachusetts. It was a feeling that was hard to duplicate, until his next assignment of course. Maybe it was the thrill of the chase, matching wits with the criminal mind, or the excitement that comes with the danger and the fear of the unknown. Or maybe it was just the satisfaction of serving American society by putting away another bad guy. He had indeed become Captain Marvel, the comic book hero whose heroics saved America and captured the minds and souls of the young and old.

For the next nine years (1956–1965), this was the lifestyle Special Agent Gittens lived, traveling from state to state at a moment's notice, sometimes even out of the country, chasing down the bad guys. Wherever people, who lurked in the underworld, would dare to venture, Special Agent Gittens was there to follow. Life as Charlie knew it would be forever changed. Gone were the days of standing in front of a safe and cozy classroom where he talked about life and prepared his students for life. Gone, were the lazy days of fishing in Aunt Ollie's pond or hunting in the woods of North Carolina. Gone were the days of hanging out at Hymie Rudolph's corner store in the Village. He was now in New York City, and as a special agent for the Secret Service, it was now his job to help protect the integrity of America's currency.

Protecting the integrity of America's currency and economic system entailed finding and arresting criminals who participated in the manufacture, possession, or sell of counterfeit currency, check and bond fraud, stealing government checks, financial institution fraud, computer and telecommunications fraud, false identification documents, access device fraud, advance fee fraud, electronic funds transfers and money laundering as it relates to the agency's core violations. Today, identity theft and computer fraud are major issues that are highly visible and have great impact on America's population. Counterfeiting, however, has always been a major problem and one of the main concerns of the Secret Service. It had to be dealt with swiftly. When counterfeit bills got circulated in a community in large numbers, it would often devastate unsuspecting citizens and ruin businesses and lives. It is illegal to possess any counterfeit bills, and once a legitimate business or an unsuspecting person realizes they have one, they are required to turn them in to the Secret Service. Counterfeit bills were usually circulated in the form of five- and ten-dollar bills because they were easier to move. There has been a historical connection between counterfeiting and the selling of illegal drugs, which has made the capturing of counterfeiters a more hazardous job for law enforcement agents.

Charlie did not start his New York experience arresting key figures engaged in major counterfeiting cases, however. As a rookie, the brunt of his caseload was filled with interviewing witnesses, writing reports, and conducting the never-ending check forgery investigations. His immediate supervisor was Al Whitaker, who was the special agent in charge of the New York office. Whitaker was a tough, no-nonsense boss who required the best out of his agents, pushed them tirelessly, and demanded excellence. He assigned each agent a ton of cases and demanded that each agent closed at least twenty cases per month (the national average for closed cases was sixteen per month). Every month Whitaker would bring in each agent and grill them on why assigned cases were not closed and help them develop strategies to close those cases. Whitaker was a large man in stature and had a sense of humor that to some may have seemed insensitive, but he was straightforward, to the point, and let you know what was on his mind. He was an experienced agent and surrounded himself with the very best. There were only twelve to fifteen agents in the New York office when Gittens got there (that number vacillated between twelve and fifteen, taking into consideration that agents were often sent out on special details that lasted various lengths of time). Today there are over four hundred agents in that office alone.

There have been unsubstantiated rumors that Whitaker did not want Gittens in his office when he learned an African American had been hired and assigned to the New York office. "In the deepest part of the Secret Service, they weren't too happy to have a black guy as an agent especially in New York," Gittens stated. "But boy, you don't get any higher than being a member of the United States Secret Service. When I reminisce about those times, I think it caused more excitement, more conversation, or more controversy maybe within the Secret Service or whenever people saw me." Whitaker wanted the best, however, and it didn't take long for him to realize that Charlie was indeed one of the best and became very comfortable with the situation.

Charlie took on every challenge and every assignment with the same zeal he had demonstrated all of his life. He started in the New York office on March 5, 1956. He was assigned primarily to check forgery cases in the East Harlem area of New York City because of his familiarity of the Spanish language. After assisting other special agents in forty-eight investigations during March and April of his first year, Charlie was assigned forgery cases on his own. For the period of May through October, he completed seventy cases, of which thirty were solved and handled ten arrests. During that same period, he spent six weeks in the Treasury Law Enforcement Training School, or his numbers could have been even higher.

With each successful case, Charlie demonstrated that he was ready, willing, and able to take on more responsibility. He received a stellar ninety-day progress report from Whitaker. In that report, Whitaker stated that "each special agent with whom Special Agent Gittens has been assigned reported that he appeared to be alert, energetic, well-mannered, and able to handle himself in the required manner with police officials and the general public. He is neat and conservative in dress and appears to be a well-adjusted individual with a high aptitude."

Each report Charlie completed was reviewed with great interest by Chief Baughman, who was responsible for hiring Charlie and who kept a close eye on his progress. Baughman indicated in several memos and letters sent to SAIC Whitaker that he was pleased with the development and work of Special Agent Gittens. In a memorandum dated October 24, 1957, Baughman stated,

Memorandum

October 24, 1957

To: SAIC Whitaker, NY
From: Chief
Re: Jake N. Kane, et al, Check Case
    Heywood Edward Brown – Forger
    I have read with great interest the October 15th report of Special Agent Charles L. Gittens giving the details of the investigation which led to the arrest of multiple forger Heywood Edward Brown in the Jake N. Kane, et al, check case.
    It is past performance of this character which has earned for this Service the outstanding reputation it holds among law-enforcement agencies and I am grateful to note that Special Agent Gittens is doing his part to uphold that reputation.
    Please convey to him my commendation for his excellent work in this case. A copy of this letter is being placed in his personnel file.

U.E. Baughman
Chief

On January 7, 1960, Whitaker sent another memo to Chief Baughman with a list of agents who had done an outstanding job by making numerous arrests and solving the cases. Whitaker requested that the agents listed receive recognition for their stellar arrest records. The agents' performances were more than double the national average. This list placed Charlie in the top three agents with the most arrests by December 1959. The list of agents included Paul Scanlon – 58 arrests, Alfred Wong – 50 arrests, Charles L. Gittens – 49 arrests, Jack H. Phillips – 40 arrests, Charles J. Marass - 39 arrests, Bernard J. Mullady – 37 arrests.

As a result of his performance, Gittens got the opportunity to demonstrate his acquired skills by investigating major counterfeiting cases. To accomplish this task, he had to dig deep within himself and do something that had been a part of his wildest imagination—he had to become somebody else. He had always been the outgoing, gregarious person who always had a smile on his face, wore his emotions on his sleeve, had a funny story to tell and had an easygoing demeanor. Now he had to practice the art of duplicity by going deep undercover in order to catch criminals. He was a voracious reader, and his personal library included books like Machiavelli's *The Prince*, Plato's *Republic*, Herodotus, the Classics, and James Baldwin (e.g., *The Fire Next Time*, *Go Tell It on the Mountain*). Instead of reading nursery rhymes to his daughter at night, he would lull her to sleep with stories from Shakespeare's tragedies. The classical stories filled with protagonists and antagonists provided a platform for him to develop the various characters he would use in the dangerous underworld of drugs and counterfeiting. Gittens recalled,

> My next assignment was in the big city. I went from Charlotte, North Carolina, to New York City. That was quite a move. New York was where you really got tested. I was stationed in Manhattan, and we bought a house on Long Island, in the suburbs of New York. I learned a lot about law enforcement in New York. Working with the New York City police was quite an experience in itself. Of the nine years I was stationed in New York, I probably only spent half of the time in New York proper or around New York. Much of the time I was on assignment out of New York in different parts of the country. Sometimes I would go on special details or special assignments. Once I got called into the office and was assigned to a special detail in Cleveland, Ohio. When I asked how long I would be there, I was told "maybe a week or two weeks." That assignment lasted almost a full year. There were some assignments that took me to other countries like Bogota, Colombia, and Toronto, Canada.
>
> The only place where I felt I was in real danger on my job was in New York City, however. There were a couple of situations, which were routine investigations dealing with counterfeiting, that got a little "dicey." *Dicey* to me meant that you had to display firearms, or you had to chase somebody when making an arrest and there was a little physical stuff. There were times when I had to display my firearm, but I never had to shoot anybody.
>
> For example, one of my partners was named Paul Scanlon. We were out one Saturday morning scouting an area of surveillance. We were "fishing" the area for counterfeiters. We went into a house and started knocking on doors. We had gotten some basic information, and we knew that there were some major counterfeiters in the area, and we were scouting them out. We went, fully armed, and knocked on one door, and a guy came to the door and his girlfriend was with him. We were let in, and when we were satisfied that they were not persons of interest to us, we just turned around and said,

"Sorry to bother you, folks." We turned to leave, and at that point I saw that the guy had a gun hidden under the covers of his bed. After he shut the door, I said to Scanlon, "I think that guy had a gun!" We decided to go back, and when we knocked on the door, we realized that he had gotten the gun and pulled it out on us. He thought he had us cold. So we did what any agents would do and what we had been trained to do and pulled our weapons and did what we had to do to affect the arrest. They took off running, and we took off after them and made the arrest.

We had a special detail called SD that was made up of agents who were the top of the line. We were used for undercover work, especially counterfeiting work. That meant these were the big boys, the Italians. They were tough and would throw you in the East River and not even bat an eyelash. A lot of our agents were Italian as well. Everybody could not do undercover work in counterfeiting because you had to be knowledgeable about Italian life. I went undercover to infiltrate these counterfeiting rings. I worked on some cases against major underworld figures who did major crimes and were sent up for long prison sentences. I also had some cases that were not major but were interesting.

One assignment made the front page of the New York Daily News but for the wrong reasons. The headline read, "Hunt Dope Addict; He Duped Feds, Fled." It was a routine investigation in Brooklyn. I, my partner Paul Scanlon, and two postal inspectors, James Oliver and Arthur Danning, went to arrest Heyward "Sonny" Yates for narcotics possession and mail theft. Oliver and I went to his second-floor apartment while Scanlon and Danning waited on the ground floor as our backup. When we knocked on the door, Yates threw open the door with gun in hand and stuck it in my face.

"If either of you move, this guy is dead," Yates snarled.

"His girlfriend [Jeanette Coy] had a gun as well. They took my gun and forced Oliver and I down the stairs at gunpoint. When we got to the bottom of the staircase, Yates forced Oliver to join Scanlon and Danning and used me as a hostage so they could get away. Yates told my partners to stay in the hallway while he forced me to leave with him and his girlfriend. We left the building and walked a block away when he shoved the gun in my back and told me to "get lost." They walked another block, and Yates then got into a cab, leaving his girlfriend behind.

Mrs. Coy was arrested later that day at her home and charged with acting in concert with Yates in assaulting a federal officer, but Yates eluded capture for several weeks. Yates started a series of stickups in the Brooklyn area. He would stick up drugstores week after week and committed a total of ten robberies (six cab drivers, two rent collectors, and two druggists). He was identified as the person who took my gun.

That was one of those incidents where I was a little frightened and something could have happened, but that was a part of the job. You knew what you were getting into when you took the job. Fortunately, no shots were fired and nobody got hurt. The local police banned together, and everybody made up their minds that they—local and federal law enforcement agents—were going to get Yates, no question about it. And they did! He was set to be put on New York's Ten Most Wanted List when two Brooklyn police officers caught him and a friend Frank Williams trying to rob another drugstore.

Secret Service agents employed various tactics in order to combat criminals as they engaged in counterfeiting. One tactic was called fishing, where agents would scout out an area where counterfeiters were known to hang out just to see if any criminal activity was going on. "Basically we found out guys were passing bad bills from tips from your informants," Gittens stated. "We called them CIs, which stood for confidential informants. They would just pass the word along, and we would hang out in the area. Sometimes we also hang out where people had connections with counterfeit money or drugs, or any kind of illicit products just to see if we could catch something."

Another tactic Chief Baughman referred to was roping. Roping was a technique in which agents passed themselves off in the underworld as criminals in order to gain the known counterfeiter's trust, the object being to get them to sell their contraband to the agent. To play the game, the agent had to take on the persona that would convince the criminal that the agent was a legitimate criminal as well. This is also known as going undercover. If the criminal was tough, then you had to be tougher. If he served time, then you'd served twice as much. If he was a drinker, then you had to be able to drink him under the table.[32]

"Going undercover basically meant that you worked in an undisclosed way as a law enforcement officer," Gittens explained. "When I was a young agent, being undercover was called 'working the streets.' The basic reason you worked undercover was so you could have access to the criminal element. Often you had to do some illegal things yourself in order to gain their trust. You posed as a drug dealer, or whatever persona you needed so you could make your job easier and make an arrest. That included anything else you had to move along, including marijuana, pot, all classes of drugs and stuff like that. We used to get real money from the Federal Reserve Bank to use as flash money to buy counterfeit money or drugs or any illegal product. Sometimes I went into the Federal Reserve Bank in New York and came out with a suitcase packed with money to use as flash money. The counterfeit money never got out to the public, and it was never recirculated as far as we knew.

"It would come out in a trial that we, undercover agents, were responsible for passing along some counterfeit bills. The agent would describe how he got into an illicit counterfeiting ring and sold it to real drug dealers and then got into their group. It would be hard to say how much money was passed along. Some defense lawyers would argue that the government was complicit in putting counterfeit money into the hands of illegal users to complete their purchase of illegal drugs. Those kinds of things always came up in trials, but to no avail. We did what we needed to make this arrest. That was the purpose of the agency. Whenever you made a counterfeit buy, you were doing your job! It was very interesting. I enjoyed undercover work. I enjoyed the excitement of it, and it was the reason we were hired."

Time and time again, Special Agent Gittens went undercover in an effort to apprehend suspected counterfeiters. He reveled in the idea that he was a part of the Secret Service, and his accomplishments weren't spectacular but just examples of an agent doing his job. He was just as much oblivious to the danger that came with doing his job as he was with the attention he received being a black agent working for the Secret Service. In response to a statement in the *Jefferson City News Tribune* article (December 29, 1974) that working for the Secret Service was a dangerous job, he stated, "I have never been involved in any shooting situation. I'm a hell of a lot safer being a Secret Service man than I would be driving a cab in New York or Chicago!" He felt that counterfeiters were different from the hardened drug dealers. "Often you'll find among counterfeiting people that once it's over—when the jig is up—there is little malice toward the undercover man," Gittens once said. "The attitude is this: it is a test of wits and you came up the winner!"

His approach, as explained by Victor Gonzalez—an undercover agent who rose to the position of special agent in charge of the Secret Service in the Puerto Rico and Toledo offices and after leaving the service became a successful lawyer—was a little different than most agents. "Charlie was one of the best Secret Service agents the United States ever had. He was thorough, he knew what he was doing. He was tough, but not abusive. He was very professional and was really proud to be an agent. He had the type of personality where he could talk to a defendant or suspect and kind of establish this kind of relationship where if they had met under different circumstances they could have been very good friends. He would have respect for the bad guys, and not just calling them scumbags like some other law enforcement agents did."

In spite of his insistence that his job was not dangerous or he was not doing anything out of the ordinary except "just doing his job," Charlie received accolade after accolade from not only his immediate supervisor, but from the director of the Secret Service, U. E. Baughman and his successor, James J. Rowley, who took over the Secret Service when Kennedy became president and dismissed Baughman. Below are letters of acknowledgment from both Baughman and Rowley:

October 27, 1960

Dear Al,

The Royal Canadian Mounted Police has informed me that Joseph Skulsky and Joseph Raymond Gauthier have been convicted in Toronto, Canada, and sentenced to prison for possession and uttering counterfeit United States currency.

I am sure the arrest and conviction of these two men has resulted in the substantive decrease in the number of offenses in the United States relating to $20 FRN (1840). The successful conclusion of this important case is due in large measure to the excellent undercover work performed by Special Agent Charles L. Gittens.

Special Agent Charles Gittens displayed initiative, aggressiveness, and physical courage in carrying out a potentially dangerous assignment in Canada, and demonstrated his ability to work harmoniously with officers of other jurisdictions.

Please commend Special Agent Gittens on my behalf and inform him that copy of this letter will be placed in his official personnel file.

U.E. Baughman
Chief, U.S. Secret Service

****

May 3, 1962

Dear Al,

During February 1961, the serious counterfeiting situation in Cleveland necessitated the use of a special squad in that city. As you know, Special Agent Charles L. Gittens was assigned to this detail, and he immediately infiltrated the criminal element of Cleveland; assumed various identities, and convincingly portrayed his role while alone with many of the most notorious racket figures in that city.

As we look back, several months and many arrests later,

it is apparent that the most difficult tasks and most dangerous assignments were those of Special Agent Gittens. Since he so willingly assumed the burden of the work, he must now accept a proportionate share of the credit.

Please inform Special Agent Gittens that I sincerely commend his performance in which he and the entire Service can take exceptional pride.

A copy of this letter will be placed in Special Agent Gittens' personnel file in this office.

Sincerely,

James J. Rowley

Director, U.S. Secret Service

****

Going undercover to rope a suspect could often be a very harrowing and dangerous experience, especially if you were not used to being in the streets or trained to go undercover. Usually, the Secret Service looked for individuals who had some experience in law enforcement in their resume before hiring them. This, however, did not necessarily qualify them for the intricate task of being a successful undercover agent. Training for new agents, for the most part, was a short introductory course held at the Treasury Law Enforcement Officers Training School that agents attended at the beginning of their career which covered general law enforcement procedures. It was U. E. Baughman who felt that agents needed better training and started the United States Secret Service Academy on November 6, 1953, in a small unpretentious building, that agents referred to as the Little Red Schoolhouse located on Twelfth Street in northwest Washington, DC. The indoor firearms training was held in the basement of the treasury building, and outdoor shooting was conducted at the US National Arboretum in northeast Washington.[33]

Most of the survival and real-life training, however, was done on the job with the aid of senior agents who were often paired with rookie agents. Each rookie was paired with a senior agent for a short period of time (one to two weeks) and then paired with another senior agent who worked at a different part of the city. Gittens was paired with Special Agent Deckard, who worked in East Harlem, for several weeks because of his knowledge of the Spanish language. Often agents were sent out on their own with only a surveillance team somewhere nearby and an informant.

Victor Gonzalez worked for the IRS before joining the Secret Service. He recalled his training and first experience going undercover for the Secret Service, "I came into the Secret Service in 1962 and came into an office where there were all of these senior agents. They were all very good agents. I was moved around. I had the chance to move around with different agents who gave me on-the-job training. The Secret

Service, in those days, required you to go to a training school before you came on the job. You would go into a field office and would have on-the-job training and then anywhere from six months to a year later they would send you down to Washington, DC for training at the US Treasury Training School. You were trained with other US Treasury agents in general law enforcement things that you had to do, whether it was fingerprinting, report writing, photography, or things that were just common to all federal agents. After you finished that, which took about six weeks, you'd go back to your field office and then you would go back to Washington and finally to the US Secret Service Academy. That's where you would learn about the specific jurisdiction of the Secret Service, and since you had been working in a field office, you had an idea and it wasn't like starting from scratch. You basically knew what it was all about, and now you were getting the fine points of the job and how it was supposed to be done.

"My first experience as an undercover agent was just to sit at this bar to hear what was going on. They suspected that there was some counterfeiting activity going on at the bar. Although I grew up in New York City, I was not a street guy. I went to school and to college but I didn't hang out or anything like that. I never drank, and all of a sudden they put me in a bar. I had two drinks, and my head started spinning around. I called in and said that I had to get out of there because I was getting drunk! I had only been there a short time, and I had to sit there and drink that stuff! I would be with some of the patrons there, and I didn't last long. I was told that when I went back in to take my time and just hold the drink and buy drinks for the others. So I had to be trained in these things. I was nervous about it. In some cases under certain circumstances I was scared although I didn't show it. I was worried because most of the time you went in on your own. You had covering agents, but they might be a block away. I was successful on many of the assignments."

As difficult as undercover work was, by its nature alone, it was even more difficult for black undercover agents, who often had to deal with law enforcement agencies who either would not believe they were agents or did not care. In many cases, there was an unfounded assumption that because of the fact the agent was black, then that meant the agent automatically knew about street life or life in the criminal world. Donald Tucker, who worked both for the Federal Bureau of Narcotics (1961–1965) and the Secret Service (1965–1990) and rose to the position of special agent in charge of the USSS Arizona office, states in his book, *The Two-Edged Sword*, that he was sent on an undercover assignment on his first day on the job in Chicago. He wrote that he showed up for work in a three-piece suit and was given two hundred dollars and told to make an undercover buy of heroin. When he complained that he was not dressed for the part, he was told not to worry about it because he would "fit right in." When the *buy* did not go off because the suspect refused to meet with whom he thought was a cop, the informant stated that the failure was Tucker's fault. Tucker was then instructed to grow a beard and buy some "hip" clothes so that he would look the part.

Art Lewis, who was a special agent for the Bureau of Narcotics and later became the first black agent to rise to the position of special agent in charge, often worked cases on loan to the Secret Service because the Secret Service had a shortage of black agents needed to infiltrate the numerous criminal organizations. He recounted his experience of going undercover as a black agent, "I heard the story that they wouldn't let Charlie use the front door when he came to the New York office, but I cannot authenticate that. I feel confident that it was not beyond the scope of imagination. Maybe they wanted to keep him undercover. Of course I would sneak into the federal building in New York when I started my career because I was doing a lot of undercover work. I wanted to make sure, for my own safety, that I wouldn't get pinpointed as to who I was, being an agent.

He had the same experience that I had. I was working undercover in New Orleans, and I had made a buy of heroin and I had it in the car. The informant who took me into the group was in the car with me. I was driving and looked in the mirror and could see three policemen in a car following us. I said, "Hmmm, this looks like a setup or something." What I did was stop the car so they couldn't say that I was trying to escape or anything. I got out, and the police didn't like that. As you know, when the police stops you, they always tell you to stay in the car. So I got out of the car so they couldn't do an illegal search—they didn't have a reason to search the car. I got out, with my smart self, and the informant got out as well. They started asking me my name, and I asked them, "What can I do for you, Officer?"

"Stand over there!" the guy said. "Where are you from?"

If I told him I was from Mississippi, I probably would have gotten hit in the head because I had a New York accent.

So I said, "Well, were we just driving . . ."

And this guy said, "Who are you, and where are you from?"

I said, "Officer, did I do anything wrong?"

He said, "Well, who are you? I want to know who you are!"

I said, "Well, I want to know why you are stopping me."

Our instructions were that you were not supposed to tell who you were and just take the bust. So this big tall guy thought I was talking back to him, so he punched the stuffing out of me. I fell to the ground, and it was hot. I put my hands on the ground, and my hands started burning!

The informant said, "To hell with this stuff. Arthur, tell him who you are!"

I told him that I was Art Lewis and I was on special assignment from the justice department. This guy pulled me up and hit me in the stomach and started to hit me again. He then said that there was no such thing as a black agent. It really ticked him off that I had the audacity to challenge him in the middle of the street. So he took me to jail because it was my car and I had a gun in there.

They took me to this prison, which was a big white building in New Orleans. I will never forget it because I had on a nice pair of pants and a shirt with an alligator on it. We pulled into this very narrow space, which was so narrow you couldn't run out of there.

I said to myself, "Well, okay, I'll just have to handle it."

We were walking down the hall, and I heard an inmate say, "Oh, that guy in the red shirt is cute!"

They put me in a cell and left me there. I kept saying that I was a federal agent and it seemed that they had never seen that kind of attitude from a black man in prison. So they called my office, and an agent came down to get me. They let me go, and I made them give me my gun and called them a few names . . . I was really ticked off. They continued to say that I was a drug dealer and I had a gun in the car even after they found out that I was an agent. I stayed down there and finished off my work, but it was tough!

When he was not working on an assignment and had time to spend with his family, Charlie found living in New York to be very intriguing. Living in New York City provided a drastically different social lifestyle for Charlie, his wife Ruthe, and daughter Sharon. Ruthe was able to find a job working for the treasury department's Internal Revenue Service, and that helped to increase the family income which put them in a different socioeconomic bracket. Because of her ability and work ethic, she rose to a position of international investigator and was also responsible for auditing the taxes of very wealthy individuals, which included Dionne Warwick and James Brown. Her job would send her overseas at times. She was always on planes going to Europe and different places, investigating residents in relation to their tax liability. Most of his life, Charlie had lived in a small town with small-town values and lifestyle. Both Oxford, North Carolina, and Cambridge, Massachusetts, were classic examples of small-town America, where they lived in close-knit communities and where everybody knew everybody and everybody got along. The major difference was that in Oxford you had racial segregation while in Cambridge you had cultural pluralism. New York City was a different animal altogether and had a combination of everything anyone could ask for.

"Going to New York was like heaven, and I loved living in New York," Charlie exclaimed! "I loved going to the movies and the theaters. Ruthe and I used to go out a lot when possible, and we had a lot of friends. New York was the city of entertainment. The best thing about being in New York was that I could go in and out of any movie I wanted and didn't have to pay. They were well prepared by the New York police. The cops were something else. The local people didn't tell New York City cops you can't go in here! What I hear is that cops in New York have not changed from my early years as a young agent. That's how things were done in New York.

"Starting in North Carolina was unusual in itself. The reason they kept me in North Carolina was because that was where I was hired, plus it saved me a bundle of money. They wanted me in New York because I could speak Spanish. Had I taken the job in New York, where they wanted me to start, there would have been moving fees and all kinds of expenses associated with the move. But starting me in the Charlotte office removed a big financial burden for me because after I was hired, I was transferred to New York, and they paid for all of my moving fees.

"When I reported to the New York office, the first thing they did was to assign a good sensible senior agent who would take me out to find a house. I had difficulty finding a place for me and my family. I had to stay with relatives until I found an apartment. Then a white agent took me to this area where all of the black entertainers lived. It was located in Long Island and was called St. Albans. It wasn't close-knit as living in the South, but everybody lived there. People like Sam Cooke, Duke Ellington, Cab Calloway, Billy Eckstine, Ella Fitzgerald, Lena Horne, John Coltrane, and James Brown, to name a few, lived there. My daughter used to go trick-or-treating at Count Basie's house. There were a lot of other people who dealt with entertainers, like drug dealers, who lived there as well. I didn't have any favorite entertainers. I liked them all because I was a musician. After I got out of the army, I didn't play anymore. I gave it up because I just didn't have the time.

"Every community in America has those kinds of areas where firemen or cops congregate and live together. The people who lived in these areas have a certain income that enables them to afford living in those areas. So I used to brag about living up there with those rich black folks. And they were all rich! There weren't any musicians or entertainers who were on the stage at that time that didn't live there. There was a racetrack that part of the town, and everybody would go there. That wasn't because of racism, but it was like that because people felt that you had 'arrived' if you lived in that town. It was very prestigious to be around the horses. On racing days, it would be crowded with people from all over. That was fun!"

Life in New York was indeed a great experience, but as usual, all good things must come to an end. The end for the Gittens' New York experience came with a letter from Director Rowley, stating that Special Agent Gittens was being transferred to the office in San Juan, Puerto Rico.

CHAPTER 8
Dark Clouds Rising

The Spanish I knew you could put on a postage stamp, and this Spanish—for our purposes—one does not learn in school. I cannot work here without having a better command of the language, and it is not going to come from "on-the-job" training. When I'm out by myself, I may as well be in Japan or Vietnam or Indonesia or someplace. Fooling around with a language is one thing, but trying to do investigations, dealing with police who at best can hardly say good morning in English, and trying to question suspects and prisoners is another. It can't be done! I am going to ask the chief if I can attend the language training school. If I don't get a favorable reply from the chief, then I'm going to ask the fellow at the state department point-blank whether or not he can use me in his outfit.

—Charles Gittens

It has often been said challenges in life will either strengthen your character or expose your lack of character. To date, Charlie had faced every challenge thrown at him and met the challenges with flying colors. He had dealt with segregation in the armed forces and refused to let it dampen his enthusiasm or spirit of patriotism. He had come face-to-face with the rigors of officers training school, managed to succeed and went on to lead soldiers, both white and black, when so many others fell by the wayside. He looked in the eye of the overt racism that existed in the South and managed to not only survive but to thrive. He was able to join the Secret Service in spite of the forces that did not believe a black man worthy of such a lofty position. He had gone into the underworld, in search of those who would besmirch the integrity of our financial institutions in search for a quick buck, and come out unscathed and satisfied that he had done his job well. But his toughest challenge was yet to come, and it was hidden on an enchanted island whose beauty was breathtaking, warmth inviting, and atmosphere intoxicating.

His nine-year run in New York City abruptly came to an end on March 1, 1965, when he was permanently transferred to the Secret Service office in San Juan, Puerto Rico. He was assigned there for numerous reasons. He had a working knowledge of Spanish. He had demonstrated his ability to function under pressure. His knowledge concerning investigative procedure and report writing was exemplary. He had demonstrated the ability to work well with the law enforcement community. Seniority put him next in line for promotion. And the office in Puerto Rico was in a state that required an overhaul due to a backlog of unsolved cases.

Puerto Rico is a beautiful island surrounded by the beautiful waters of the Caribbean to the south and the Atlantic to the north. It is the smallest of the islands in the Greater Antilles, which includes Jamaica, Cuba, Haiti, and the Dominican Republic. It was claimed by Spain following Columbus's second voyage to America in 1493 and was ceded to the United States in 1898 following the Spanish-American War. Puerto Ricans were granted US citizenship in 1917. With its turquoise blue water, sandy white beaches, warm tropical weather, and beautiful people, Puerto Rico seemed, on the surface, like it would be an attractive assignment for Charlie and his family. However, that was far from the case, which he would soon discover shortly after his arrival on the enchanted island.

The problems in the Puerto Rican office were vast and not necessarily a result of poor management. The office in Puerto Rico was responsible for a vast amount of space covering various jurisdictions in numerous foreign countries, but only had a staff of three agents plus one supervisor. The office covered all of the islands in the Caribbean, including the US Virgin Islands, the British Islands, and the countries in Central and South America. This meant that four agents had to cover an area from Guatemala to Argentina and from Jamaica to Trinidad. Each agent had to do quite a bit of traveling and was virtually on his own when performing an investigation. Not only was the office short on personnel, but it was short on equipment and supplies as well. All of these shortcomings gave rise to an alarming backlog of unsolved cases that brought about an unfavorable pool rating after the office went through its annual inspection. To make matters worse, in addition to catching counterfeiters and forgers, it was the responsibility of the Secret Service to keep a very close eye on the Puerto Rican Nationalist Party, whose main objective was to seek independence from the United States. This was the organization that spearheaded numerous revolts in 1950 and to which assassins Oscar Collazo and Griselio Torresola (both men died in an attempt to assassinate Pres. Harry S. Truman in 1950) belonged.

Charlie was transferred to the Puerto Rican office as a replacement for Special Agent Harry Hastings who was being transferred to another office. However, everyone in that office knew he was more than just a replacement for Hastings, but was sent there to replace the boss of the office, Special Agent in Charge

(SAIC) Frank Leyva. Charlie's arrival, therefore, created a great deal of tension and emotional reaction. Leyva, who was a very competent agent and who Charlie believed should not have been held personally responsible for the backlog, had been working diligently to correct the problems in the office, but was angered by the inspection rating because he had identified the problems and had been asking for more support from the main office for some time. Leyva was ready to leave the Puerto Rico office but did not want to leave under the current circumstances. He felt that the office should have sent Charlie two years earlier, and in that time, they could have worked together cooperatively and maybe Charlie would have been better prepared to take his place. Leyva was not happy about the fact that the main office had to send somebody here to straighten out his mess.

On the same day Charlie arrived in Puerto Rico, another agent from the Miami office, Ernie Aragon, arrived for a sixty-day temporary assignment. Special Agent Aragon had been in the service for eight years and had worked around the Cubans in Florida for several years. He had a fair command of the Spanish language, and his parents were from Spain. He believed that he would be selected to take command of the office in Puerto Rico, but when he found out his assignment there was only temporary and Charlie's assignment was permanent, he realized he would not be selected. This was a major disappointment, and Ernie expressed his desire to leave as soon as possible. He stated that he would quit first if the service assigned him there permanently under those circumstances.

Another person who felt he would be selected to run the office was Special Agent Victor Gonzalez, one of Charlie's close friends when they were in the New York office together. Gonzalez was a very talented and competent agent, and he was a native Puerto Rican. He knew the language and the culture, and people on the island knew him. Even though he was relatively a young agent and lacked the seniority, he felt the office should have recognized the outstanding work he had done and promoted him. He also requested to return to the special detail in the New York office.

This created a huge dilemma for Charlie because he was in a foreign country, did not have a clear understanding of the culture and the community, and had to work with senior agents who he needed to provide the on-the-job training necessary to do his job, but who were emotionally upset and wanted to leave. In the short time he was on the island, Charlie became convinced that the running of the office was no job for an outsider, especially in his type of work that depended on information from and collaboration with informants. Special Agent Hastings had made it there because he was accepted as a Puerto Rican and the people liked him. In fact, agents didn't even have to identify themselves as agents wherever Hastings was known. All they had to say was that they were *compañero* (partner) of Harry Hastings, and right away people would open up and say welcome. Charlie was new and was there officially to replace the popular Hastings, coupled with the fact that Frank, Ernie, and Victor wanted out.

To add to this dilemma, Charlie thought he had command of the language. After all, he graduated from college with a degree in Spanish, had taught it at the high school level in Greensboro, North Carolina, and had to use it in his work while in New York, but he found that the Spanish spoken in Puerto Rico was vastly different from the Spanish he learned in school. Spanish and English were the official languages in Puerto Rico, but the Spanish in Puerto Rico had evolved into having many idiosyncrasies in vocabulary and syntax which differentiates it from the Spanish spoken in other Spanish-speaking countries. It includes occasional Taino words (the Amerindian culture that dominated the island when Columbus arrived) as well as African words from the slaves that were brought in to work the plantations.[34] Charlie arrived in Puerto Rico on March 1 and was set to take over the office by August 30. This meant he had six months to acclimate himself into the culture and environment well enough to take command. He didn't see how he was going to be able to become proficient enough in the language in order to handle the slightest exigency by himself.

Charlie's first inclination was to look at all of the other federal agencies on the island to find out if they had the same issues he was facing and how they were able to resolve the problems. He found out that the FBI had at least fifty-five agents on the island and all of them had six months of training at the language training school prior to arriving in Puerto Rico. The FBI agents all worked in pairs and had well-paid informants to help them get their work done. He found that the deputy marshals, US attorney, customs agents, and other federal agents were all native Puerto Ricans. He realized that he had a huge disadvantage. He felt sorry for SAIC Leyva because he had to deal with this huge disadvantage and got an unfavorable inspection report against his record. Leyva knew everybody on the island, had given lectures at the police academy, chamber of commerce, and the Kiwanis Club and was president of the Puerto Rican Law Enforcement Officers Association. Charlie began wondering how he was ever going to be able to fill the shoes of Leyva or even survive on the island. For the first time in his life, self-doubt and his insecurities began to creep into his psyche. Charlie talked to Leyva about his language dilemma and about the fact that he wanted to inform Washington about his problem and request that they send him to school for language training. Leyva insisted that Charlie spoke better Spanish than most of the FBI agents and that, in time, he would have no difficulty in getting along. Leyva felt that while formal training was worthwhile, Charlie had all of the background necessary to improve his Spanish on his own. He suggested reading the Spanish newspaper daily and watching movies and television in Spanish. Leyva was very encouraging, but Charlie was a perfectionist. He knew, from his undercover days in New York, that the slightest slipup could endanger his life and his assignment.

Charlie went to a party at the officers club at Fort Buchanan given by the FBI. It was quite a moral builder for him because in talking over mutual problems, he found that almost all of the FBI agents he talked with were experiencing some of the same difficulties he was going through. One of the guys told him a story of an incident that occurred several weeks before when in his very best Spanish he started an interview with a Puerto Rican woman which went something like this:

"Perdón señora, mi nombre es John Jones, Agente Especial del FBI, etc."

Well, the agent was real proud of his introduction; he just knew he was *hablaring mucho Español* until the lady responded, "Lo siento, pero yo no hablo a Inglés." (I'm sorry, but I don't speak English.)

"Hell, lady," the agent quickly responded. "I'm not speaking English. I'm speaking Spanish!"

The agent had Charlie laughing hard, something he hadn't done for a while, and he desperately needed.

The way Charlie saw it, he was inheriting a mess, and this would be a major test of his managerial skills and abilities. In order to resolve the difficulties facing him, he knew he needed help, but soon realized he had to use his own wit and training to get out of this jam. He only had six months before he would become the boss, and in that time, he had to demonstrate to his team that he could do the job, that he deserved a leadership position, and must convince his disgruntled team that without teamwork, nothing could be accomplished. He also needed to begin to address the numerous problems that plagued the office prior to his arrival and have working knowledge of the language so he could function on his own and not put himself in a position that could get him or his teammates injured. He did have another option. He could just walk away from the whole situation and let somebody else handle it, but that was not his way. He knew he had to come out a winner because in his mind, failure was not an option!

Charlie decided to write an informal letter to Mr. Anderson, chief of personnel, explaining his difficulty and the need for language training and requested to be sent to the language school. He felt his request would be denied but wanted them to know from him about his deficiencies as opposed to them finding out from someone else. He decided to try and enroll in the University of Puerto Rico or at the school at Fort Buchanan in order to get formal language training but couldn't enroll until August, which was too late to help him. He understood the basic language but knew that was not enough, especially if he had to work undercover or do investigations on his own. He was a perfectionist and set the standard high for himself and everyone who worked with him. He found a Spanish tutor in an advertisement in the newspaper and went to get lessons from her. She was surprised he wanted a tutor because she felt his accent and command of Spanish was excellent. She felt he was being overly critical of himself, and all he really needed to do was to learn a few colloquial phrases and he would be able to handle a regular conversation. He realized he knew just as much Spanish grammar as she did and decided there wasn't very much she could teach him, so he decided not to use her services. He took Leyva's advice and listened attentively to the radio and voraciously read everything he could get his hands on that was in Spanish and practiced his Spanish on everyone within earshot. His sister Thelma's husband, Jorge Munoz, was Puerto Rican, and Charlie would write letters to him so they could communicate in Spanish.

Charlie went to bed one night, and about midnight a loud knocking on his apartment door woke him from his sleep. He was surprised and more than a little concerned by the knocking, for he did not know anyone on the island. He felt this had to be the police, firemen, or some bad news. Much to his surprise and delight, it was his friends from New York, Enid and Josephine "Josie" Quinones, who were staying in Ponce and decided to visit him in San Juan. Enid, who liked to be called by his middle name *Ricardo*, was a postal inspector. He met Charlie while they were in New York working on joint cases. Ricardo's job was to apprehend criminals who were stealing mail from the mailboxes in Brooklyn. Criminals would steal private checks, food stamps, and anything of value out of those mailboxes. If they stole government checks, then the Secret Service became involved in the investigation. Charlie and Ricardo became close friends and would often engage in a friendly competition to see who could make the most arrests. They would often go undercover together and worked as a team on joint investigations. The post office in Puerto Rico needed a bilingual investigator; and so Ricardo, who was born in Puerto Rico, applied for the position, took the test, and in September 1964 got reassigned to that office.

Since Charlie's family would not arrive in Puerto Rico for another five months, it was good to see familiar and smiling faces. They would all go out together, and they took Charlie to different places, helping him to become acquainted with the island. They went to bars, restaurants, and on tours where Charlie would practice the nuances of the language and met the people. They would drive him to Ponce, which was a long arduous trip. San Juan was about seventy-one miles from Ponce, but it took about three hours to make the trip. In the 1960s, there was no superhighway going from San Juan to Ponce like there is now. It was a long, curving one-lane road over the mountains, and it was very scary. They visited Ricardo's aunt in Santurce, had drinks at the Caribe Hilton Hotel in San Juan, and dined at the La Concha Resort. Charlie had an opportunity to use the language and began picking it up quickly.

Charlie fell in love with Ponce and, in his senior years, would often talk about returning to either Oxford, North Carolina, or Ponce to live out the rest of his life.

"Ponce was more like a seaside town with fishermen and boating," he recalled. "That was their thing. The people were very basic and simple, and I don't mean that in a negative way. They fished. That's what they did. When you took that drive over the mountains and started heading down, you got that beautiful view. It was by the sea with fishing boats docked by the harbors that were all around. The water was a pretty blue, and the atmosphere was serene. I did a lot of fishing whenever I got the chance. San Juan was a place to fish too, but it was more commercial fishing. In

Ponce, you got the local guys fishing on their small boats, some just for fun. It was very family oriented, and the environment was made for procreation. It was the rural part of the island on the water. I liked Ponce! San Juan, on the other hand, was more urban. If you wanted to find crime in Puerto Rico, you could find it in San Juan. There were a lot of bars, and a lot of drinking. This is where the sailors would come to town. They would never go to Ponce. They would go straight to San Juan and find as many girls as they could find."

While trying to master the language issue, Charlie knew his next major task was to try and keep his seasoned agents on the island with him and to get them to work together with him. He was there to replace Frank Leyva, and Ernie Aragon was there on temporary assignment. He could have written to Washington and asked them to make Ernie's assignment permanent, but Ernie had already expressed his feeling that he would quit the service if that happened. The key now was to get Victor Gonzalez to change his mind about wanting to leave so they could work together. He knew that if Vic and Frank left at about the same time, his chances for success would leave with them. He could have asked the chief to require Vic to stay, but that was not his way. He wanted Vic to stay willingly and completely on his own rather than trying to make him stay. He and Vic were good friends, and Vic was a top-notch agent.

Vic was born in Puerto Rico and came to the United States when he was eleven years old. Before joining the Secret Service in 1962, he had worked for the Internal Revenue Service in New York where he met Charlie's wife Ruthe, who was a coworker. He had wanted to become a lawyer but couldn't get into law school directly after college and needed a job. He would often complain to Ruthe about how boring it was sitting behind a desk auditing people's taxes. Ruthe told him she knew of a job that was "very interesting" and introduced him to her husband, Charlie. Charlie talked to him about joining the Secret Service and invited Vic to come and meet Al Whitaker, Charlie's supervisor. The fact that Vic spoke Spanish and was already a part of the treasury department made him an attractive candidate, and Vic became a member of the Secret Service after he passed the intensive background investigation.

After only a year on the job, Vic was selected to be a part of the special detail where he went undercover to catch counterfeiters. He was a quick learner and had several agents who showed him the tricks of the trade.

"Charlie was a tremendous agent, and I learned a lot from him," Vic stated. "When I came on the job, he was my big brother, and he was a person I could always go to and depend on for answers. Having said that, we always had a brotherlike relationship where we were always arguing about one thing after another. I had a great deal of respect for him, however. There were other great undercover agents I learned from as well. There was one agent named Lenny Vickione who was unbelievable in dealing with the criminal element."

After fifteen months on special detail in New York, Vic was transferred to the office in Puerto Rico (July 1963), where he spent four years working undercover. Ruthe had indeed been correct when she said that this job was not boring! Being an agent in New York was exhilarating, but he was really put to the test when he got to Puerto Rico.

"I had some situations where my life was in danger," Vic recalled. "I was doing undercover work in Latin America, and I remember one particular case because there was a high government official in Country X who had some information about counterfeiting for us and the US embassy requested that an agent be sent down. I was sent down, and I was on this assignment by myself. I was in a foreign country, so I was not carrying a weapon with me. This government official decided that he would meet with me, but he decided that I would have to meet him at midnight by some bridge in the park. The embassy drove me out in a regular car accompanied by a US Marine guard. He stayed back on the street while I went into this dark, isolated park by a little bridge that went over a creek waiting to meet this guy at midnight. I was alone, and it was a scary situation. It was times like that when you worried about being shot or something like that.

"I was in Chile when they had their problems with Allende [the twenty-ninth president of Chile who was opposed by the Nixon administration and who mysteriously died during a military coup]. I was there when they had curfews. I got caught up in Ecuador in a general strike, and they had tanks and military people all over the streets. In those days as an agent, I'd be all alone, and it was left to me to figure it out on my own.

"I was in Columbia, one time, on a counterfeiting investigation and was staying at the main hotel there. I was sleeping when all of a sudden I heard gunshots. I got up and started running to the window to see what happened and tripped over this chair and hurt my knee. I got to the window and looked down and saw this guy sprawled out on the ground and then I heard another shot. I went back to the phone and called the people that I was working with there. I was working with them supposedly on a certain assignment, but I was doing other things. They had no reports about the shooting and told me not to worry because they would send somebody up there and call me back to make sure I was okay. I saw some police units come to investigate the crime scene. My contacts called me back in about fifteen minutes and said that it was just the guards at the hotel. One shot the other and then committed suicide, and that's what you saw. I said, 'Okay.' But I was still shaking. It was the anniversary of the Cuban Revolution. I was there, and it was interesting and somewhat frightening."

Charlie planned to talk to Vic to try to get him to see the advantages that would accrue to both of them if he stayed. Charlie knew from experience, however, that it would mean nothing unless he demonstrated he could carry his own weight and perform as well as or even better than any agent on the island. In fact, he was

SAIC Gittens meets heavyweight boxing champion Rocky Marciano (center) and El San Juan Hotel's assistant manager Jack Bolivar in San Juan, Puerto Rico (1968)

Gittens participates in the INTERPOL Conference in Rio De Janerio in 1965

determined to not only demonstrate to Vic and the other agents that he could do the job, but he was determined to prove it to himself. This wasn't the first time in his life that he was faced with trying to convince others he was worthy of leadership. He knew from his days in the military that leadership could take many forms, but a more effective leadership style was when you lead by example. He remembered the time he wrote a letter to his mother (February 6, 1950) to try and calm her nerves about his desire to join the paratroopers once he found out what was to be his first assignment as an officer. In that letter he wrote,

> Mom, will you please stop worrying about my joining the paratroopers. There's absolutely nothing to it. Nothing whatsoever to worry about. Besides, it'll probably be quite some time before I know whether or not I'll be accepted. You see, the detachment I'm going to command is with the Eighty-second Airborne Division, and most of the men are paratroopers. And as detachment commander, my prestige and respect will be greatly raised if I also am a paratrooper. Paratroopers are a very haughty and proud group of individuals, and they don't like to have anything to do with people who aren't paratroopers. So since I'm going to be right down there with them, I may as well become one of them. Besides, as a military policeman, I wouldn't have to make many jumps.

Charlie knew he had to gain the trust and respect of the agents in Puerto Rico, and to do so meant he had to go out on his own and do the job. He accepted assignments that took him to Bogota, Colombia, Managua, Nicaragua, Peru, and Panama.

"I did exactly what I did in the States," Charlie exclaimed. "I worked in all of the Latin countries and countries in Central and South America. I was able to go out on my own and independently make arrests, dealing with counterfeiting and forgery. I think it shocked a lot of people that a non-Spanish-speaking Yankee could make a trip around the island alone without a 'native guide' and still get a credible portion of the work completed. I was determined to do it!

"I made my first arrest on a PRS [Protection Research Section] case when I had to take in this guy who made remarks against President Johnson and his wife. The guy was nutty as a fruitcake although you'd never know it to talk with him. He had just started work as a trumpet player with the Paul Anka Show, which had just opened at the El San Juan Hotel. He was supposed to be playing in the band at an exclusive tourist hotel, but instead he spent the night *en el cárcel* (jail), so I don't know how the show got along without him. I guess a trumpet player wasn't that important when Paul Anka was singing. I really felt sorry for the guy. He was quite likeable and intelligent. All he had done was enjoy his freedom of expression. He had written a two-word message to President Johnson—*fuck you!* Really it was a little more than that. He wrote two such messages and said that he also sent a similar greeting to Lady Bird Johnson. I felt a little guilty about locking him up by myself, because using the criteria that got him in his jam, he should have had about three hundred Secret Service agents after him."

Another dark cloud on the horizon that caught Charlie totally off guard dealt with an issue he had absolutely no control over and fewer answers for. In fact, it was an issue for many federal agents whose obligations to the job disturbed the harmonious growth of the agent's personal life. The wives and children of federal agents, especially in the early days of the service when there were so few agents trying to do multiple tasks that required long hours away from the family, had to adjust to a life that was marred with fear, absenteeism, and infidelity. Wives had to come to grips with the fact that their husbands were not only married to them but married to the service as well, and more often than not, the wife came in second in this three-way relationship.

"The one problem with the job was my wife," Agent Victor Gonzalez stated. "When I was working with the IRS, she was used to me coming home from work every day at 5:00 p.m. I would take the bus and be home in fifteen minutes. When I joined the Secret Service and started working undercover, she never knew when I was coming home. Every morning you had plans, but you never knew what was going to happen that day. Every day something new would pop up, and you were mobbed with that. It was pretty tough on the wife because that was not what she had signed up for. It took her a little while to get used to it. I don't think she ever got used to it."

Special Agent Clint Hill, who achieved notoriety for jumping on the back of President Kennedy's car and shielded Mrs. Kennedy from harm during the assassination of President Kennedy, expressed similar concerns regarding how his responsibilities with the Secret Service influenced his family life.

"I was assigned to Mrs. Kennedy for four years and realized that I was away from my family 90 percent of the time," he recalled. "In the time period from 1960 to 1964, I didn't spend any Christmas or Thanksgiving with my family or any birthdays. I had two sons, and they really grew up without a father. My wife and I don't even live together anymore. For all intents and purposes, home was just a place to go to change clothes and take a shower. My first son was born while I was still in the army. My second son was born while I was in the Secret Service. I was in Newport, Rhode Island, while he was born in Alexandria, Virginia, so I wasn't there for his birth. It was really tough on the family. My sons don't talk about my days in the Secret Service at all. I think they resent it because they didn't have their daddy. My emphasis was on the job and not the family. It was just like being in the military, doing a service for my country. Now they didn't want for anything because they were well taken care of, but that's not the point. I just wasn't there."

Wives often lived in fear not knowing whether their husbands were coming home or whether they would get that dreaded phone call in the middle of the night saying that their husband was not coming home at all.

"I know what it is like being the wife of an undercover agent," lamented Josie Quinones. "He [Enid Ricardo] did a lot of undercover stuff. I was so sorry that he did because I was so afraid. One time he was down at the airport after some people for bringing in some kind of contraband, and he was out all night. Sometimes he wouldn't come home for dinner. Sometimes he would come in real late and wanted his dinner. So I would put the dinner under a double boiler, but by the time he got home, the stuff was dried out anyway. You couldn't contact him either, God forbid if you had an emergency. In those days there was no way to contact him. I guess now they have walkie-talkies or cell phones or something, but then there was nothing. I had nightmares about that. Thank goodness I had kids and relatives who were very supportive. When we went to Puerto Rico, however, it was tough because I wasn't around friends and relatives. I was kind of isolated."

The danger did not always just impact the agent, but sometimes the agent's family was placed in harm's way. Agent Art Lewis, who worked for the Federal Bureau of Narcotics and worked on joint assignments with the Secret Service, recalled an incident where his family was placed in jeopardy.

"I had a tough career, and it was hard on my family," Lewis said. "When I was an agent in Detroit, I had to put my family in protective custody because I had made an undercover case against a pretty bad group out there. An informant, who was in prison in Michigan, said that he wanted to get out and that he was willing to trade something in order to get out. He said he had information that some of the criminals involved in a case had put a 'hit' on me. He said he would tell me who it was if I could get him out of prison or lessen his sentence. We took the guy [Therland Crater] and his girlfriend [Carolyn Ann Newman], who had introduced us to the gang, and sent them up to Canada and put them in protective custody with the Royal Canadian Mounted Police in Toronto. I got a call in the middle of one night that Crater and his girlfriend had been murdered in Toronto. They were shot, and his head was cut off while her throat was cut from ear to ear. In the meantime, I had put my wife and children in protective custody back in New York. My wife was a sturdy woman. She took the children to New York, which created a lot of concern and took time out of their personal lives. But such was the life in undercover work."

"I can vividly remember lying in the bed when I was thirteen and thinking, I don't ever want to marry a man like that!" Charlie's daughter Sharon reflected. "He was getting ready to go to work, and it seemed like life was just about work! He was a work-a-holic. He was always gone. We were sad because he was always packing, and we were always taking him to the airport. Sometimes he'd come back, stay about a week, and then he'd be gone again. We had to live on his letters and phone calls.

"It wasn't until the third or fourth grade that I even knew what he did. I thought he worked in the post office like his friend Enid Quinones. My mother found out when I told her that I had to do 'show and tell' at school and needed something from the post office to show. That's when she told me that he did not work for the post office, but that he worked for the Secret Service. I didn't know what that was. People knew about the FBI, and people knew about the local police, but what was the Secret Service? Well, maybe it was a secret, I thought.

"Even when he was home he was working. He started to learn how to bug stuff, and when he came home, he would practice bugging things around the house. I came in from playing one day, and my mother met me on the sunporch and pushed me back out of the door. She said, 'Your father is bugging everything in the house. I think he bugged your Chatty Cathy doll, and I think he bugged the toy stuffed Llama that he brought back from Peru. I just want you to know.' I think she felt that it was an invasion, but she knew that he had to learn to do it. A few weeks later, I was playing with my Chatty Cathy doll, and I guess it had a two-way transmitter in it because his voice came back through the stinking doll! Ha-ha-ha, I guess it was supposed to be funny, but it scared me to death."

Charlie's wife Ruthe was used to him being away from her, but up until this point was able to handle it. When they first got married, he was in the military. Even when he resigned his commission in the active military, he joined the reserves and was a part of a military intelligence unit that took him away during the summer months. Then when he got his job as a teacher at Dudley High School, he lived in an apartment in Greensboro, North Carolina, during the week while Ruthe lived and worked in Durham, North Carolina. She was not the typical stay-at-home mother that was characteristic of professional women during the 1950s and '60s. She had a master's degree and had worked most of her life, often with very influential individuals. When Charlie got transferred to the New York office, she got a job working in the IRS as an international auditor. She would often fly to Europe or Canada or the Caribbean to interview celebrities and influential subjects. She had her own career along with being a wife and mother.

The move to Puerto Rico was devastating to Ruthe. She not only had to give up her career and became a stay-at-home housewife, but she left the lights, the action, and the hustle and bustle of life in New York for the isolation of the suburbs of San Juan. To make matters even worse, she couldn't speak a lick of Spanish and was now in a country where that was the major language. She even tried to enroll in the University of Puerto Rico to take a couple of classes in Spanish but to no avail. Her gregarious personality enabled her to get help with the personal daily living issues, but it was very difficult. When she and her daughter, Sharon, got to Puerto Rico, they first lived in a place called Santurce, which was a suburb of San Juan. Soon after, they moved to a place called Bayamón, which was also a part of the metropolitan area of San Juan, and finally moved to an upscale gated community in Guaynabo.

They lived in an area where there were no other Americans nearby. They may have been one or two Americans in the general area.

"She didn't like Puerto Rico," Sharon stated. "She loved New York! New York was a big city, and we were close to relatives. We had relatives in New York, we had relatives up and down the East Coast. We were close to Boston and could get to North Carolina when we wanted or needed to. We had relatives in Philadelphia and New Jersey, so that was convenient. In Puerto Rico, however, we had no relatives, no friends, and there was a language change. We were isolated. Dad had been there ahead of us, so he had a few friends and he had his work. She just had me. She would keep telling me that it was going to be alright, and that it was important for my father's job. She would tell me that I was going to make new friends and learn a new language. I was twelve when we moved to Puerto Rico, and I hated Puerto Rico. It turned out that she didn't like it either. That was when we really began to bond into a sisterhood and not just a mother-daughter relationship. She was an only child, and her mother left her when she was young to join the mass migration of blacks from the South to the North. Her father joined that migration a little later, and Ruthe ended up staying in the South and being raised by her Aunt Ollie Johnson. Aunt Ollie sent her to Mary Potter Academy and later to North Carolina College. She was determined that I be raised in a home with love and discipline, but she had to become my mother and father.

"We would laugh about how crazy everything had become. I'd get frustrated, and she would talk me through it. I remember when we first had to go to the grocery store and we didn't know how to catch the bus or get a cab. People didn't stop to help us, so we would walk that long walk. She would laugh and say she should have worn different shoes. Then we would get into the store and found out that the men would pretty much shop with the family. She let my dad know and would say, 'We looked strange, just a woman and her child in the grocery store, so you are going to have to go to the grocery store with us!' He would say, 'Go to the grocery store for what?' And she would say, 'So we would look normal! I don't want to be the odd person.'"

Even when her husband was promoted to run the office and was able to come home on a more regular schedule, his travel schedule was still full, and he was constantly absent from the home. His responsibilities now included developing friendly relationships with leaders of other countries, delivering speeches or conducting workshops for police organizations, and helping other police organizations resolve some of their problems in addition to running the San Juan office. He was also sent back to New York from time to time to testify in counterfeiting and forgery cases and to report on the political activities of the Nationalist Party.

There was one assignment where he spent a month (May 10–June 18, 1965) assigned to the personnel and training section of the Secret Service for the purpose of conducting a recruitment program for qualified minority group applicants for appointment to special agent positions within the US Secret Service. He coordinated the recruitment program that included fellow African American special agents Ronald Meriwether, Robert Faison, and Philip Struthers. They travelled to forty-four Negro colleges and universities located in the southeastern part of the United States. They gave presentations to seniors, outlining the advantages and requirements of becoming an agent and generated a list of potential candidates.

The constant fear, loneliness, boredom, isolation, and the discovery of an indiscretion of a social nature started Ruthe down a path of self-destruction that caused her to slip into the abyss of cigarette smoking and alcohol. She and Charlie always wanted a large family, but as hard as they tried, Sharon turned out to be their only child. Sharon spent most of the waking day in school, and with Charlie away so much and her coming to grips with being a housewife, Ruthe's only activity was keeping the house clean, listening to music, and waiting . . . waiting for her daughter and husband to come home. The smoking was a habit she had developed early in life but had curtailed until now. It ultimately led to a devastating battle with cancer that she fought hard, but would ultimately lose.

The much-anticipated memo arrived in the Puerto Rican field office on July 6, 1965. The memo was from Secret Service Director James Rowley and addressed to Special Agent in Charge Frank Leyva. Regardless of what the other agents thought or felt, Charles L. Gittens was promoted to special agent in charge (SAIC) of the field office of San Juan, Puerto Rico, to take effect on August 30, 1965. He was now responsible for everybody in that office as well as the operation of the office. He had to sign off on reports and make assignments for the agents. The mess that was the San Juan field office was now his mess and his job to straighten out. He began tackling each deficiency one by one. He had the ability to request agents that he wanted or needed and got his bilingual partner from New York, Joseph A. Gasquez, reassigned to San Juan. Charlie was also able to convince Vic Gonzalez to renew his agreement to extend his tour of duty in San Juan for another two years. By June 8, 1966, they were able to reduce the caseload of unsolved cases from eighty-five to eight. He sent memo after memo to Director Rowley requesting an increase in the number of men to handle the numerous incidences of counterfeiting, an upgrade of equipment that was outdated and archaic, a reevaluation of operating procedures in San Juan that he felt were antiproductive, and a stern sixteen-page retort to an inspection report that he felt was unfavorable and unfair in light of his many request.

Director Rowley sent Charlie a memo dated September 22, 1966, acknowledging the many deficiencies of the San Juan office, but made it very clear what was expected of the San Juan office and what he expected Charlie to do in spite of the deficiencies. In the memo, Director Rowley stated,

> *We are not unmindful of circumstance in your and some other offices which pose unique problems and require special consideration. The special requirements of San Juan are of concern to me. The history of*

*violence in the Nationalist Party, the proximity of Cuba, and the social
unrest in Latin America require constant reevaluation of the role which
the San Juan office plays in protective intelligence. THIS SHOULD BE
YOUR PRIME CONCERN. To the extent of your limited resources, which
we hope to implement as soon as additional personnel are available,
you should give first priority to protective intelligence matters. If this
requirement results in an inability to handle matters of lesser priority,
the situation in San Juan will be taken into consideration by this office
in evaluating the performance of your office.*

*Your efforts to recruit a suitable agent in Puerto Rico who could
be assigned to the San Juan office to increase our intelligence capability
should continue.*

In other words, protection of the integrity of the national currency had been
the primary reason for the development of the Secret Service, but following
the assassination attempt on President Truman on November 1, 1950, and the
assassination of President Kennedy on November 22, 1963, the main focus of the
Secret Service shifted to the protection of our political leaders.

CHAPTER 9
We Live in the Shadows

The only time anyone knew about the Secret Service is when we messed up. Very few people knew what we did. You didn't want to be known; you wanted to be Mr. Anonymous. The only way we knew we were doing our jobs was when nothing went wrong. That was our gratification. As long as nothing went wrong, you were happy because you knew you had done the job right. When something goes wrong, it usually ends up in death. We lived in the shadows, and that was acceptable.

—Clinton J. Hill, US Secret Service

Charlie walked proudly into a bar in Cambridge, tagging along with his popular brother Sonny. All of the regular fellows were there and were very pleased to see Charlie. His return to his quaint little community was like that of Caesar returning to Rome or MacArthur riding in a New York City ticker tape parade . . . a conquering hero. He was now a celebrity, and everyone wanted a piece of him.

"Show me your gun Charlie," one patron exclaimed.

"I saw you on the tarmac when Khrushchev came to DC," shouted another.

"Did you actually talk to President Kennedy when you were guarding him?"

"What was Mrs. Kennedy like?"

"Was Nixon as mean as everyone says he was?"

"Was that really Shirley Temple I saw you with?"

Question after question came pouring out before he had an opportunity to respond to one inquiry. Sonny stood proudly in the background as if he had done these things himself. He was happy for his little brother and listened intently as the conversation bantered back and forth. To please the crowd, Charlie took out his Secret Service identification and his .357 magnum handgun, took out the bullets, and let the onlookers touch them as if they were a handful of gold, while he spun stories that had the whole establishment erupting in laughter. Charlie was a gifted storyteller and mixed in a great deal of fiction that had the hint of truth. He was careful not to mention too much, for most of what people wanted to know he could not reveal because he was sworn to secrecy. But he couldn't help but bask in the glow of the moment. He held an important position that carried with it a certain amount of prestige and honor. He remembered how he felt about the treatment veterans returning from WWII received and how he wanted to be so much like them. He had accomplished that dream and so much more.

Most people knew very little about what he actually did or knew much about the Secret Service except for its role as protector of the president. They didn't know about his ability to go undercover and become different characters so far removed from his own personality that they would not even recognize him. They didn't know about his role as a supervisor and organizer who was placed in charge of other agents all over the world. They didn't know about the countless hours he spent investigating, interrogating, and testifying against check forgers, counterfeiters, and other criminals. When one thinks of the Secret Service, the popular image is that of the stone-faced, deadly silent, sunshade-wearing professional talking into his sleeve and watching everything that moves with piercing eyes and catlike reflexes.

The assassinations of presidents Garfield, McKinley, and Kennedy, the attempted assassinations of presidents Theodore Roosevelt, Franklin Roosevelt, Harry Truman, Gerald Ford, and Ronald Reagan, along with various films like *In the Line of Fire* and *Guarding Tess* have made the protection of the president synonymous with the Secret Service. But it was the assassination of Pres. John F. Kennedy in 1963 that had a major impact on the Secret Service, how it operated, and how it was viewed. The countless conspiracy theories surrounding the assassination of President Kennedy, some of which included the Secret Service as either supporting culprits or incompetent protectors, have thrust the Secret Service into the limelight of the American political and historical conversation. Historically speaking, the Secret Service has had a relatively good track record trying to accomplish an almost impossible task (i.e., preventing a crime before it happens) with limited resources. There have been countless attempts on the lives of our elected officials, many of which the public are unaware and will probably never hear about—some thwarted by fate, luck, or circumstances and many that have been thwarted by the Secret Service. The Secret Service chooses to keep the number of threats or attempts secret because of fear that this knowledge would stimulate many more attempts. Since the assassination of President McKinley in 1901, the Secret Service had successfully thwarted numerous assassination attempts for sixty-two years before President Kennedy fell to an assassin's bullet. Each failure, however, had devastating effects and has highlighted the importance of the men and women who are members of the Secret Service.

It was an unusually cool spring evening in Washington, DC. People of all races and nationalities were out on the streets strolling around in a carefree manner which disguised the turbulent times that plagued the nation and had thrown it into a cauldron of violence for so long. There was an eerie calm in the air that seemed to indicate better days were on the horizon. The president and first lady had decided to take a break from their usually busy schedule and ease the tension with some light entertainment. Everyone seemed to be having a wonderful time. Suddenly, out of the darkness, a darker figure appeared, crept into the president's box, pulled a .44 single-shot derringer, and squeezed off the trigger, blowing a gaping hole in the back of the president's head. They rushed the president across the street and tried to save him, but everyone in attendance knew that on that fateful night in April 1865, Pres. Abraham Lincoln was no more. Lincoln's bodyguard, John Parker of the metropolitan police force, had left his post of duty that night and was having a drink at Taltavul's Star Saloon, which was located next door, when the fatal shot was fired. The irony of this situation was that earlier that morning, Secretary of the Treasury William McCulloch had met with the president and suggested that a special organization be created to combat counterfeiting. President Lincoln agreed, and three months later, the United States Secret Service was born . . . three months too late unfortunately.

The Secret Service was not there thirty years earlier when in 1835 Richard Lawrence walked up to Pres. Andrew Jackson, aimed a derringer at his chest, and pulled the trigger. Fortunately the gun misfired, and an infuriated Andy Jackson tried to beat the man to death with his walking cane. Nor was Pres. James Garfield afforded the protection of the Secret Service in 1881 when Charles Guiteau walked up to an unprotected Garfield and fired two shots into his shoulder and back. Garfield died three months later of blood poisoning. Tragedy was avoided in 1912 when former Pres. Theodore Roosevelt, who was running for reelection, was the victim of an assassination attempt. It was Theodore Roosevelt who gained the presidency following the assassination of Pres. William McKinley, and as fate would have it, an assassin was now after him. While on his way to give a campaign speech, John Schrank fired a bullet from a .38 revolver into the chest of TR. Though struck in the chest, TR decided to give his speech anyway, telling the audience that he had been shot and exclaiming, "It takes more than that to kill a Bull Moose [the name of the political party he was representing]!" After the eighty-minute speech, TR went to the hospital where the doctors decided the bullet posed no threat to his internal organs and left it in his chest. It was believed that it was the speech's thick manuscript, folded in his breast pocket along with a metal glasses case that absorbed most of the bullet's force. It may have been luck or fate that saved President-elect Franklin Roosevelt in 1933 when Giuseppe Zangara fired six shots into a crowd that had come to hear FDR. Five people were hit, including Chicago Mayor Anton Cermak, who later died from his stomach wound.[35]

It wasn't until after the assassination of Pres. William McKinley in 1901 by

Leon Czolgosz at the Pan-American Exhibit in Buffalo, New York, did Congress give authorization for the Secret Service to protect American presidents. The Secret Service thwarted one of the most dramatic assassination attempts on a US president when in 1950 two Puerto Rican nationals (Oscar Collazo and Griselio Torresola) tried to shoot their way into the Blair House [the temporary residence of the president while the White House was being renovated] in an attempt to assassinate Pres. Harry Truman. In a raging gun battle that took place on Pennsylvania Avenue, the two assassins shot and killed Secret Service White House Police Officer Leslie Coffelt and Joseph Downs and wounded Officer Donald Birdzell. Before succumbing to his wound, Officer Coffelt got off a shot that hit assassin Torresola in the head, killing him instantly. Special Agent Floyd Boring and Officer Joseph Davidson joined the gun battle, wounding Collazo and ending the attempt.

Pres. Gerald Ford was able to escape two assassination attempts when Lynette "Squeaky" Fromme, a follower of Charles Manson, pointed a gun at the president and three weeks later when Sara Jane Moore fired one shot at him. Even popular Pres. Ronald Reagan was the victim of a deranged gunman, John Hinckley Jr. Reagan was shot in the lungs before Secret Service agents wrestled Hinckley to the ground and subdued him. All of these assassins and would-be assassins were either arrested and sent to prison, a mental institution, or executed for their crimes.

Winter in America was an album written and recorded by famous jazz musicians/ poets Gil Scott-Heron and Brian Jackson. It was also used by them to describe a period in American history between 1963 and 1974. Scott-Heron used winter as a metaphor: "a term not only used to describe the season of ice, but the most depressing period in the history of this industrial empire marred with threats of oil shortages, energy crisis, political corruption and the murder of our political leaders." During this cold season too often our television programs were interrupted by Walter Cronkite or Tom Brokaw with the infamous words, "We interrupt our regularly scheduled program with a bulletin special. . . . President Kennedy has been shot!" In what seemed like a very short span of time, we witnessed the assassinations of President Kennedy and his brother Robert F. Kennedy, as he ran for the presidency, the shooting and crippling of Gov. George Wallace as he ran for the presidency, the assassination of Martin Luther King Jr. as he fought for social and economic justice, and the attempt by the Nixon administration to maintain their power by committing crimes against the Constitution and committing political suicide in the process. It was indeed, to coin a phrase from Shakespeare's *Richard III*, "the winter of our discontent."

The publicity surrounding the assassination of President Kennedy caused a major reorganization of the Secret Service. The Secret Service that existed before Kennedy was small, and agents where hired to accomplish its primary task, going after counterfeiters and check forgers. There was a permanent division within the Secret Service, then known as the White House detail, whose main purpose was to protect the president and his family. That detail was small in comparison to what exists today. If the president, however, traveled to a particular city, then agents in the field office of that city were taken off whatever assignment they were doing at the time and assigned to temporary duty to help with protection. According to Special Agent Clinton Hill, there were only 269 agents worldwide in the Secret Service when he entered the service in 1958. Today, there may be 269 agents on one protection assignment at any given time.

"It was an extremely small organization at that time," Hill reflected. "The only way you got into the Secret Service was if someone retired or died; otherwise there were no vacancies. There was a branch of the Secret Service called the Protective Research Section (PRS), which was the intelligence arm of the service. This division was abolished after the reorganization in 1966–1967. This is where all of the files that were kept on threats to the president were received and analyzed. An advance team usually had to go out to check on the location the president was going to visit. If you were going to do an advance research on a particular city or area, this is where you would check first to find out what was going on in that area. If there was something that was going on that you needed to know about, the guys in the PRS would know and be able to tell you who were the cases in that area that were of concern. It is hard for me to think about it today because we had three-by-five cards with the information on threats; we didn't have computers then. The cards would have information about a suspect on one side and his/her picture on the opposite side. It was really primitive. You sorted everything by hand and there weren't many people working in that section either. So if the president was going on a big trip that included a lot of stops, you had to gather the information together for all of those places, and you really had a problem.

"We didn't have very good equipment either. We got leftovers. Whatever we got that was any good, we got from the military. We got those big radios; there weren't any personal radios or anything like that. When I came into the service, I was issued a four-inch .38 Colt revolver, a set of handcuffs, a handcuff key, a commission book, a badge and a Secret Service manual, and that was it. We had so few people, and Congress wouldn't let it get increased. You were stuck with what was available to you. When something bad happened, then Congress would allocate the necessary funds. That happened every time. I remember when I became the assistant director, we wanted to install big electronic gates at the White House complex. Congress wouldn't give us the money. One Christmas Eve, a guy comes down Pennsylvania Avenue, turns right, and drives through the gate. He knocks down the closed gate with his truck, drives up close to the North Portico, and gets out. He has his entire body covered with what looks like a bomb with tape and all that kind of stuff. We defuse the situation, and about a week later, Congress approved everything we asked for. Nothing adverse happened with this guy because he was crazy, but that was the only way we could get things approved. Something had to go wrong before they'd finally say okay. The FBI got whatever they wanted, however, and that probably was because of J. Edgar Hoover. He even had an armored car! We didn't have an armored car, and we were protecting the president!"

Protection of the president, according to the Warren Commission investigating the assassination of President Kennedy, was an "extremely difficult and complex task. It was unlikely that measures could be devised to eliminate entirely the multitude of diverse dangers that may arise. The protective task was further complicated by the reluctance of Presidents to take security precautions, which might interfere with the performance of their duties, seriously or accept security procedures which may inhibit their desire to have frequent and easy access to the people." Confrontations between the agents guarding the president and presidential aides, who want maximum exposure, are historic. An example of one of these classic confrontation occurred when presidential aide H. R. Halderman wanted spontaneous crowd scenes at one of Nixon's infrequent presidential campaign appearances. There were reports that during an appearance in Providence, Rhode Island, Halderman wanted to drop the barricade to permit the airport crowd to swarm around the president. The special agent in charge (SAIC) of the White House detail, Robert Taylor, remembering the shooting of Governor Wallace of Alabama during a primary campaign, ordered tighter presidential security. It was reported that Taylor threatened to arrest Halderman if he lowered the ropes. The end result was that after the confrontation, Taylor was demoted and transferred to the SAIC of the visiting dignitaries' detail.

Pres. Lyndon Johnson relied heavily on the Secret Service, and yet at times he would become furious with his agents. He even fired one of them thirteen times.[36] "President Johnson was odd, a little different," Charlie recalled. "The guys really close to him, I mean his staffers, seemed to be able to get him to do whatever they wanted him to do. You could tell, however, that he really loved being president, or it sure seemed that way. He would like to make decisions that should have been left to someone lower on his White House staff. When it came to his relationship with the Secret Service, you kind of got the feeling he was determined to get whatever he wanted. He was president of the United States and felt that he should get whatever he wanted."

Charlie stood outside of a major hotel in Manhattan in New York City. The dark shades seemed somewhat silly at first because it was an overcast day, but were necessary to hide his true intentions. For while everyone's eyes were straining to get a glimpse of President Eisenhower, all of the Secret Service agents trained their eyes on any potential danger that could befall their protectee. The purpose of the sun shades was not to protect the agent's eyes from the sun, but to hide the intense wandering gaze of the agent as he looked for anyone with their hands in their pockets, or if someone was wearing a bulky overcoat on a warm day, or if one of the thousands of faces that were labeled as threats and placed on the bulletin board in the Secret Service office appeared in the crowd. Every agent in attendance was trained in hand-to-hand combat, could shoot the head off a needle, and was prepared to use deadly force at the sight of any attempt on the "general's" life. Charlie was no different. Eisenhower was his first presidential assignment, but he would not be his last. In fact, Charlie worked with every president—either as a special agent assigned to temporary protection duty or as the special agent in charge, whose responsibility it was to ensure the protection detail went off without a hitch—from Eisenhower to Jimmy Carter. He felt that he did not play a significant role in the protection of Eisenhower because he was such a "low man on the totem pole and there were a ton of agents used for the presidential appearance." Agent Clint Hill, however, had a different recollection of Charlie's significance. Hill recalled,

> I went to New York occasionally when President Eisenhower went to New York, and in that process, I met Charlie because Charlie was assigned to the New York field office. When we would come up there to New York with the president, the entire New York field office would assist us. It was in 1959 when I first met Charlie. My first impression of Charlie was that he was quiet, kind of reserved, and always had a smile on his face. It was obvious that he was well regarded by all of the agents who worked with him by the way they respected him. It was just infectious. You got that same impression as soon as you met him. He was a guy you could trust, and you could depend on him. My impression just got better after I knew him a while. You never had to worry about anything if Charlie was involved. If he was involved, you knew things were going to be done right. That's the way he did things. He was a perfectionist. Everybody recognized that.
>
> He probably got some of the toughest assignments because of that, especially in the investigative field. I know that he worked a lot of undercover work, and that's not easy to do. When you are undercover, you can't be yourself—you are playing the part of somebody else. You are running a risk, and he was willing to do that for the organization and for the country. He did a fantastic job of it. And we needed Charlie. There were circumstances in investigations when nobody else could do the job. This was because he was black, for one thing, and he was smart and knew how to handle himself. He was a lot smarter than they were. He took some risks, and he came out the top dog. I didn't know the exact cases, but I know they were counterfeit cases. He was working undercover in New York with an Italian agent name Carmine Motto. Charlie did everything right; he was meticulous. If you

gave him an assignment, it was thoroughly done, you never had to worry about it. You didn't have to second-guess him because he did it right the first time. He was someone who got along with everybody. I don't know anybody who didn't like him. The only people who didn't get along with him were the few agents who came from the South. There was this one agent from Mississippi who didn't get along with anybody from the North, especially if you didn't eat grits.

Whenever we came to New York, Charlie was a part of our operation. I recall going to New York in 1960. President Eisenhower had not done any campaigning for Nixon who was running against Kennedy. I was put on a team of four agents that were sent to set up the trip for Nixon and Eisenhower to come to New York to campaign. I was in charge of the motorcade and the speech at Terrell Square. I remember Charlie helped me a lot because he knew the guys at BOSSIP (Bureau of Special Service Private Investigations) in New York, and they were kind of a pain in our sides because they wanted to do things their way and we wanted to do things our way. Charlie knew how to finesse them. It was very good to have him on our side in those situations.

He got in more so during the Kennedy administration because Charlie was fluent in Spanish—Mrs. Kennedy's personal assistant, Providencia "Provi" Paredes, who was not too fluent in English but very fluent in Spanish, and she and Charlie would talk. I couldn't understand one word that was being said, but they really got along. They would have long conversations, and they'd be smiling. I don't know what they were talking about half of the time, but he was really helpful to me as the special agent in charge of Mrs. Kennedy. He knew people in New York, he knew places. He would tell us where to go and, more importantly, where not to go, and that was most beneficial.

In 1966, President Johnson went to Punta Del Este in Uruguay, and Charlie, who was the special agent in charge of the San Juan office at that time, helped us out with that. His ability to speak Spanish was a godsend because we didn't have many people who were bilingual.

In his short time in the Secret Service, Charlie had had enough experiences to last him a lifetime, but participating in the protection of the president of the United States was the most exciting and memorable experience he had in his life, especially working with President Eisenhower and later President Kennedy.

Charlie exclaims proudly:

My first presidential assignment was with Eisenhower. There I was, a young agent in his twenties out protecting one of America's foremost five-star generals, and here I am in the room with this guy and other agents! It was my principal assignment to be close with him and watch every move that he made in order to protect him. He was a very popular guy. The funny thing about Eisenhower was that he would talk to me. He asked me what it was like when I became an agent. Was it something I always wanted to do? How did it feel when I was out there? Was I ever in the army? He seemed to know my personal feelings. I didn't see him talking to any other agents like that, so I assumed that he was questioning me because I was a black agent, or maybe because I was just a great guy! Eisenhower was such a war hero. Whether you liked him or not, he was still a hero.

Most of being on a protection detail would be boring. You couldn't slack off at all because you would have to keep your eyes and ears open. But most of it was figuring out how you were going to keep yourself awake for the next ten, twelve, or fifteen hours. You just never knew what was going to happen. Anybody who would pose a threat to the General, which is what we liked to call him, became a person of interest. The detail leader and all of the key position persons would be on the lookout for anything that could represent some kind of threat. It could appear maybe when you were going under a bridge where they were constructing something. You wouldn't even get that far. You wouldn't even go into a place like that because it presented a danger. You stayed far away from anything like that. The lead agents would get the president's itinerary and check that stuff out way in advance. The lead agents were even involved in the writing of that itinerary before it was submitted up the ladder for approval. And then tons of people would have to read the plan.

We used to practice protection scenarios where we were given situations to see how we would handle an attack on the president. The basic job of protection was the same for all the protectees, regardless of who they were. So many people would be involved from the planning stage to the advanced details that would go out to scout the areas, to the protection detail that was assigned to the president. I don't know how they did it in the early days because I didn't go out on all of those details. They would use agents with a lot of experience to go out on advanced details and then the pre-advanced details, and they would go over it again to the point that they were worn-out and bored to death by the time they got to wherever they were going.

The details in the Presidential Protection Division or PPD were made up of guys with certain experiences depending upon where the president was going and what he'd like to do. When I joined the Secret Service, the maximum number of people assigned to a presidential visit would be around 200 to 250 people. Today you can't even count the number of people who would be involved and the experiences they would have. Most are highly trained. I was assigned to the PPD just like everybody else. I was a good marksman, but not better than some of the guys who were put on the rooftops along the presidential route. They could shoot the head off a pin at a distance you could barely see. They were really good, and that's all they did. They trained every day for long hours. When I was special agent in charge, it was my job to pick people for those details. I picked more people than people picked me.

I served every president since Eisenhower. That included Kennedy, Johnson, Nixon, Ford, and Carter. I didn't do it full time because that was not the only thing I had to do in the Secret Service. Those assignments were generated as they were needed so that on any particular day, a supervisor could check the roster and see who's on the Nixon detail today, for example. Sometimes those agents might have been on that detail for any number of years. A detail didn't normally last that long. It wasn't until after the Kennedy assassination that there was a major change in the way agents were trained and who was selected or assigned to a particular president. Agents were selected sometimes based on the particular skill set they possessed. We needed agents who could swim, ride horses, participate in cross-country running, or play golf. It was based on what the president liked to do for recreation. When we were up at Cape Cod with the Kennedys, we had to select agents who knew how to swim. President Johnson liked to go to his family home in Texas, his ranch. He'd stay about two weeks. He liked to ride horses and stuff like that. I never rode with him. By this time there were a lot of guys that went with him. You'd be out there. And if you were needed, you'd be used, and if not you just be around. He had his own detail, and he had his favorite guys who'd be with him. I wasn't one of his favorites. I played just a minimal role on his detail. There wasn't a lot to do out there. The guys were like on vacation when they went there.

The assassination of President Kennedy was a major tragedy, and it caused the reorganization of the service. We might have had 300 or 350 agents at that time, but after the assassination, the organization hired hundreds of employees and agents. There was a major overhaul of how the agents operated and how they carried themselves with their personal behavior. There have been so many changes since Kennedy that I would not even recognize the service today.

I wasn't in Dallas at the Kennedy shooting because I was at a training facility in Delaware. When it happened, an alarm went out. When I say alarm, I really mean a notice went out clear across the world that all Secret Service agents had to report into headquarters no matter where you were or what assignment you were on. It was because of the shooting. It was a very stressful time."

As popular as the Kennedy administration was to the American people, it was a very turbulent time and highlighted the dilemmas faced by the Secret Service from the very beginning. According to U. E. Baughman, chief of the Secret Service in 1960, the close race between Kennedy and Nixon created a dilemma on election night of when to start protection and whom protection was to be given. By law, the service was required to give protection to the current president (i.e., Eisenhower) and his family as long as he was in office. The Secret Service was also supposed to provide protection for the president-elect and his family from the second it became clear who the winner was. On election night, Senator Kennedy was on the East Coast while Vice President Nixon was on the west coast so a contingency of agents had to be dispatched to both locations until a winner was declared. At that time candidates were not afforded protection (a law that would later be changed) so the agents had to stay close by and be on alert until election results were in. The election was so close and dragged on until the next morning that Chief Baughman took a chance and made a precarious decision to provide protection for Senator Kennedy, who seemed to be the winner and whom he felt could not go unprotected a moment later. If Baughman was wrong, there would have been dire consequences, both politically and personally, but it turned out he had made the correct decision.[37]

In December 1960, before the inauguration, an assassin attempted to take the life of President-elect Kennedy while he was on his way to Sunday mass. Richard P. Pavlick sat in a parked car in front of the Kennedy residence in Palm Beach, Florida. The car was rigged with dynamite, and his intention was to ram his car into the Kennedy car and kill everyone within walking distance, which included a contingent of Secret Service agents. Pavlick had been on the Secret Service "person of interest" list, and there was a manhunt out for him because it was reported that he had made threats against President-elect Kennedy's life. But there he was, sitting in plain sight, with every intention on carrying out his heinous plan. When Kennedy came to the door, however, his wife Jacqueline and their children came out to say good-bye; and Pavlick, as he later stated, decided that he did not want to take the life of Mrs. Kennedy and the children, so he aborted the plan at that time. Before Pavlick was actually able to attempt his plan, he was captured in the Secret Service manhunt that was looking for him.[38]

A major disaster that could have had huge repercussions on American history was avoided on the inauguration day. Thanks to the Secret Service and members of the DC fire department. President-elect Kennedy and former President Eisenhower stood on the inauguration platform along with many important and influential leaders of our country with heads bent and eyes closed while Cardinal Cushing of Boston gave the solemn invocation that always preceded the president's oath of office. Everyone participated in the prayer except members of the Secret Service, who had to keep their eyes focused on the crowd for potential threats. Suddenly a puff of smoke appeared from below the lectern. The smoke was a sign that something had gone disastrously wrong and, if not corrected, could have entrapped everyone on the wooden platform in a fiery grave and caused a panic that would have hurt many others. The wooden inaugural stand was attached to the Capitol building with only a narrow aisle leading to the building, too small to safely evacuate the numerous guests in the event of an emergency. Below the stand there was a river of radio and television cables connected so the world could witness this historic occasion. Though the wires had been inspected numerous times by the Secret Service before the inauguration, one wire developed a short and began to smolder before erupting into a major catastrophe. Chief Baughman had to make a decision to either interrupt the historical proceedings or try to clandestinely locate the problem and resolve it. While America basked in the security of the democratic transition of power, Secret Service agents frantically searched for the faulty wire and, with the aid of the fire department, put out the blaze.[39] Again, Kennedy flirted with potential disaster but came out unscathed. His luck would run out in 1963 when an assassin's bullet tragically ended his life.

To Charlie, as well as many Americans during that period, Kennedy was a very cordial and charismatic president. "He was a real human," Charlie reflected. "He was very concerned about the agents and their wives and families. It was nothing for him to talk to an agent or invite him and his family to the yard. He would strike up a conversation with you and then later would ask how things went and if you were okay. He knew who you were and would call you by your first name. This caused an embarrassing but funny moment for me once. We had gotten off the plane at Hyannis Port, and a group of us were walking to the place where we were going to be staying. We had just settled in the presidential home, and President Kennedy, as usual, sank into his rocking chair. As we were walking and keeping an eye on our surroundings, I heard the president say, "Charlie, Charlie, come here, Charlie." I looked and saw the president looking my way and immediately started moving toward him. He started waving me back and smiling, and then I saw his little dog Charlie run up and jump into his lap. Everyone got a good laugh at that one."

The Kennedy assassination and its worldwide notoriety, along with the rash of assassinations and attempts during the 1960s and '70s had a direct effect on the number of agents that were hired in order to be able to handle the volume of protection responsibilities the service inherited. Congress had extended protection to former presidents in 1961 and vice presidents and vice presidents-elect in 1962. Now the Secret Service was given the responsibility to protect former presidents' spouses and families (1965), presidential and vice presidential candidates (1968), visiting heads of state (1971), vice presidents' families (1974), foreign diplomatic missions (1975), and spouses of foreign heads of state (1986).

Times were beginning to change, and it was inevitable that the attitudes America had toward hiring minorities in highly visible, prestigious, and important positions were changing as well. Blacks, Hispanics, Asians, and women began filling the ranks of the Secret Service in increasing numbers. As the president traveled around the country and the world, he was accompanied by the Secret Service. Wherever he stayed, they stayed. Wherever he ate, they ate. The changing faces of Secret Service created a situation that challenged some of the entrenched social customs, laws, and attitudes especially in the South with respect to equal rights and equal protection. Charlie and other African American agents like Robert Faison, Hubert Bell, Abraham Bolden, and Donald Tucker met that challenge head-on, took the abuse and insults, and paved the way for other minorities to be able to travel with the president and not be harassed.

Segregation in the South posed serious problems when it came to assigning agents to the protection detail. The service sometimes dealt with this problem by not assigning black agents to certain details because they knew they would not be accepted in the hotels and dining facilities. But as the requirement for more agents to serve on protection details increased, making assignments based on color became cumbersome, inefficient, and against the ideals the service was trying to adopt.

"When Charlie came into the Secret Service as the first black special agent, it was inevitable; everyone just had to accept it," recalled Clint Hill, who became the special agent in charge of the presidential protection detail in 1966. "It was a different time, and things were different with respect to minorities, but times were changing rapidly and society had to adjust to those changes. The service recognized the need for minority agents back in those days. Charlie was just one of us who looked a little different. We didn't think a thing of it. He was just one of us, just one of a band of brothers, one of the guys. And so were the other guys like Bob Faison. Now there were certain individuals in the service, I won't deny that, who were very, very bigoted. Most of them came from Mississippi or Alabama or somewhere in the South. Sometimes we had problems with them. They didn't want to work with a black agent, and they certainly didn't want to take orders from them, but they learned they had to. It was either do it or you were out the door because the service wasn't going to put up with that. I think for the most part the hierarchy in the service recognized the fact that including minorities was now a way of life, so you had to just get used to it. Bob Faison was the first black agent permanently assigned to the presidential detail. We had some problems because certain hotels would stop him because he was black. Then we would tell them either we stay here or the president doesn't, and that kind of changed their mind. Most of the time we were in New York, and accommodations weren't much of a problem at that time."

Charlie lamented,

> It would make me mad when I was denied access to a facility because of my color, When President Johnson made his first trip back to Dallas after the assassination of President Kennedy, to attend a football game or some athletic event, I was on the trip with him. It was really interesting. The detail was made up of agents from the presidential protection detail and supplemented by other agent from other field offices. There was a whole group of us, maybe about fifty guys along with another fifty local guys. There was a group of us from Massachusetts and New York, and we all traveled together. I was the only black guy.
>
> During this particular time, segregation was alive and well in the South. We stayed in a hotel, and there was no problem with me staying with the white agents because the Secret Service blocked off a large number of rooms in the hotel for the agents and the support people who were coming in the town for the event. When the event was over, we started to check out of the hotel when one of the agents from Dallas decided they we should all go out for breakfast instead of eating at the hotel. There was a small restaurant just a block from the hotel, and we decided to go there.
>
> We left our luggage in the lobby and walked down there. I was the only person of color with this group, and most of the guys were from New York. There might have been ten or fifteen of us at the time. There was a sign out front saying, No Negroes Allowed. I didn't pay the sign any mind because at the time I was not a Negro. I was a special agent for the United States Secret Service.
>
> The local people would look at us and say, "Hey, there's a black guy. I wonder what they are doing."
>
> Somebody must've said, "The president is coming."
>
> When we walked into the store, the clerk walked up to us

and the situation exploded. He said something like, "That guy is a Nigger!"

The senior agent among us said, "Don't you know who we are?"

The clerk was so scared that he was calling me and everybody else sir. I guess it must have caused quite a scene. The clerk said, "It's not me, it's the law, and that is how it is down here. We think this is terrible, but there is nothing we can do about it. It's the law."

One of senior agents said that we were agents sent here to protect the president of the United States. Everybody knew that President Johnson was in town attending a function. The guy was really scared. He didn't know if the president was going to come in and do something awful to that city. He didn't serve me, and some guys were very upset and wanted to do something so he would never forget this. You've got to understand, some of those guys were from New York, and they don't take a bunch of junk from anybody. New Yorkers in general and especially New York law enforcement officers were like that. Some of them said that they had better serve us.

But some of the senior agents said, "No, let's get the hell out of here! We represent the president of the United States."

I thought that it was best for us just to leave there. I had dealt with segregation before, both in the army and when I was in Oxford, but I also felt that this had to change. We later laughed about it, but it made me feel terrible. Here I am, representing the president of the United States and got treated like that. It made me feel like they have to break this stuff up. But for the most part, everybody [the agents] was opposed to what they witnessed, and they felt bad for me. We knew it was happening in other parts of the country, especially in the Deep South, but we didn't expect it to be happening in the home of the president of the United States.

Though Charlie had dealt with segregation and the dehumanizing effects of Jim Crow laws before, having to face this form of discrimination now created an emotional and occupational dilemma. Blacks, as well as other minorities, had been striving to be accepted into the mainstream of American society, and Charlie thought he had achieved that by being accepted as a special agent for the Secret Service. He would soon find out that the Service had accepted him, but all of America still had not.

Charlie once said,

> The Secret Service did not stand for that kind of stuff [racism].
> Not that we didn't have discrimination, we sure did, but it wasn't
> blatant. The country was in pretty bad shape with regard to racism
> and segregation. Here goes an agent going somewhere below the
> Mason-Dixon Line, and he runs into trouble whether it is on a
> plane or a train. How the hell are you supposed to deal with it?
> That's a pretty tough thing to deal with when you think of it. It's
> not just stopping some guy when you're trying to get a cab or a
> train. I've been stopped on both trains, planes and cabs, but what
> do you do? Do you get into a fight with the cab driver?
>
> He's been told, "Don't pick up no black folks!"
>
> They were told that. I would show them my credentials and
> tell them, "I am a federal agent, a United States Secret Service
> agent. Are you going to stop me from doing my job? That really
> wouldn't look good for your company!"
>
> You try and handle it the best way you could, except you knew
> they weren't going to fire anybody because segregation was the
> law of the land. So it was a touchy situation and a touchy one
> for the way our agents handled it. The agents knew that the US
> government wasn't going to arrest the guy for carrying out his
> instructions.
>
> Some would be very blatant about it and say, "Can't do it, pal.
> I'd lose my job. What you ought to do is lock me up, and that might
> make them change the law."
>
> Most of them would say, "Sorry, pal, I can't do it" and would
> give the agent the name of their boss.
>
> I've been with white agents in other cities, and the same thing
> would happen. I would get stopped . . . It didn't happen every day,
> but frequently enough to make you conscience of the fact that
> if you started anything, the cops wouldn't be on your side. The
> cops would say, "What do you want this guy to do? It's a federal
> law. He's got a family and makes his money picking people up."
> So federal agents were in a situation where they had to follow the
> law, and the law was clear, and that was the way it was. So what
> do you do? Do you obey it, or disobey it? Do you arrest the guy?
> Depending on what state you were in, what were you supposed to
> do? Take him down to the local police station, and what do you
> charge him with?
>
> Do you think some redneck cop is going to say, "Yeah, we'll

take him, but what are we going to charge him with? He didn't break any law!"

That was a real dilemma, a real honest-to-God clash. They were enforcing the law of the land that I was hired to uphold. Many of those guys would pick you up anyway in spite of the law because they were getting paid. And as agents, we knew where the hotspots were, so we tried to avoid them. This kind of discrimination happened more so on trains, where they wouldn't let you get on, so we found other ways of getting there.

Some guy would joke around when assignments were being made. They would say, "Nah, we can't send Charlie down there." Or they would joke around, when we were marching in a parade, about people taking a shot at me, and say, "Man, I'm not walking on the side with Charlie!" We would joke about it, and that's how I was able to deal with it. I could have gotten upset about it, but I didn't let it bother me. I had been a part of a segregated army, so it was not new to me. I also knew that being the first carried a certain responsibility. I think the first of anything was a great stepping stone and opened the door wide open for others. As the first black agent, I felt it clearly meant a lot to other black agents. I don't think people have any idea what it was like, but I knew that just feeling uncomfortable was not enough to make me quit.

Charlie didn't quit. He also knew, from his army days, that rank has its privileges, and being in charge puts him in a better position to do something about how things are done. He discovered that just being a special agent was not enough . . .

Gittens greets the president of Liberia (William Richard Tolbert Jr.) along with Ambassador Shirley Temple Black. President Tolbert was assassinated weeks after this photo was taken.

SAIC Gittens is in charge of the Washington field office

CHAPTER 10
Changing Times

I was livid. I wasn't that close to Gittens at the time, and immediately I knew that the Secret Service had gotten to him. "Charlie, do you like being somebody's lackey? Do you like shining shoes? Straightening bowties? The Secret Service is using you like an Uncle Tom—can't you see that?"
—Donald Tucker, United States Secret Service

Ike Hendershot and John Myers sat patiently in the outer office at the Secret Service headquarters in downtown Washington, DC. George Benson's soulful song *Breezin'* was playing on the radio, quietly serenading the office before being interrupted by an advertisement about the new hit film *Rocky*. The Secret Service was aggressively hiring new agents as a result of the increased need for agents to support the numerous upcoming bicentennial events scheduled around the country as well as the 1976 presidential elections. They both had just been hired and were about to meet the special agent in charge (SAIC) for the first time. They had heard that Mr. Gittens was a tough boss who expected perfection from each of his agents, but was a fair man. Throughout the entire interview process, they had only met with the assistant SAIC, so this was a big day. Both men were ushered into the main office, and behind the desk sat a tall, physically intimidating black man with a stern look on his face. He came from behind his desk, strolled over to the young recruits, and, with his huge hands, shook each recruit's hand before sitting down with them at the small conference table.

He smiled at John and said, "Welcome to the Secret Service. What did you do before coming here?"

"I was a Fairfax County police officer, and I spent my last two years in the police academy as an instructor," John confidently replied.

"That's great! We have a lot of former law enforcement officers here," he replied. "You'll do well."

Then he turned and looked at Ike and said, "Ike, what did you do?"

Ike took a big swallow and quietly replied, "Well, Mr. Gittens, I was a bartender. I painted apartments, and I fashioned myself as a rock-'n'-roll singer."

A very serious look appeared on Mr. Gittens's face, and after a short period of reflection, he took off his glasses and said, "Ike, I think your application got by me! Keep your nose clean and we will see what happens."

Charlie began to wonder to himself how a guy like Ike Hendershot was able to get so far in the process of becoming a Secret Service agent. Charlie had a high expectation for incoming agents and looked only for the most experienced and qualified applicants, and he probably would not have even considered Ike for an interview. But there was something about Ike's confidence, perseverance, quick wit, and positive attitude that appealed to Charlie. Maybe it was Ike's imposing physical stature that made Charlie think he would be good for the presidential protection detail. Or maybe it was the gleam in his eye and the excitement in his voice that made Charlie remember his own attempt to join the Secret Service while working as a teacher in Greensboro, North Carolina, so many years ago. He would later find out that Ike had been a marine and had a degree in criminal justice. Eleven years of serving as the SAIC in both San Juan and now the Washington field office had sharpened Charlie's skill for identifying potential talent. He may have made some mistakes during his tenure, but in this case, his gamble on Ike paid off big dividends as Ike ended up serving twenty-five distinguished years in the Secret Service.

Ike spent six months in the Washington field office doing background investigations before being transferred to the Presidential Protection Division where he became an assistant team leader on the Counter Assault Team (CAT), a new concept for the Secret Service. The CAT provided aggressive offensive protection for all of those protected by the Secret Service based on threats. He later went on to become the deputy special agent in charge (tactical) on the PPD, then on to the role of SAIC of protective operations in headquarters, and finally the SAIC of all Secret Service emergency preparedness.

Charlie indeed kept his eyes on Ike, as well as all of the agents and employees under his supervision of the very busy Washington field office. Even though he was now relegated to working behind a desk, from time to time Charlie would go out on assignments to make sure the people under his charge were doing the job correctly or sometimes just to satisfy the urge to be back on the streets. "There was a counterfeit case once where there was a buy in Silver Hill, Maryland, and Mr. Gittens went out to watch," Ike recalled. "Well, the buy went down and the suspect took off running. Mr. Gittens jumped out of his car, ran the suspect down, and threw him on the ground. When I and the other agents finally caught up, he said, 'Take this guy to jail!' That was Mr. Gittens. He was that kind of guy—very active and engaged and he stayed in great shape. He was always ready to praise, always ready to counsel, always ready to talk. He was also a great storyteller."

Mr. Gittens had been appointed as the assistant special agent in charge (SAIC) of the Washington field office on August 24, 1969, where he worked closely with SAIC H. Stuart Knight. Special Agent Knight would later become the fifteenth director of the Secret Service. It didn't take long for Knight to recognize Charlie's talents, propensity for hard work and administrative skills, and they soon became close friends. In January of 1971, Knight sent a memorandum to Director Rowley recommending that Charlie get a pay increase due to his outstanding performance of his duties. In that memo, Knight wrote,

> *Mr. Gittens has an understanding of all the function of the office that exceeds the average. His administrative ability is excellent. Time and time again, his keen insight has forestalled problems that would have been most difficult to cope with had the situation been allowed to develop. This office has an abundance of new agent appointees and others in a training status. The counseling and guidance given these young men by Mr. Gittens is a contribution difficult to measure. Because of my supreme confidence in his abilities, I have delegated many functions to him, which he carries out in efficient and expeditious manner. He is performing at a level well above that could be expected from an incumbent of his position.*

Following the departure of SAIC Knight, Charlie was promoted to the head position (SAIC) on March 16, 1971. Being put in charge of the Washington field office was a major step in his ascent up the corporate ladder. This office covered the Washington region, which included the nation's capital, northern Virginia, and parts of Maryland. It had become the principal field office that supplemented Secret Service details all over the world. There were a million things going on in the Washington office all at once, and Charlie was responsible for them all. Not only did he have to help coordinate protection for the president and vice president, but all of the foreign heads of state and all of their family members who came to Washington, DC. With Washington being the seat of the national government, which required numerous government workers, the number of cases of theft of government checks along with the usual counterfeiting, check fraud, and food stamp fraud cases created a workload for the Washington office that never seemed to end. The office was often depleted of personnel to handle the counterfeit and forgery cases along with the overabundance of request for protection details.

Actually, the Washington field office was tailor-made for Charlie's skills set and experience, and it seemed he had been groomed for the task. He had been selected to assist Inspector Dahlquest (office of inspection) with the inspection of the Pittsburgh field office in February 1965, even before being transferred to the San Juan office. Inspector Dahlquest wrote that Charlie had "exhibited better than average knowledge as to the requirements of good administration and thorough investigations" and that the experience would "enhance his training." Charlie also received commendation from SAIC Howard Anderson (personnel and training) for the way he coordinated the forty-four Negro college and university recruiting program in 1965. Agent Anderson stated that "Special Agent Gittens served as the coordinator for the program and demonstrated that he is especially well qualified as an administrator and supervisor." Charlie was selected by Director Rowley to attend the Secret Service administration and management institutes in January 1967 and selected to assist in the inspection of the New York field office in June 1970.

As a leader of the San Juan office, it was important for him to learn the cultural idiosyncrasies of law enforcement organizations in other countries and how they operated. He found it extremely helpful to give speeches and workshops to these organizations on how the United States identified and handled counterfeiting issues. He did a great deal of international traveling and was able to forge numerous friendly relationships with many heads of state. He was selected to represent the United States at the INTERPOL (International Criminal Police Organization) conferences in Rio de Janeiro, Brazil (1965) and Lima, Peru (1968). INTERPOL was the organization established to facilitate assistance and cooperation in criminal matters between countries. He was instrumental in helping then governor Nelson Rockefeller make four trips to countries in Latin America and Caribbean during his presidential mission excursion. His connections and experience with foreign dignitaries made him an ideal candidate for the Washington field office where contact with foreign heads of state was a constant occurrence.

His tenure as SAIC in the San Juan office at first seemed like a burden but, in fact, turned out to be a blessing in disguise. It was in San Juan that his leadership ability was put to the test, and he managed to handle some of the very same issues that plagued him now, which included having an extremely large workload, inefficient number of agents to handle the massive number of cases, inadequate equipment, the importance of protection versus counterfeiting, and working cooperatively with foreign dignitaries and international law enforcement agencies. He had become a tough task master and demanded respect and hard work from his colleagues and workers. He set a high standard of excellence for himself and his workers as well, and when his decisions were challenged, as they often were in the beginning of his tenure, he made sure that everyone knew that his word, as long as they remained within the guidelines of operating procedures, was law. He chose to use his wit and gregarious nature to foster an atmosphere of camaraderie in the office, but when his directives were not followed, his kind demeanor would quickly turn cold and hard, and he was quick to resolve the problem. He documented everything, and writing was one of his particular gifts he used to get his points across. In one particular instance in 1968, when an agent refused to follow one of Charlie's directives and verbally responded to a reprimand, Charlie sent the agent a memorandum of admonition, parts of which stated,

> *When I mentioned to you that a certain number should have been used on the reports, your response and behavior within the hearing of other employees was not only disrespectful and discourteous, but bordered dangerously close to intentional disobedience.*
>
> *I am proud of your work here. You are doing an excellent job, and I have made this known to headquarters both orally and in writing. However, I cannot and will not tolerate from any employee the kind of behavior that jeopardizes the orderly operation of this office. You must certainly realize that in any organization, large or small, the ultimate decision and responsibility therefore rests with only one person, i.e., the person in charge.*
>
> *While I by no means intend to stifle initiative or imagination on the part of anyone in this office when it comes to getting the job done, all operative and administrative questions are purely my responsibility and mine alone. There will be no deviation from this policy.*
>
> *I am fully aware that you were perhaps a bit disturbed at the time due to your current personal situation. I am also aware that the very nature of our duties as Secret Service agents precludes the luxury of such emotional releases.*

His point was made very clear, and when written reprimands were not enough, Charlie was not afraid to utilize other disciplinary measures in his attempt to operate and maintain an efficient office. Such confrontations were few and far between, but Charlie sent his message out loud and clear that he was in charge.

Another issue developed after he took over the Washington office that had clear racial overtones and had to be addressed forcefully and immediately. Charlie recalled,

> One of my agents was out in the field on a temporary assignment in another office in the Midwest. I got the word back that he had been using some racially colorful language. So my boss said to me, "So I guess you heard what happened? What do you want to do about it?"
>
> I then asked him, "What do you want to do about it?"
>
> And he said, "Well, I'll let you handle it any way you want. I'm not getting involved in that."
>
> It seemed like the issue had received a lot of attention, and

everyone seemed to be waiting to see what was going to happen. I made the agent travel all the way back to Washington, DC and let everyone know why he was being called back to my office. I figured this would give me the psychological edge. His offense was calling another agent a nigger and disrespecting him in public. To some, this may have seemed to be a small offense or indiscretion, but for many others and especially me, this was too much to let go. The Secret Service was supposed to be above this kind of stuff, and I would not stand for it. Not that we didn't have discrimination, we sure did, but it wasn't as blatant at this time.

When the agent arrived at my office, I asked him what did he have to say for himself and what he thought should be done about it.

His first response was, "What did I have to say about what?'

"I said, 'We're not here to play games!"

Then he responded, "Well, I guess you'd have to take some kind of action."

I said, "Yeah, not only do I have to, but I will! I could do any number of things. It could be your job, or you could be reassigned to a tougher office. It could mean be reassigned to a detail that requires more traveling, it could be any number of things."

He responded by saying, "Well, I've got some things going on at home, and I would really hate to be on a trip at this particular time."

I said, "You put yourself in this spot. You put your wife in this spot. You put your little kids in this spot. Now they are going to be without a daddy for a while because he was sent someplace he didn't want to go."

I didn't hurt him too badly, but I did give him an assignment away from home and told his bosses he was being sent there as punishment. I'm sure he would have much rather had a white guy issue out his punishment because the word got out that Mr. Gittens issued his punishment, and he probably got chastised. There was a lot of reaction to this incident, and it turned out to be a good way to send the word out about what would not be tolerated.

Charlie's attempt to send a message that racial intolerance was not to be tolerated was clear, but the problem was far from resolved. After all, the development of racial attitudes in this country was forged over decades of hate, misinformation, and mistrust, and it would take much more than the punishment of an individual to alter such ingrained learned behavior. As more and more reports of incidences of this nature reached the office of the director, H. S. Knight finally wrote a memo on November 21, 1977, to all employees addressing the issue. In his memo, he wrote,

> *I have received some disturbing reports regarding some members of our organization. These reports come to me from a variety of sources. The reports center on what are perceived to be racist remarks and comments made to fellow employees or uttered in their presence . . . by co-workers.*
>
> *I know all of us deplore racism and bigotry. All of us desire to be treated as fellow human beings . . . with courtesy and dignity. Sometimes we speak or act before we think. Sometimes old habits persist and we fail to recognize how our utterances and actions are received or perceived. Often the 'receiver' of a message does not know the intent or state of mind of the 'transmitter' of the message. Comments made in jest or in a jocular vein may be perceived by the receiver as intended to be insulting, degrading and debasing.*
>
> *At the very least, racists remarks, no matter how intended, are in extremely poor taste! Such comments can, and sometimes do, engender extreme resentment which naturally leads to hostility. Unchecked hostility, as we all know, fosters divisiveness and is counter-productive to both the organization and the relationships of all involved.*
>
> *I charge all of you to raise your consciousness and sensitivity to these situations. I charge all of you to demonstrate (1) that you personally do not engage in this type of activity yourself, and (2) that you will not condone or tolerate such activity on the part of others. I specifically charge supervisors, at all levels, to deal promptly and firmly with any comment or action of the nature I have discussed. Disciplinary action can and will be taken in appropriate cases. I will take a personal interest in assuring that appropriate sanctions are employed.*
>
> *I also feel that there are only a limited number of our colleagues who either willingly or unwillingly engages in the activities I have discussed. I want all of you to be aware of the matter however, and lend your effort to completely eliminate it from the United States Secret Service.*

The Secret Service had tried its best to create an environment that was tolerant of cultural differences and void of overt racial discrimination and bigotry. Like so many other American institutions during the early and middle parts of the twentieth century, however, integrating African Americans into the mainstream of the organizational structure was slow and beset with growing pains. Charlie came into the Secret Service in 1956, but it took another four years before another African American was hired when Abraham Bolden joined the service in 1960. Even when African Americans aspired to join the Secret Service, they had to pass a litmus test, so to speak, to even be considered. Like Jackie Robinson, who integrated professional baseball in the 1940s, African Americans had to not only be the best of the best of their race, but had to have the emotional strength to stand up to the racial hatred and prejudice that existed without responding in a manner that would "embarrass the Secret Service." This was the price of being a pioneer. Charlie knew that in order to open doors so others could come in, he had to not only be the best, but he had to battle segregation, stereotypes (a belief that because he was black, he was supposed to automatically understand the nature of crime and poverty, or that he was intellectually and mentally inferior), as well as innuendos that he was given the job and promotions because of his race as opposed to his credentials, accomplishments, and experience and not be so emotionally upset that he could not do his job.

In 1964, Congress passed Public Law 82-352 (78 Stat. 241). The provisions of this civil rights act, which was lobbied for by Pres. John F. Kennedy in 1963 at the urging of black political and religious leaders and signed into law by Pres. Lyndon B. Johnson, forbade discrimination on the basis of race as well as sex in hiring, promoting, and firing. In the final legislation, section 703 (a) made it unlawful for an employer to "fail or refuse to hire or to discharge any individual, or otherwise to discriminate against any individual with respect to his compensation, terms, conditions or privileges or employment, because of such individual's race, color, religion, sex, or national origin." Title 7 of the act created the Equal Employment Opportunity Commission (EEOC) to implement the law.[40] President Johnson was adamant about making sure that all government organizations complied with the new law swiftly.

As a result, the treasury department, of which the Secret Service was a part, created an equal employment program to ensure that the directives of the president were met. Charlie was selected by Chief Rowley to be a member of the treasury department's employment policy review board, representing the Secret Service, at its meeting held in Washington, DC on January 19, 1965. At that time, Charlie was still a member of the New York field office. The meetings were supposed to be held two or three times per year. During the first meeting, it was revealed that the treasury department, as of June 30, 1964, had "173 Negro employees in the GS-12 category compared to only 35 in January of 1961, and 2,473 in the GS-5 group compared to 1,437 or an increase of 1,174 Negroes in the middle and higher level positions." The Secret Service, however, was lacking far behind and had to catch up with the rest of the treasury department in terms of hiring and promoting African American agents. It was Charlie who suggested that the Secret Service initiate a recruitment program where the service went to black colleges and universities in the South to locate qualified candidates, and he also suggested that the service would get more exposure if more blacks were assigned to protect the president when he went on trips, especially in the South.[41] Charlie was selected to organize and coordinate that recruitment effort.

Other African American agents like Robert Faison, who became the first African American to be permanently assigned to the presidential protection detail; Ronald Merriweather, who guarded Vice Pres. Hubert Humphrey and later became a municipal court judge in Philadelphia; Hubert Bell, who became the first African American to serve as the special agent in charge of the vice presidential detail and who later became inspector general of the Nuclear Regulatory Commission; Donald Tucker, who became the assistant inspector at Secret Service headquarters and later SAIC of the Arizona field office; and others bore the brunt of the fight to ensure that the Secret Service operated on a racially equal playing field.

As more and more minorities entered the Secret Service, the struggle to dismantle institutional overt racism and discrimination seemed to be having some success, but sexism and covert racism was entirely a different matter. Even though the 1964 Civil Rights Act prohibited discrimination against women, it wasn't until September 15, 1970, that the Secret Service set a precedent among federal law enforcement agencies when its Executive Protection Service (predecessor to the Uniformed Division) appointed its first female officer. Additional female officers were hired shortly thereafter, and one year later, on December 1971, five of those women (Laurie Anderson, Sue Baker, Kathryn Clark, Holly Hufschmidt, and Phyllis Schantz) were transferred from the Executive Protection Service to special agent positions.[42]

Charlie fondly recalled,

> I had the pleasure of bringing into the Secret Service the first women agents. Women sometimes take a beating too because in the workplace, these women were all well qualified to be special agents, but just because they were women, they weren't allowed to be employees of the Secret Service or the FBI or the Bureau of Narcotics. We had a number of women assigned to the Uniformed Division of the Secret Service, but they couldn't be plainclothes special agents of the Secret Service. Being the kind of person that I am, I said, "Those women needed to be special agents." We needed female agents in the Secret Service for practical purposes and not only for operational purposes. Not just because they were women, but many of the assignments called for women. There were some assignments that women could do better. For example, there were a lot of people that we protected in addition to the president, like foreign dignitaries when they came here. Those dignitaries usually

came with their families, which included women and kids. It didn't make any sense to me why you couldn't have women agents protecting women protectees. Ultimately, I convinced my bosses that it really was time to bring women into the Secret Service as special agents. The bosses above me finally agreed and selected six women—and assigned all of them to my office. I was their first Secret Service boss. My bosses told me that "since you wanted them, we're assigning all of them to your office."

The women had some trepidation about being the first women agents, but I told them that they didn't have to worry about it because they had the best boss in the world. I explained to them that I started as the first African American in the Secret Service, and I could probably understand what they had to go through and how they felt. I assured them that things would work out and there will be no problems. They had the advantage of serving in the Uniform Division of the Secret Service, so they were familiar with the requirements of protection, but now they were going to be special agents. I didn't treat the women agents any differently than the men. They could come in dead tired from an overseas assignment and would be sent straight out on another assignment on the street. They were just as tough as men agents and extremely intelligent.

We did have some problems when they first entered the Service. Some of the male agents had problems with it because they weren't used to taking orders from women. In addition, they suffered through discrimination just like black agents when dealing with the public. There was one particular situation that occurred at the Congressional Country Club in Maryland. Congressional was an all-male club, and absolutely no women were allowed on the premises. President Nixon was going to the country club, and my office got heavily involved with the movement and protection. We would do advance surveillance and security setup. Part of the team that went up there included one of those women. The team leader called me back, after he had gotten up there, and said, "Mr. Gittens, we've got a problem up here."

I said, "What's the problem?"

He said, "They won't let Holly into the club because she is a woman and she's got an assignment."

The young lady's name was Holly Hufschmidt, I'll never forget that. I couldn't believe it, but that's the way it was. I told the team leader not to shoot anybody up there, but we've got our job to do and they have their rules. I told him to give her an assignment on the outside of the grounds at the arrival point or some place, but she is going to stay on that detail and we will deal with their rules later. We had to work around their rules until we got the chance to change them. And that's the way it was back then. At first, we didn't have any African American agents for a long while, and we didn't have any woman. Now we have women in very high places running things. We've got a ton of black agents who are pretty big bosses in the Secret Service, even higher than I was. We now have a woman assistant director, we have women agents in charge. We have an African American woman who is the first woman in charge of one of our offices on the African continent. I am very proud of that!

Donald Tucker, an African American special agent, was promoted to a supervisory position at the Washington field office. He was involved in several projects that were designed to improve the agency and its relationship with all of its employees. In his book *The Two-Edged Sword*, he wrote about the struggles of bringing women into the Secret Service and how it was done. He stated, "I was assigned to an exploratory committee to examine the feasibility of hiring female Secret Service agents. Although it was the 1970s and the women's movement was in its infancy, I could understand why such a committee was necessary. I traveled with other agents throughout the country, interviewing personnel from the field offices and protection details. It soon became obvious to me that female agents would not be welcomed with open arms. Usual objections were, 'We've done the job without them for so long, why do we need them now?' This was probably the same type of pretzel logic that had been expressed before the United States Secret Service hired Charles Gittens and opened the door for other black agents like myself to be hired. Some of the most interesting comments came from wives of the agents. One of the standard responses was 'I don't want my husband to be working late hours in close surveillance with female agents. Only bad things could happen and romantic liaisons could occur.' [43] We also had to deal with the issue of single rooms for agents on assignments. It was the normal practice to assign two male agents to a room. It didn't matter if the agents knew each other or were compatible. It was common knowledge, however, that some agents refused or were reluctant to room with black agents. To avoid unequal treatment, all agents, male or female, were given single rooms."[44]

Special Agent Clint Hill was also on the committee that was responsible for hiring female agents. "I was one of the people who were in the process when the decision to include women was made because I was moved to headquarters," Hill said. "The decision was made that we would start having female agents. We had employed seven females as uniformed officers in the Uniform Division. At that time, the service had two divisions in the Uniform Division: the White House division and the diplomatic division. We needed women badly. I sure could have used them back in 1961, '62, and '63. I was with Mrs. Kennedy, and there were certain circumstances when you had a female protectee that it would have been really advantageous to have a female agent with you. When the decision was made to hire women, we said we already had seven that we could transfer over right now. They were all qualified, in so far as education was concerned, but we could not move one of them. We couldn't move her because she was pregnant, and we couldn't put her through the strenuous training process. From that point on, I was considered a 'pig' because I raised the point that we couldn't put this female through the training process while she was pregnant. Boy, oh boy, she hated me ever since. One of the first female agents was Phyllis Schantz who was previously a DC police officer before she came to us. Lori Anderson was another. They helped out a lot. I was the assistant director for protective forces at that time, and we were still protecting the Kennedys, Caroline and John. We also had to protect the vice president's wife, which was an addition because we didn't used to do that. He had a daughter going to school. Then you had the two Nixon daughters. So to bring these female special agents in was really advantageous for us, especially on trips. The female agents were assigned to the Washington field office because they were already here, and so that was the logical thing to do. Charlie took them under his wing and made sure they were taken care of and not abused."

Where it was easy to identify and address the issue of sexism in the Secret Service, dealing with covert racism and prejudice, on the other hand, was more difficult to identify and even harder to address. As more and more minorities entered the Secret Service, as well as other federal law enforcement agencies, the voices of discontent began to sing louder in opposition to discrimination, actual or perceived. The passage of the Civil Rights Act of 1964, coupled with the continuing civil rights movement, the reemergence of the women's movement, the public anger over the Vietnam War, and the vocal and free spirit of Americans who were disenchanted with the status quo during the 1970s forged the emergence of a different type of minority worker whose approach to resolving issues of discrimination was less passive and more aggressive. African American Secret Service agents wrote letters, registered complaints through the chain of command at first and then directly to the director, and demanded that a list of concerns be addressed. Many of the complaints centered on discrimination practices in recruitment, hiring, assignments given, performance evaluation, promotion procedures that created a ceiling above which blacks were not allowed to advance beyond, and retaliation for reporting discrimination. Other complaints included employees refusing to work cooperatively with African American supervisors, supervisors not giving African American field office manager the same support that non-African American field office managers received which was needed to run the office efficiently, and the continued use of language that was racially offensive. Some example cited in a memo sent to the director included,

(a) As of December 31, 1973 there were only thirty-six African American Special Agents out of 1,209 total Special Agents in the United States Secret Service. This counted as less than three percent of the entire force. Out of that number of thirty-six agents, twenty-nine worked in the field offices and assigned to the check forgery cases, which was considered the lowest job in the Secret Service and provided the least opportunity for advancement. Some supervisors expressed a disdain for the minority recruitment program making statements like, "I don't think it is right to lower the standards of the agency just to fill racial quotas", and even refused to hire "qualified" black applicants.

(b) African American agents, as a group, were expected to work more undercover assignments without consideration for the experience, age, or grade level. They were directed to work undercover for case agents – often their subordinates and although the successful investigation of the case was often the direct result of the Black agent's undercover efforts, the non-black agent was the employee who received the credit for the case while the black agent was evaluated poorly for failure to maintain his caseload.

(c) In order to attain a promotion African American agents, as a group, had to spend longer periods of time within a grade level than non-African American agents. The Secret Service used a performance evaluation system that was excessively subjective. As a result, performance evaluation scores were arbitrary and capricious. Even in those instances were African American special agents received high scores, the scores were not sufficient to secure their promotion (e.g. SA Reginald Moore received a score of 98.57 out of a possible 100 but did not get promoted to GS-14 position; SA John Turner scored 98.10 but denied promotion; SA C. Yvette Summerour scored 93.31 but was unable to obtain a promotion, etc.).

(d) One African American agent was a member of three law enforcement organization one being the Black Peace Officers Association (BPOA). He was warned by his supervisor against affiliating with BPOA, but encouraged to participate in the all-white groups. He was told that he could get into trouble for belonging to BPOA.

(e) There were instances when agents posted Swastikas with the word *nigger* on the walls of the Secret Service field offices.

(f) An African American female special agent was assigned to the Presidential Protective Detail and held the number two "whip" position. "Whip positions are leadership positions. The whip is the immediate backup to the shift leader as it pertains to all aspects of the shift. To obtain the maximum points for a promotion to GS-14, a candidate must receive a whip position. She was set to be promoted into the number one whip position when she was reassigned and transferred. She was told that the Secret Service was not yet ready for a black female leader. As a result of this transfer, she was unable to obtain the promotion.

These were only a few of the incidents that showed a pattern of racial discrimination African American agents tried to bring to the attention of management. When efforts to get these issues resolved did not receive the appropriate attention, nine agents filed a class action lawsuit against the Secret Service in 2000, highlighting 124 specific documented instances of racial discrimination dating back to 1974.

The struggle for racial equality in the Secret Service was waged on many fronts and was not met without resistance. There was a backlash of complaints that the service was "lowering its standards to recruit minority candidates to fill a racial quota," which was harmful, unfair, and divisive, and that affirmative action programs (a term first used by President Kennedy in 1963 referring to measures used to hire and promote women and minorities who had been the victims of decades of discrimination and exclusion] would tear the country apart. The end result, however, was that the Secret Service was able to evolve into an organization that is culturally diverse and where a purer meritocracy exists. Many young men and women were afforded opportunities to demonstrate their abilities and to participate equally in American society as a result of these struggles. One such person is Keith Prewitt.

"I've often been asked if I have ever encountered racism as a member of the Secret Service, and I can personally tell you that I have not encountered any problems," stated Keith Prewitt, an African American who began his career with the Secret Service in 1983 as a special agent and retired as deputy director in April 2012. "That is not to say there might have been some people who said some things that weren't too kind or challenged some things that I had done operationally, but if they did, they did it behind my back. They never did it to my face. I've never ever been in a scenario in my professional career, and that's thirty years now, where I felt discriminated against, whether it was a white agent or a Hispanic agent that they came after me because I was an African American agent. And quite honestly, if it had occurred, I wouldn't have stood for it. I think, when you first see me you will find that I am pretty intimidating, and that helped to deter a lot of that. I also think that I developed a reputation for being pretty competent, and I was there to get the job done. I wasn't there to be anybody's friend. We had to work together, and I was civil and always professional to everyone. It has always been my position that you didn't have to like me, but you had to respect me, and I was going to respect you until you showed me otherwise. When I would answer questions about discrimination in the Secret Service, I would tell young people, and I told members of Congress the same thing. There is no institution or organization in America where prejudice does not exist. But there is a difference between an individual being prejudice and institutional discrimination. For example, if an organization like the Secret Service, or any organization for that matter, is fostering a pervasive environment of discrimination, racism, and bigotry, that's institutional discrimination, and that is unacceptable. Prejudice will always exist and is difficult to address, not even all of the brothers get along for one reason or another! I make the distinction between individual prejudice and blatant institutional discrimination, whether it is sexism or racism, but there will always be some form of prejudice."

For Charlie, the struggle against racial discrimination in the Secret Service created a different dilemma, one he had not anticipated. The color of his skin had never been an issue when he was growing up in Cambridge as a young adolescent. That world and belief system was turned upside down when he entered a segregated army and later when he lived in the racially segregated South. Most of his adult life, he and members of his generation had struggled to be accepted in the mainstream of American society as individuals; to be judged not by the color of their skin but by the content of their character. They fought to be viewed as equal partners in the struggle for truth, justice, and the American way. They were taught that in order to make it in society, you had to prepare yourself academically, obtain academic credentials, set a high standard for excellence, and there was no substitute for hard work. He knew that if a black man was going to advance in a white dominated society, he had to be better than average and twice as good as any white person. He wanted to be viewed not just as a black Secret Service agent, someone who was different from the rest, but as a Secret Service agent, someone who was proud of his service to this country. His strategy for survival and advancement, in a situation where he had no power, was to learn the system, work your way through it, and rise above the petty attitudes and small-minded people to a position where he had the power to effect change. This strategy worked for him because he had risen to a managerial position. The problem now was that the struggle for racial equality was against management, and he was a part of management. He was now placed in a position where he had to walk a very thin line.

Following World War I, African Americans returning from the war to save democracy felt that they would be the benefactors of that international effort at home. Unfortunately, this did not occur, and in fact as economic times worsened and fell into the abyss of depression, violence and racial discrimination grew all over America. When America entered WWII, black Americans again thought they would reap the benefits of their involvement to end tyranny abroad by being accepted as first-class citizens at home. Again, when this did not happen, black reaction about this sort of treatment began to change from literary and verbal dissatisfaction to social and legal action, which led to the development of the modern civil rights movement. By the 1960s and early 1970s, the movement became influenced and energized by young adults who began drifting away from passive resistance and started demanding change. As the movement started infiltrating the northern cities, attitudes about what it meant to be black changed; and what they would accept or not accept, in terms of treatment, changed as well. *Black* became a metaphor for beauty and power, and phrases like "by any means necessary" began to be adopted as the new approach to gaining civil rights. Blacks who entered the Secret Service were of the mind-set that they were not going to tolerate racial discrimination, actual or perceived, and, as a result, took measures to address it. In some cases, especially when they felt that he was not doing enough to further the cause of racial justice, Charlie got caught in the line of fire and received the brunt of their anger.

For example, in the effort to recruit minorities from the South during the 1970s, an issue developed with the treasury enforcement examination for agents (TEA). Many black applicants from the South were unable to pass the math portion of the test, not necessarily as a result of their aptitude, but as a result of the fact that math was not a basic requirement in the high schools they attended and therefore had not taken any math courses. The public education system had historically viewed the education of black students differently from that of white students. A memorandum was sent to the assistant director seeking to revamp the examination. Charlie's position was that the examination was fair, and that if blacks were allowed to get in without passing the same requirements other agents were required to do, then the proponents who were against allowing minorities to enter the Service would have ammunition to fuel their arguments. Furthermore, as a result of his experiences with the highly educated and accomplished community in Oxford, North Carolina, Charlie had been conditioned to believe that in order for black people to advance in this country, they had to go through rigorous academic training in order to be prepared for what they would encounter in the white man's world. For him, there was no substitute for a stringent and advanced education. This conundrum and Charlie's response drew the ire of many blacks in the Secret Service who were working feverishly to get more minorities hired.

In situations where matters of race and racial discrimination were involved, Charlie was often thrust in the forefront as an example of the fairness of the Secret Service or as a buffer between disgruntled black employees and management. When African Americans complained that promotion procedures were unfair, management would respond by saying, "But what about Charlie?" Even though he had struggled and sacrificed through hardships alone, Charlie was now looked upon as a *token* by both white and black agents. Whites, who didn't have close personal contact with Charlie, felt that he was the recipient of the hated affirmative action program while blacks viewed him with distrust and contempt. In a memo sent to Director Knight, a group of concerned African American agents listed their grievances concerning racial discrimination and wrote,

> *A group of us Blacks recognizing the injustices toward us, drafted a memorandum which was a document supported by each of us with*

one exception. There was one Black none of us trusted to the extent of cutting him in on any of our plans. He, by the way, has risen very high in this agency and doesn't identify with us or relate to our problems.

Of course a copy of this memorandum was given to Charlie by management, and it hurt him deeply.

When African American Special Agent Abraham Bolden was arrested and put on trial for counterfeiting, a charge that to this day he vehemently denies, Charlie was asked to sit at the prosecution table, a ploy used to circumvent any notion that Agent Bolden was being persecuted as a result of his race. This was something that Charlie regretted doing. Before being arrested and charged by the Secret Service, Bolden was set to testify in front of the Warren Commission, claiming that Secret Service agents were complicit in the assassination of President Kennedy. When the first counterfeiting trial ended in a mistrial, Charlie was again asked to sit with the prosecution during the second trial, but he refused. Even though he felt Bolden was guilty, based on the evidence he had seen, he realized that his presence was only for appearances, and he did not want to be used in that manner.

Another situation developed when Charlie was asked to speak with Special Agent Donald Tucker about his attitude. Tucker was irate about the way he was being treated by his temporary supervisor. Tucker had been serving on a thirty-day detail to guard presidential candidate George McGovern in 1972. On two separate occasions during the detail, Tucker was called back to Chicago to testify in a criminal trial on a case he had been working. When he returned to the presidential detail, the detail leader, who was upset that Tucker left, told him he had to stay on the detail longer than the thirty days he was assigned. When Tucker asked for more specific information as to how long he had to stay, the detail leader told him that he "was not going home and that he would stay until he decided Tucker could leave." When Tucker pressed the detail leader for a more definite time schedule so that he could inform his wife and tie up the loose ends on the trial he was working on at home, the detail leader snapped and said, "You will go home as soon as I am good and ready!"

Tucker was a highly decorated special agent who had worked for the Federal Bureau of Narcotics before coming to the Secret Service. He was also very outspoken about the treatment black agents received in the Secret Service and was not the type to accept disrespect from anyone. After the encounter, he wrote a memo to the detail leader, stating that "effective on a specific date he was leaving the detail and returning to his office in Chicago." After reading the memo, the irate detail leader told Tucker to report to Jim Burke's (the assistant director for inspection) office in Washington, DC effective immediately. When Tucker arrived at the headquarters and explained the detail of the situation and the reasons for writing the memo, Burke listened attentively and asked Agent Tucker if he could stay on the presidential detail for one more week and then return to his home office. Tucker happily agreed and left the office to return to the detail. On his way out of the hotel, he received a phone call at the hotel clerk's desk. When he picked up the phone, it was Charlie asking him to go out for a drink and chat. Charlie began telling Tucker that it was important for him to be careful and watch his attitude before he "got into trouble." Tucker was furious. He felt that management had asked Charlie to talk to him to settle him down, but viewed the phone call as the white establishment using one black man to try and control another black man, and this upset Tucker even more.

"I don't know how you feel about it," Tucker lambasted, "but I don't like being treated like a second-class citizen. I will not let it happen to me! I've done too much good work for the service to be treated this way. If we don't stand up for ourselves, no one ever will! Charlie, do you like being somebody's lackey? Do you like shining shoes? Straightening bowties? The Secret Service is using you like an Uncle Tom— can't you see that?"

On that note, Tucker slammed the phone down and went back to the McGovern detail. Sometime later after Tucker got out of the Secret Service and after much reflection, he realized that there was no malice in what Charlie was attempting to do. When the Secret Service gave Charlie an award with a special tribute paid to him for his longtime and dedicated service, Tucker wrote him a letter that was read at the ceremony. Tucker wanted to attend the ceremony but was unable to come at that time. In the letter he wrote,

> Charlie, although we may have had our differences in the past, I have to appreciate what you had to go through as the first black Secret Service agent just to survive. You were in a survival mode. I'm a younger Black, and I just can't take some of the things you had to deal with.

The one thing about Charlie was that he was tough skinned and determined to persevere. Adversity had become his close companion, and he had learned how to navigate through the minefields of troubled times. Every decision Charlie made was viewed through the prism of perceptive. He was in a catch-22 and felt he had to walk a fine line and do what he thought was right. When he made a decision his white subordinates did not like, he was that "uppity nigger." When he made decisions his black subordinates did not agree with, he was that "Uncle Tom." He continued to make decisions. Never in a million years, however, would he ever have thought that he would be trapped by the color of his own skin.

CHAPTER 11
The Color of My Skin

Light skin, brown skin, dark skin, BLACK
Broad nose, big lips, your place is in the back
Dark skin, brown skin, light skin, WHITE
Straight hair, fair features, you must be alright
Light skin in the house, Dark skin in the field
Giving some a glimpse of hope while other starve for a meal
Somewhere along the way we reversed the color trend
Black became beautiful while light-bright a big sin
What we fail to realize is that this was a part of a master plan
An easy way to keep us divided, a ploy
we still don't understand
America has always used color to
control the unsuspecting mind
Granting some great privileges while
making others wait in line
Why does it seem important to keep bringing up this mess
Can't we all just get along and give the color issue a rest
It only becomes important to explain our history
And find those who rose above it all
Bringing pride and honor to our family tree
—Maurice A. Butler

There was a hint of spring in the air. The sun was peering innocently through the partially opened blinds, revealing what looked to be a glorious day in the making in their quiet White Oak community in Montgomery County, Maryland. Charlie sat back on the couch reading his newspaper and drinking a hot cup of coffee. With his busy schedule, he very seldom had time to just sit back and relax, but this was one of those mornings. Ruthe ambled lovingly through the living room, stopping briefly to give her husband a kiss on the forehead before fixing a tantalizing breakfast. She gazed out of the front window and noticed that the mailbox, which usually stood guard perfectly erect on the curb, was missing, and she went outside to investigate. When she got outside, she realized that it had been knocked off of its perch and smashed on the ground. She called to Charlie to come out, and when he got there, he thought to himself that it was probably a childhood prank. When they turned around to go back inside, however, they realized that this was much more than a prank. They gazed in horror at their innocent home. The garage windows had been knocked out, and their house had been spray-painted with the ugly message Niggers, Go Home!

To Ruthe, this ominous message was typical and something that she had experienced most of her life growing up in a racially segregated community in Oxford, North Carolina. To Charlie, however, it stimulated a range of emotions that frustrated and haunted him, making him realize that as much as he tried, being a normal American citizen was more difficult than he could have ever imagined. Since leaving the warm and cozy womb of a racially and culturally pluralistic community in Cambridge, Massachusetts, where the color of his skin did not seem to matter, it seemed as though no matter where he went, how important he became, or what he tried to do, the color of his skin seemed to always be an issue. Here he was, running one of the most powerful offices in the land with hundreds of workers under his supervision and responsible for protecting one of the most powerful leaders in the world and to some he was nothing more than a *nigger*—an inferior, subhuman being not worthy of the rights of an American citizen. And when he tried to exercise his own individuality and make decisions that he felt were the best for him, the Secret Service and his people, he was labeled an Uncle Tom by members of his own race—a subservient black man who caters to every whim of the white man.

Most of his adult life, Charlie tried to view himself not as a colored man or a black man but just a man. He didn't want people to think that he was anything special because he was a black Secret Service agent, but because he was proud to be a Secret Service agent. He came from a generation of people who desperately wanted to be recognized and accepted as American citizens after years of suffering through slavery, segregation, and disenfranchisement. He was able to get a job in the Secret Service, rise through the ranks to a position of influence in spite of the color of his skin, felt that if he could do it, anyone could if they were academically prepared and worked hard enough. He understood the role race played in how things operated in the world but refused to let it serve as a reason for not obtaining his goals, or to be used as an excuse for everything bad that happened to black people. He would constantly discuss or debate the issue of race with his friends and colleagues in an attempt to get others to see his point of view or maybe to convince himself that racism wasn't as debilitating as it seemed.

"Charlie and I would often have big debates about the existence of racism in

America," stated Yvonne Gittens, one of Charlie's nieces. "I don't know why he felt he never experienced racism or why he felt that things that happened to me weren't examples of racism. I explained to him that I had gotten a professional position as the assistant director of financial aid for MIT and would talk to him about different things that happened to me while on recruitment trips. I would travel to different parts of the country with the admission team. We'd be in the line at the hotel to get our rooms for which we had confirmations. When I would get to the front of the line, I was often told that there weren't any more rooms, or I was put in an isolated part of the hotel where the rooms had not been refurbished, and yet my white colleagues would talk about how nice their rooms were and how wonderful they were treated. Sometimes I'd be in the line and when I finally got to the front of the line, the clerk would say that she was going on break and I had to go to the back of another line. This was in the 1980s, and we didn't go into the Deep South. This would happen in places like New York and Washington, DC. I would tell Charlie these things, and he would say, 'Oh, you must be making these things up.' I would say, 'Why would I make that up?'

"He and I would have some heated discussions. He would say, 'Well, why do you think that happened?' I would say, 'It's racism!' Then he would say, 'Why do you think everything is racism?' I would reply, 'Oh, Charlie, I don't think everything is racism. I'm just looking at it point by point.' He'd say something outlandish like, 'Well, it could have been because the sky was orange!' I used to tell him that he was often the only black person in the circle he worked or traveled, and so he was not a threat to his white colleagues and they tolerated him. I think a lot of northern Blacks never felt discriminated against, or if they did, they didn't know what it was. I worked at MIT from 1965 through 2007, and there were black students who had never been called a *nigger* until they got on that campus and didn't know how to handle it. They would say, 'Are they talking to me?' They probably never felt that they experienced overt racism because they were the only black in their little private school, or they were the only black in their little neighborhood and was always accepted. Now they were being discriminated against for the first time, and it devastated them to the point where some of them stopped functioning. You had to go dig them out of their room and get them over to mental health so they could function again. I would say to them, 'This is America. I don't know what rock you've been living under.'"

In retrospect, however, the color of Charlie's skin color had always been an issue that stimulated reflection, question, and discussion, even going as far back as his experiences growing up in Cambridge, Massachusetts. His brothers Sonny and John and his sister Grace all participated in WWII and came back with shocking experiences and stories of racism and prejudice in the military. When Charlie had a difficult time accepting or believing the stories, his sister Grace would say, "Poor, Charlie, he doesn't know that he is a Negro, but he is going to find out!" Charlie did observe that there was a difference in the treatment one received based not just on your race but also the shade and tone of your skin color. While there was no segregation in his neighborhood, most of the few black families that lived in his neighborhood were light skinned, whereas those who were trapped in the community not too far from him referred to as the Coast were dark-skinned blacks and seemed to be "struggling to make it economically." Even though he had very little shared experiences with his father, because his father was put in a mental institution when Charlie was very young, he knew that visiting his father on the job was forbidden, and it had something to do with the color of his skin (his father was *passing*).

Passing was an assimilation tool used by African Americans, who had physical features similar to white Americans that enabled them to avoid the economic, political, and social disenfranchisement in American society. For example, when Charlie's brother Sonny, his wife Millie, and son David would travel to Oxford to visit him, Millie, who was fair skinned and whose physical features made it difficult to the unsuspecting eye to see that she was African American, would sit in the back while Sonny and David would sit in the front of the car. The ruse was to make anyone who had a problem with a black man and "white" woman traveling together think that the black man was a chauffeur. Millie was able to go into the restaurants in the South that would not serve black people and use the White Only restroom as well as order food and bring it out to the car for Sonny and David to eat.

Another example was one of Ruthe's relatives and high school classmates in Oxford, North Carolina, named Patricia Tyler Knight. Patricia's father was a very successful businessman who would often employ this tactic because he was very fair skinned and looked white.

"My father was a veteran of WWI, having served in Verdun, France," Patricia recalled. "He was an owner of a lucrative taxi business. We lived near Butner, North Carolina, in Camp Butner during WWII. The camp has since been turned into a correctional institution, where Jack Johnson [the first African American heavyweight boxer in the United States who was convicted of violating the Mann Act—transporting a white woman across state lines for "immoral" purposes] requested to serve his time. During WWII with Camp Butner there, which is halfway between Oxford and Durham, my father ran a very prosperous taxi business with the GIs. Afterward, he worked and built some of the most beautiful houses in Oxford, and he built his own house in 1921. My father would work on his regular carpentry jobs and then go up to Butner to check on his taxi service. One day a white man asked my father, who was in one of his taxis, for a ride. My father told him that the taxis were over there and the white man said no that he wanted a white taxi. My father said, 'Okay, come on.' The man thought my father was white. We used to tease my father because he went to his grave with *white* on his driver's license. His belief was that if color was so important to the white man, then he should be able to tell the difference. And if he doesn't, then I'm not going to tell him!

"I have had incidences like that for myself. After I left the University of Maryland, I started working in the Woodward and Lothrop's in Wheaton, Maryland. This person I was working with started talking about black people using words like *nigger this* and *nigger that*. I said, 'Wait, just a moment please. You don't ever know who you are talking to, and I don't approve of this language that you are using.' After that, she quieted down and stared at me. I did not have a sign on my back saying that I am black because I had the same philosophy that my father had, even to this day. If they don't know the difference and it is that important, *daggone it* I'm not going to school them! Once, when I was in the maternity ward having my third child, this woman said, 'How did you get that beautiful tan?' I said, 'Well, I was born with it!' And that's all I said. Of course they wanted me to be Portuguese or anything except black. I don't feel that I have to explain anything. If you saw me, of course, you would know that I was black. You would almost immediately know that I am not white, but as you know, whites come in so many different colors. You've got dark Italians and dark Jews. I have two Jewish friends, one who is the same color I am and one who is darker than I am. That's the irony of this colored junk that the English started."

There was a dark side that existed in the black community created by the desire to appear as close to white as possible. The fact that light-skinned blacks received preferential treatment by whites in terms of employment opportunities, social acceptance, to a certain level, and freedom of movement created a belief that black skin and black features were something negative and undesirable. This issue created a great deal of emotional drama within the black community, with respect to developing positive self-image and pride, until the late 1960s. The use of the term *black* even became an insult if used in certain context. For example, if a black person wanted to hurt another black person's feeling or insult them, they would say things like, "don't bring home anyone that was the color of the top of the stove, or you're blacker than that car." To call someone black was an invitation to a fight. Blacks tried various tactics to appear more white and less African. For a black person to have light skin with "good hair" (i.e., hair that was not nappy or kinky) was a desired trait. Light-skinned girls were called red-bone or high-yellow and were considered very attractive candidates for jobs and marriage. Dark-skinned girls were often referred to as jigaboo or pickaninny and became the subject of ridicule. Blacks began spending millions of dollars on products like lightening cream, to make their skin appear lighter, or products like *congoleen* to make their hair straight in an attempt to appear as close to white as possible (this was called conking).

More importantly, this issue created resentment and division within the black community and created a social dilemma for the light-skinned black person.

"As we walked by the white school, the white kids used to tease and taunt us as if we were absolutely nothing," Patricia Tyler Knight reflected as she reminisced about the dilemma of being black, but looking white in a rigidly segregated Southern community. "Our family was a little bit different than the other black kids because we had very fair skin. We were taunted by both the white kids and the black kids. One day we were coming home from school, and the black kids would walk behind us and shout, 'Issue, issue, issue.' I was in the fourth or fifth grade at the time, and I heard it all of those years and just ignored it. So I finally went home and asked my mother what it meant. She said, 'You can't talk about black, and you can't talk about white.' My mother said we were free issues. The Tyler freedom was issued to our family long before the Emancipation Proclamation. Then I figured out what it meant. My family was free issues. My siblings and I have a piece of property that was willed to my father in the Tyler name since 1776. Some of our relatives actually owned slaves. One of my great-grandfathers had a couple of slaves. One of my friends, Karen Franklin, the daughter-in-law of John Hope Franklin, said, 'Pat, I wouldn't brag about it.' I said, 'No no no, I'm not bragging about it, I'm just mentioning it. Since I talked about the white kids teasing us and calling us niggers and saying we had no business going to school and all that kind of foolishness, I remember how we got it from both sides, the whites and the blacks."

The term *issue* has evolved into an entity that carries economic, legal, and social connotations. According to Black's law dictionary, the term *issue* and *descendants* have been held to be coextensive and interchangeable. The word *issue* in a will is sometimes said to be equivalent to *heirs of the body*. The general rule in most states is that the illegitimate child may inherit from the mother but not from the father but if legitimate may inherit from both parents. The definition of the term *issue*, according to Webster's Dictionary is *to descend from a specific parent or ancestor*. The term *free issue*, which was a term commonly used in Virginia and North Carolina, meant a black or mixed race person free by manumission (set free) or birth, especially the child of a white woman and a black man. In many parts of the South during slavery, the race and status of a child was determined by the race and status of the mother. This meant if a black female slave produced a child with a free white male, the child would be considered a slave, and conversely, if a free white female produced a child with a black slave, the child would be considered free. Through time the term took on negative social connotations and was used to taunt offspring of mixed racial parents (Is you white, or is you black?).

Color and race has been a divisive factor in American history ever since the institution of slavery became engrained in the economic and social fabric of our society. The long-term impact that *the peculiar institution* had on black and white Americans has kept the conversation about race at the forefront of our political and social consciousness even to this day. One would think that the election of an African American president in the twenty-first century would be evidence that this nation had finally put to bed the hatred, mistrust, and bigotry produced by racial differences, but unfortunately, it seems it has not. It seems that Willie Lynch's training was very thorough, and his self-fulfilling prophecy has been very accurate.

Willie Lynch was a slave owner living in the West Indies during the early 1700s. He wrote a dissertation, a slave owner's handbook, if you will, outlining how to break the mind, body, and spirit of black people (slaves were considered the property of the owners) during slavery, as well as strategies to help the landed aristocracy (plantation owners) maintain control over the masses of middle- and lower-class whites and blacks. If these strategies were applied correctly, according to Lynch, blacks would continue to exhibit the self-destructive behavior that would keep them subservient to whites for "hundreds of years." In addition, the working-class whites would accept their position in society, placing the blame for their lot on blacks. This would create an atmosphere of hate and distrust between members of the lower classes and thus enable a small minority of rich, powerful leaders (landowners) to maintain power and control.

According to the 1860 United States Census, less than one-third of all Southern families owned slaves at the peak of slavery prior to the Civil War. In Mississippi and South Carolina, the figure approached one-half; in Virginia, one out of every four families (25 percent) owned slaves. The total number of slave owners was 385,000 amounting to approximately 3.8 percent of the Southern and border states population. While most Southerners were not slave owners, and while the majority of slaveholders held ten or fewer slaves, wealthy plantation owners (i.e., planters) were those who held a significant number of slaves, mostly as agricultural labor. These planters are often spoken of as belonging to the *planter elite* or *planter aristocracy* in the antebellum South. Many of the wealthy and influential men in colonial Virginia were tobacco planters. A number of America's first presidents were members of this landed aristocracy.[45] Therefore, the majority of Southern whites were in direct competition with slave labor and lived a meager existence at best. In order to stay in power and control the enormous number of slaves, who, contrary to popular belief, were not "happy" with their lifestyle as slaves, as well as the majority of working-class whites, who were not happy trying to survive economically, this group of planters turned to Lynch for guidance.

Lynch came to Virginia in 1712 and gave lectures to Southern planters, explaining his philosophy and approach. In his book entitled *Let's Make a Slave: The Origin and Development of a Social Being Called "The Negro,"* Lynch copiously detailed the seasoning process for enslaved Africans and their future generations. His plan included the following suggestions:

- Both a wild horse and a wild or natural nigger are dangerous even if captured, for they will have the tendency to seek their customary freedom and, in so doing, might kill you in your sleep.
- Take the female and run a series of test on her to see if she will submit to your desires willingly. If she shows any signs of resistance in submitting

completely to your will, do not hesitate to use the bullwhip on her to extract that last bitch out of her.

- Take the meanest and most restless male nigger, strip him of his clothes in front of the remaining male niggers, the female, and the nigger infant. Take a bullwhip and beat him to the point of death in front of the female and infant. Don't kill him, but put the fear of God in him, for he can be useful for future breeding.
- By her being left alone, unprotected, with the male image destroyed, the ordeal caused the nigger female to raise her male and female offspring in reverse roles. For fear of the young male's life, she will psychologically train him to be mentally weak and dependent but physically strong. She will train the female offspring to be psychologically independent. Now you've got the nigger woman out front and the nigger man behind, scared, mentally dependent, and weak.
- To prevent them from reverting back to their former mental state, shave off the brute's mental history (take away the knowledge of self, former customs, and accomplishments).
- Cross-breed the niggers for purposes of creating a division of labor. Cross-breeding niggers means taking so many drops of good white blood and putting them into as many nigger women as possible, varying the drops by the various tones that you want, and then letting them breed with each other until the circle of colors appear as you desire.
- Completely annihilate the mother tongue of the nigger and institute a new language. If you teach a slave all about your language, he will know all of your secrets and he is then no more a slave, for you can't fool him any longer and having a fool is one of the basic ingredients and incidents to the making of the slavery system.
- Use fear and envy for control purposes. Distrust is stronger than trust, and envy is stronger than adulation, respect, or admiration. You must pitch the old black male versus the young black male, the dark-skinned slave versus the light-skinned slave, and the female versus the male. You must also have your white servants and overseer distrust *all* Blacks. These are your keys to control.[46]

One would be hard-pressed to believe that every Southern plantation owners followed the directions of Willie Lynch or even heard of him. Lynch was not the originator of brutality, miscegenation, or the "divide and conquer" theory. He did, however, popularize these social tools during a time period when the dependence on African slave labor was increasing and fear of revolt was on the rise. Ideas, especially those written down in books, are powerful and have a way of translating into patterns of behavior, especially when those ideas are helpful. Many did, however, listen to

Lynch, purchased his books, employed his strategies, and the impact has been long lasting and staggering. Words like *nigger, colored, Negro* and even the word *black,* which were used to identify slave owner's property, evolved into divisive, derogatory, and offensive terms especially after slaves were emancipated and Southern leaders tried to reestablish their political, economic, and social control over the South. The term *nigger* was used not only as an identifier but as a label for someone who was inferior to other whites regardless of their socioeconomic status. The breakdown of the African American family structure, the denial of education with regard to the teaching of reading and writing, the systematic stripping of positive stories and accomplishment of Africans and African Americans from early history texts, the creation of mistrust and envy between blacks based on skin shade, the creation of hate and distrust of whites toward *all* blacks, and even the negative self-image attached to the word *black* were legacies produced by the teachings of Willie Lynch and further popularized by terrorists organizations like the Ku Klux Klan and the Knights of the White Camellia.

The response to slavery, disenfranchisement, and racial discrimination by African Americans was as diverse as the many differences that existed in the black community which was impacted by geography, culture, and experiences. To think that the black community as a whole is a monolithic society is a mistake that is often made. African Americans come in many shades of black, a wealth of different experiences and different points of view, but are often expected to think, respond, and act alike. Slavery again was the culprit for this phenomenon. When black Africans were captured and thrown on the slave ship, they came from different tribes, with different languages, religions, customs, and experiences. Some were political leaders, some scientists, mathematicians, farmers, kings, queens, and laborers. Despite their many differences, they were all thrown into the same boat and viewed through the same prism—*slave,* an inhuman piece of property. Even when slavery officially ended, they were viewed through that same prism, but this time the label was *nigger,* an inferior second-class citizen. They had one common denominator—the color of their skin. In order to control this ever-growing population, skin color became the broad brush that painted them all into a racial caste system.

Even though the problems were similar (i.e., racial discrimination), there was an expectation that all blacks would respond the same way. A black man born and raised in Cambridge, Massachusetts, is expected to apply the same logic and strategies to the race issue as a black man born and raised in Oxford, North Carolina, even though the experience set and circumstances may be different. Since the inception of American slavery, however, blacks resisted in numerous ways, varying from covertly grinding up glass and putting it in the slave owner's food, to escape, to leading violent revolts. The fact that there were differences in strategy on how to resolve issues that plague the African American community is nothing new. There have been numerous examples in history where very public debates between African American leaders over the best approach to resolving common issues of racial discrimination were thrust into the limelight. The differing approach to resolving issues in the black community of Booker T. Washington, a Southern African American leader, and W. E. B. Dubois, a northern African American leader, was a classic example. Nor did Martin Luther King Jr., a Southern, Baptist minister, advocate the same solutions to the race problem (total and peaceful integration) as did Malcolm X, a northern, Muslim minister (total and peaceful separation). Marcus Garvey, another noted black leader, had a different solution altogether— leave the United States and return to Africa.

As the participants in the civil rights movement became younger and younger during the early 1960s, they began to move away from the strategies of passive resistance to that of active engagement. Cries of Black Power and Black is Beautiful began to creep into the revolutionary rhetoric of the movement. A new sense of pride in the African heritage of black Americans forged to the forefront of the psyche of the black community. Members of the black community began to embrace the idea that the term *black* was inclusive of all people of African descent regardless of skin shade or tone. The terms *Negro* and *colored*, labels that were given to African Americans, were replaced by the terms like *black*, *Afro-American*, and finally *African American*. Blacks even took ownership of the hated word *nigger* and turned it around using it as a term of endearment in certain contexts, creating a firestorm of reflection and discussion.

Charlie was not naïve about the race question and the impact that race had on the development of this country's history and had very strong opinions about it, which he shared in many of his letters to family and friends. At one point during his experience in the segregated army, he decided that he no longer wanted to live in the United States as a result of the treatment he and other members of his race received. While stationed in Yokohama, Japan, following WWII, he wrote a letter to his mother (March 18, 1947) expressing his displeasure with the treatment of the colored soldiers. In that letter he wrote,

> Now that I've started my travels, I really do want to travel again. I don't believe I want to live in the United States for the rest of my life now after seeing how rotten these white people can be. Yokohama base is just about made up of all colored soldiers. In fact, when we had the Armistice Day Parade, they had to send for some white troops from another area so that the colored soldiers wouldn't be dominating the photographs. Now that the war is over, these high-ranking officers don't have anything better to do but harass the troops, and they certainly are giving the colored boys over here a hard way to go. They don't have any colored troops in Tokyo, and now they are trying to push us out of Yokohama. You see, it burns them up to see the colored fellows living

so nice in these two large cities, walking down the street, especially the big black ones, with a cute little yellow girl. For almost no reason at all, they'll discharge a colored soldier as undesirable, what we call a 369 discharge. Rumor has it that the band is supposed to move down to Osaka, but so far I have heard nothing official. It's not bad down there, it's about 300 miles from Yokohama, but it's just the idea of being so far away from everything and everybody. John can tell you about the famed 24th Division (colored). Well, they're down in Osaka now.

While attending the integrated Officers Candidate School in Fort Riley, Kansas, and later while attending the Military Police School in Camp Gordon, Georgia, he had come face-to-face with the Jim Crow restrictions that limited where he could go, eat, or sleep. He realized that his rank as an officer afforded him some privileges which he tried to take advantage of whenever possible, but he resented the fact that his people were being treated this way. On June 10, 1949, he wrote to his sister Miriam "Babe" about a dance he refused to attend. He wrote,

Tonight the company is having its midterm party at the Junction City Country Club [Fort Riley, KA]—a pretty ritzy place. I really should have gone because I know my instructor will make a remark on my report card next week saying that I was uncooperative and not sociable for not attending. We get graded for little things like that you know. But I don't care, for honestly, Babe, I wouldn't have enjoyed myself. First of all, if it weren't for the fact that I'm an officer candidate, I wouldn't be able to go near the back door of that country club.

Secondly, I can't dance, I don't have a girl, and I don't have the time to find one so there wouldn't have been any sense in going to that party. There is a college in Manhattan, Kansas, about forty miles from here, and I'm told that there are some pretty fine girls (colored) going there. Some of the fellows go down there some time to their dances, but I haven't gone yet. I ought to go down there though. I may be able to find a cute little rich colored gal, huh? They're crazy about the candidates so I hear (smile).

In a letter to his sister Grace (October 31, 1949), Charlie laments about the Jim Crow restrictions in Georgia:

I'll start class next week, Grace, and I am glad! I've got a fine job now though, and I'm working with some wonderful officers, but the sooner this class starts, the sooner I can get out of Georgia. Don't get me wrong now; Georgia isn't all that bad. But you know when one isn't

accustomed to the restrictions of Jim Crowism it is rather difficult to swallow in one big gulp. You'd be surprised, but these bars [rank of lieutenant], the Buick and those Massachusetts [license] plates have helped me immensely as far as respect and prestige is concerned. Why I received better and much more courteous service at the Buick Co. here in Augusta than I did at home, believe it or not. I was treated so nicely and so politely that it frightened me. So you see, even in Georgia, as far as business is concerned, there's only one color and that's green—the color of your money, not your face.

Charlie was not just a person who read or studied history, but as a military leader and then a member of the Secret Service, he had a front-row seat, watched it develop, and, in many cases, participated in its development. He was a lifetime member of the National Association for the Advancement of Colored People (NAACP) and felt very strongly that their work was crucial in helping black people break down racial barriers, especially in the South. He was a firm believer in Martin Luther King Jr. and felt that without his influence the civil rights movement would have had difficulty "getting off the ground." On May 26, 1954, he wrote a letter to his mother, stating,

I'll write a longer letter next time mom and tell you what I think about the Supreme Court's decision outlawing segregation. Of course, it's the most wonderful thing that could have happened for the Negroes; a real victory indeed. The next step now is the banning of segregation in housing, transportation, restaurants, etc.

Later that same year, he wrote a letter to his sister Grace (October 3, 1954), describing his feeling about social customs in the South:

We have a "quaint" lil ole Southern custom down here, as you've seen by the reaction to the Supreme Court's decision on segregation in schools. One of these reminders of the good old days (B. L., before Lincoln) is the ringing of the slave bell at the traditional time—in the morning, afternoon, and about 9:00 p.m.—the latter being a warning that all niggers were to be in their quarters. They don't ring the bells here in Durham, but in Fayetteville, the DARs (Daughters of the American Revolution) made the ringing of the bells their foremost duty. They still have an old historic landmark in Fayetteville—the slave market—from whence the bells ring. The marketplace is right in the middle of downtown Fayetteville, which creates quite a traffic hazard, but the crackers are so proud of their few reminders of the old

days that they wouldn't take it down for hell or high water. Several
attempts have been made to dynamite the place by Fort Bragg soldiers,
but all, I regret to say, have been in vain.

After being transferred to the Secret Service office in San Juan, Puerto Rico, Charlie began traveling through Latin America and began making observations and gathering information on how race impacts societies outside of the United States. To his amazement and disgust, he found that there were some awful similarities in how other countries dealt with the race question. He expressed his feelings in a letter to his wife Ruthe (June 27, 1965) while traveling through Central and South America. In that letter he wrote,

You know, this trip has been quite enlightening to me, and it sort of
proved something I've always believed about Latin America and the
race question. This hotel, La Siesta, is really fabulous. Movie-type stuff
with bikini-clad girls and all, mostly airline stewardesses on stopovers.
I'm about to die, but there is nothing I can do except suffer. Right
now I'm sitting on the patio overlooking the swimming pool, and if
I just bat an eye, a white-coated, dark-skinned waiter will break his
neck scurrying over to my table to cater to my every wish. You see, my
advantage is that being an American Negro (or just any kind of garden
variety Negro), I've got to have plenty of money to be here, and since the
American dollar is king, hence the extra special treatment. They think
they've got no race problem as such because of the economic situation.
Money is the important thing here, and dark-skinned Latinos have no
money. Hence, they know what their lot in life is, and they accept it. The
problem, of course, is much deeper and has a myriad of ramifications,
but it boils down to one thing—a dark-skinned person with anything
at all in Latin America is indeed a rarity.

Everywhere I've been there seems to be a highly and easily
recognizable correlation between color and status. For example,
in the hotels without exception, there is a relationship by startling
gradations, between the color of the desk clerk straight thru the various
jobs to the lowest laborer, who, of course, is quite dark-skinned. Do I
make myself clear? It's very interesting!

In Peru, for instance, the main bloodline is Indian. There just
aren't many Negroes. But there are enough, it seems, to supply the main
hotels and restaurants with doormen, porters, and dishwashers. Where
they come from I don't know, but they are certainly not Peruvians.

It seems, then, that for a Negro to attain any degree of affluence in
Latin America would be quite a difficult task. I've talked to many people

about this, and the standard answer is that which has been echoed a million times in our own southland—"They're happy, no problem, they don't want change, that's the way things are here etc., etc."

And right here in Panama—Central America—it's exactly the same. I can understand, now, why the African delegates at the convention were standoffish and obviously not anxious to mingle with the whites. They know the white man— they've fought for and won their independence (some of them) and they don't aim to let him get a foothold again if they can help it. Enough—I sound bitter, don't I? Well, I am!!!

Charlie was acutely aware of the fact that he was the first African American to join the Secret Service and, in so doing, was being used as a measuring stick to determine if other black agents would follow. He understood that the first of anything always opens doors for others. He was under the pressure of being constantly watched, knowing that if he "messed up" or caused any "embarrassment" to the service, it would be a long time before another African American would be hired. He knew that blacks looked to him as a source of pride, and some whites looked for flaws in his character to bring him down. He carried this burden willfully but also understood that for a black agent to make it in the Secret Service, being good was just not good enough. He knew that excellence had to be the standard and set the bar very high when recruiting other blacks to join the Secret Service and took an active role in trying to increase the number of minorities. He felt that not much was known about the Secret Service, which inhibited the recruitment of qualified candidates. He advocated for more blacks to be assigned to the Presidential Protection Division so that other blacks could see them and aspire to become a Secret Service agent. As one of the first black members on the treasury department's employment policy review board representing the Secret Service in 1965, he suggested that recruitment of qualified minority applicants could be enhanced by visiting black colleges and universities and was subsequently given the task to organize the recruiting venture. He wrote to Director Rowley of the Secret Service on June 21, 1966, with concerns that the board did not meet regularly as they original planned and wanted to know if the board was serious about the recruitment of minorities as President Johnson had mandated. In March 1971, he was selected as an Equal Employment Opportunity counselor for all Secret Service employees, with emphasis on ensuring equal employment opportunities for minority groups, women, older employees, and employees with disabilities. On February 23, 1972, he wrote to Robert Goff, an Equal Employment Opportunity officer, responding to a memorandum addressing the need to change the EEO action plan concerning the hiring of minorities. He felt that the EEO was long on planning but short on action. In that memo he wrote,

I would like to reiterate that as set forth in the Plan, the policy and the letter of the EEO Program are adequate. But the deed, the spirit of the Plan, the implementation of the Plan – these are the areas if we are genuinely concerned – that make one wonder whether a mere cursory and perfunctory updating of the Plan is what is needed. Our action plan, as written is a good plan. What we need to concentrate on is finding as efficacious solution to the implementation of the plan, particularly as it relates to the hiring of minority group members in those offices that have traditionally not given employment opportunities to such persons, and where the hiring practices are questionable, at the very least.

One need only to observe the racial makeup of our Headquarters' Divisions and any of our field offices, particularly the larger offices regardless of geographical location, and one immediately wonders whether or not we indeed have a realistic, functional EEO Program.

I have heard it said that certain Southern cities in which some of our offices are located are not yet "ready" to accept minority group employees; that the racial climate in some of these areas would render such persons, if hired, ineffective to the point that accomplishment of mission would probably be jeopardized. I have even heard it said that the personal safety of minority group employees in some of these areas would be a question of serious consideration. I submit that what more aptly ought to be a question of serious consideration and concern is that in this time of enlightened social and racial progress, we are still hearing such anachronistic expressions.

Again, these are simply my observations and it seems to me that more important to this program than the routine updating of the Action Plan is getting across to many of our supervisors, as set forth in the current plan, that "the success of the EEO program in any organization is based on acceptance and understanding of EEO by all employees, especially by managers and supervisors. This factor is particularly important where the employment of minority group members or women constitutes a change in traditional employment patterns".

He wrote to the director again on September 30, 1974, in response to a memorandum concerning minority recruitment, suggesting that the Secret Service was behind other law enforcement agencies because of the amount of money being offered to entry-level employees. In that memo he stated,

One problem area experienced and anticipated is the likelihood that the cream of the undergraduate crop – white, Black, female or whatever – from schools such as George Washington University,

*Georgetown University or Howard University generally go on to
graduate and professional schools in pursuit of higher learning. Also,
with those students interested in following a career in Federal law
enforcement upon completion of undergraduate school, we must face
the fact that beginning at the grade of GS-5 level in these inflationary
times diminishes our bargaining power, particularly when the Federal
Bureau of Investigation has an entrance grade of GS-10.*

In 1976, he became one of the founding members of an organization called
NOBLE (National Organization of Black Law Enforcement Executives), which
was established to address crime in urban and low-income areas. Sixty black law
enforcement executives from twenty-four states and the District of Columbia met
in Washington, DC to discuss issues that were common to black law enforcement
officers around the nation. The goal of NOBLE was to be recognized as a highly
competent public service organization that was at the forefront of providing
solutions to law enforcement issues and concerns, as well as to the ever-changing
needs of the black community, to unify black law enforcement officers at executive
and command levels, to conduct research in relevant areas of law enforcement, to
establish linkages and liaisons with organizations of similar concern, to evaluate and
recommend legislation relating to the criminal justice process, to establish effective
means and strategies for dealing with racism in the field of criminal justice, and to
articulate the concerns of black executives in law enforcement.[47]

In 1996, Charlie was asked to address the Secret Service Academy graduating
class, an honor that he graciously accepted. In that speech, he eloquently addressed
the issue of working in a culturally diverse environment and the need for the Secret
Service to adjust.

He stated,

*During the turbulent events of the 1960s, the Secret Service found itself
faced with even more dynamic changes that had to be addressed. The
social fabric of our American society demanded more diversity in our
social and cultural development, and progressive policies needed to be
implemented.*

*For years, America had been paying lip service to the notion that
our nation was a "melting pot" of people from diverse cultures. Then,
somebody took a closer look and discovered the truth. We did not and
we don't have a "melting pot." What we have is a "salad bowl" with
many different ingredients which retain their own individual flavors.
The most effective thing we can do is to keep pouring on a dressing of
democracy over them and hope to make them sufficiently palatable to
satisfy everyone's taste.*

As Charlie and Ruthe gazed in disgust at their damaged home, they did what they had been doing most of their lives. They rolled up their sleeves, picked up the mailbox and replaced it on its perch, replaced the garage windows, painted over the graffiti on their house, repaved the driveway, and then went back in to fix the things that were going on inside the house . . .

CHAPTER 12
All Good Things . . .

After some twenty-three years in our great organization, the time has now come for me to request that you approve my application for optional retirement effective September 30, 1979. It would be impossible for me to capture in a few words the enormous pride my family and I will always have as a result of my association with the Secret Service, so I will not try to do so. My career has been such a pleasant and rewarding one that I had great difficulty in reaching this decision but there is a time for all things and it would appear that my time to retire has arrived.

—Charles L. Gittens

To everything there is a season, and a time for every purpose under the sun. A time to be born and a time to die; a time to plant and a time to pluck up that which is planted; a time to kill and a time to heal . . . a time to weep and a time to laugh; a time to mourn and a time to dance; a time to embrace and a time to refrain from embracing; a time to lose and a time to seek; a time to keep silent and a time to speak; a time to love and a time to hate; a time for war and a time for peace. (Ecclesiastes 3:1–8)

There is an old adage that says time waits for no one, and it seemed that time was beginning to catch up with Charlie. For the first time in his life, Charlie began encountering obstacles he could not overcome, some beyond his control and some self-inflicted.

Following the turbulent decade of the 1960s in America, which saw the height of achievement when an American stepped foot on the moon, as well as the lows of the social and political upheaval that followed the assassinations of John F. Kennedy, Robert F. Kennedy, Martin Luther King Jr., Medgar Evers, and Malcolm X. In addition to America being dragged deeper and deeper into the abyss of the war in

Vietnam that seemed to never end, a new and more challenging America emerged during the 1970s or the Age of Aquarius. The American people seemed to awaken from a political slumber and began openly questioning everything its government did and said. The civil rights movement, which had been planting seeds in America's social conscious for decades, began bearing fruit from its labor that manifested in affirmative action programs, forced desegregation of public schools and public facilities, and the hiring and promotion of blacks in all walks of public and private life. The women's movement began bearing fruit as well with issues of pay equity being addressed, the acceptance of women into certain colleges and the United States service academies, and the right for women to receive abortions if they so chose. Young people began questioning the logic of being old enough to fight in a war, but not old enough to vote or purchase a beer from a store. The comfortable life Charlie had enjoyed for so long—which was characterized by rapid job advancement and a quiet, cohesive, and loving family environment—was coming to a rapid end, and it seemed there was nothing he could do about it.

Life, at the beginning of the 1970s was good, and it seemed things could not have gotten any better for Charlie and his family! He had gotten promoted to lead one of the most important offices in the Secret Service (the Washington field office), was on a fast track up the corporate ladder, was doing well financially, had a wonderful family, held a passport that said he could travel anywhere in the world, and he was doing something he loved doing. He was designated as the Equal Employment Opportunity counselor for the Secret Service field office employees in April 1971 and in September 1972 was selected by Chief Rowley to attend the Federal Executive Institute in Charlottesville, Virginia. The primary objective of the institute was to broaden the knowledge and enhance the effectiveness of federal executives who were responsible for implementing national programs and policies. His talents and accomplishments were not only recognized by the Secret Service, but other countries and organizations began to take notice. His participation in the INTERPOL conferences brought him into contact with numerous political leaders from foreign countries who sought his expertise. While he was directing the Washington field office of the Secret Service, he was contacted by Nigerian government officials in an attempt to lure him away from his current job to establish a Secret Service organization on the African continent.

"I was asked to set up a Secret Service agency in Lagos, Nigeria," Charlie recalled. "We had just left Puerto Rico, and I was in charge of the Washington field office. We had a family meeting to discuss my options. The money they were offering was huge! I remember Sharon asking if we were going to be rich and if we were going to have limo drivers. Ruthe asked what it would mean for my career. I said I would be creating a secret service on the continent, the first one of its kind. She then asked what the disadvantages were. I remember thinking that this opportunity would be a short-term opportunity because of the instability of African governments at that time and the way power was transferred from one person to another. During that time, those governments changed leaders frequently and usually by violent means. My feeling turned out to be prophetic when several years later the president of Liberia (William Richard Tolbert Jr.) came to the United States to solidify relations with his country and the United States, and I was responsible for setting up his protection detail. Not long after leaving the United States, he and his cabinet members were assassinated in a coup d'état.

"Another issue preventing me from taking on this task dealt with the value system I wanted to live under as a family. The majority of the people in Nigeria lived in abject poverty while the leaders lived a luxurious lifestyle. I remember asking Ruthe and Sharon if they really wanted to live somewhere a mile outside of the city, even for a lot of money, while the people were living in deplorable conditions. We would have gold faucets but had to wonder if water would come out. The class difference was so absolute in a lot of those countries. You were either very rich or very poor, and there wasn't much of a middle class. So I decided to decline the offer and stayed with the United States Secret Service. I also declined another large and prestigious offer from a security organization in Tennessee."

On the surface, things at home were tranquil now that Charlie was no longer in the field and had an office job. He was able to spend more time at home. Below the surface, however, the winds of time began to slowly whip into a frenzy of discontent that would ultimately tear up what was once a fairy-tale existence. His daughter, Sharon, was the love of his life, and he gave her everything she desired. She was daddy's little girl. He and Ruthe had tried to have a larger family but to no avail.

After leaving Puerto Rico and returning to the continental United States, Ruthe was able to get her job back with the Internal Revenue Service and became an international auditor. They had two incomes again and wanted for nothing. The close-knit father-daughter relationship, however, began to change drastically as Sharon grew into a teenager. The normal rebellious spirit that occurred in many families across America began to create a divide between them.

Sharon stated, remembering her days as an adolescent:

> He would come home and shout, "I'm home!" My mother would really have an apron on, and she would really put down the dish rag, and I would run to the door, and he would lift me up and say, 'How's my girls?' It was like a scene from a television show. There was a lot of routine in our house. I didn't have to guess about anything. Dinner was always going to be served; breakfast was always going to be served. When I ate lunch at school either they packed my lunch or I ate in the school cafeteria. I always had everything I was supposed to have. When we went to church on Sundays, I was always able to bring a friend because we would go

out to eat or go somewhere like to the museums. He would tell me nighttime fairy tales or read Shakespeare to me before I went to bed.

But those days were few and far between because he was rarely there. He was usually on a trip to some foreign country, and the only pieces of him that we could hold on to were the many letters he wrote, the phone calls, gifts, foreign money, and stamps he would send home. We were always sad when we had to take him to the airport to go on another one of his trips. The irony of this situation was that he grew up without his father ever being around because when he was young his father was put into a mental institution. He used to tell me that he never remembered his dad being home. All he remembered was that his mother used to dress him up, and they went to *the place*, and she made sure he kissed his father. He remembered kissing his father because he had a scruffy beard, and it would irritate his face. So I guess him not being around the family was a normal thing. As I turned into a teenager, I thought I was grown and would often get smart with him when I was angry. I would say things like, "It's not like you are actually here enough to tell me what to do," to try to trump him, as if he didn't have the right to tell me what to do since he wasn't around a lot.

It seemed like before we came to Washington he was never home, and I think I somewhat resented that. I don't know how my mother took it. My mother was there daily, and she was the disciplinarian in the house. She would spank me when I didn't do right, and she didn't play. Instead of lecturing me to death when I did something wrong, she would let me face the consequences so I would learn not to do it again. I stole something once when I was about five years old, and when she found out, she put a quick end to that. My father didn't find out until I was about seven years old. We used to go to Woolworth's five-and-dime store, and when I came home, I had stuff that she didn't buy. When she saw me in my room playing with the stuff I had stolen, she said, "Honey, where did you get that? We're going to go back to the store and tell the man that you took this without paying for it. That's called stealing." She was right down at my eye level looking right at me. She walked my behind the two or three blocks right back to the store pulling me along.

We walked in and she said, "May I see the manager please, my daughter has something to tell him." I told him that I took the stuff, but I had money to pay for it.

My mother said, "No, you don't. You are not using this money for this!" And then she asked him would he accept the merchandise back and she would pay for any damage done. Then she asked him if he had anything he would like to say to me.

I had to stand there while that white man was telling me, "Well, young lady, that is stealing, and I could have called the officer back there, and he could have taken you to jail." That was very humiliating, and I learned my lesson.

Another time she let me have a temper tantrum in Macy's department store. I was falling out, and when I opened my eyes, she wasn't there anymore. I had to go to the back room where they had to announce that they had a little lost girl. The man asked, "What was my mother's name?" and I said, "Mommy." I didn't know my mother's or my father's names. I just called them mommy and daddy. Needless to say, I never had another temper tantrum in public again.

Later, I got pregnant while I was in college, had an abortion, and I didn't tell my parents. The day it almost came out was during the Easter break. I was home, and we were in the car going shopping. It was my birthday, and she wanted to go shopping with me before sending me back down to North Carolina. I threw up in the car.

When I threw up, she looked at me and said, "What the hell. Are you pregnant?"

I said, "Pregnant, I threw up slimy eggs!"

She said, "You're going to clean that up, and I am taking you to the doctor."

And I said, "For what, Mom? It's just a cold!" She looked at me, and we pulled over so I could clean it up and then we went back home so I could wash up and change my clothes.

She said, "I ought to take you to the doctor!"

And I said, "I'll be going to the infirmary Monday morning, and I'll call you." When I went to the school infirmary, I found out I was pregnant, but I never told her. I had to get money for the abortion and all of that. Then one day when I was about thirty years old and was down South with my grandmother, everybody was talking junk about skeletons in the closet and my mother said, "You think you want to tell me now about your pregnancy? Enough time has passed now."

I looked at her amazed. I said, "Well, you evidently already know! Ain't nothing to tell you!"

She said, "I knew I should have taken you to the damn doctor."

I experimented with smoking weed during my teenage years, and when my mother found out, she addressed it immediately. She found some weed in my room and asked me who it belonged to, as if she didn't already know. I told her that it belonged to my cousin, and my mother said, "Well, tell her I flushed it down the toilet." When she flushed it down the toilet, I was in shock. Much later, when she was in the hospital suffering from cancer, I sat down at the foot of the bed. She asked me if I was still smoking marijuana and I said, "Sometimes." She gave me a stern look and said, "Just make sure you know what it does to your body!" She turned away, coughed, and didn't say anything else.

My father wasn't much of a disciplinarian. He only spanked me four times in my life, and one of the times he hit me was because I was being disrespectful to my mother at the breakfast table. It was in the morning before school when we were in Puerto Rico. I was in the ninth or tenth grade when that happened and Jimmy Hendrix was popular. My mother called us to the table, and I had on a headband and some gladiator sandals.

My father looked at me and said to my mother, "Is that what she is wearing to school?" He talked around me like I wasn't even in the room and I said, "I'm right here!"

He looked at her and said, "That's got to be some kind of violation!" He put me in the third person and just dismissed me. He treated me like I was one of his employees at work or something.

My mother said, "Well, it's just a scarf, just a teenage thing."

And then I said something to her like, "Well, I'm going to wear what I want."

The next thing I knew, my father smacked me across my face which caught me totally off guard.

My mother suddenly jumped up with a kitchen knife and screamed, "Don't hit her! That's a girl. You can't smack her in her face!"

My father said, "Did you hear her mouth?"

I was sitting there stunned, and they were arguing, which was very unusual because they were usually a united front and never overruled each other.

My father threw his napkin down and said, "I'm sick of this! I'm not eating anything here. I'll get something at work. If that's the way you want her to talk to you, then you let her do it. But she's not going to talk to me like that!"

And I had the nerve to still suck my teeth. He turned, gave me a stern look, got his briefcase, and went out of the door.

My mother looked at me and said, "Get ready!"

She checked my face for bruises, and we got into the car to go to school. I went to Antilles, which was the school on Fort Buchanan's base. We drove to school in silence. She let me out. Not long after being in class, I got called over the PA system to report to the principal's office and was told that I had to go home because I was in violation of the dress code. They called my mother and told her to please come and get me.

She came back to get me and said, "Was it worth it? You got smacked, you got into an argument, you got sent back home, you had to change clothes."

That was my mother's way. She knew all along that they were going to send me home, but instead of just telling me to change my clothes, she made me learn the hard way. I had to go back to school after changing clothes because she wouldn't let me stay home.

As Sharon got older, her interest in young men, which started as a flicker of light, evolved into a flood of sunshine. This became another source of irritation between her and Charlie. Fathers all over the world, at one time or another, have had to deal with the emotional dilemma of their daughters growing up and developing an interest in dating, and Charlie was no exception. Sharon went to college at the University of North Carolina in Chapel Hill, North Carolina. She wanted to go to North Carolina Central University like her mom and dad, but integration had opened opportunities for blacks, and her parents convinced her to take advantage of the new opportunities. She would come home during spring and summer break. She started dating and staying out late. This, of course, did not sit well with Charlie.

Sharon recalled.

One night my father called me on the phone while I was over one of my friend's house kind of late. It was around two o'clock in the morning when the phone rang. When my friend picked up the phone, my father shouted, "I want my daughter home now! Put her on the phone."

When I got on the phone, he sternly said, "I doubt he will bring you home, so get your butt in a cab and get home now!"

Mind you, I was in college and feeling quite independent at this point. We lived in White Oak, Maryland, and by the time I got home, it was about 3:30 a.m. I figured that I'd just come in the house and face him in the morning, but when I opened the door he was sitting diagonally across from the door.

He said, "Under what conditions did I raise you where you think you can come home four o'clock in the morning. What kind of date was that?"

I said, "I'm sorry."

He told me to sit down and he talked me to death, but all I remember was that he was saying that I was acting like a *whore*.

He said, "I'm never calling you again at some guy's house to tell you to come home. If you can't end a date at a reasonable hour and he can't escort you home, then you determine how you want to live your life somewhere else." So I never went out with that guy again.

He didn't seem to like any of the guys I went out with. My father was usually a gentle and jovial guy, but when he lost his temper, he could use a very nasty tone, and his tone could be so threatening and his words so volatile that it was frightening. One of my boyfriends found this out when it became apparent that I had fallen in love with him and we wanted to get married. His name was Cortez Quick, and he lived off of Florida Avenue in Washington, DC. My father didn't think that Cortez was good enough for me, and he went over Cortez's house and threatened him if he didn't leave me alone. I had only seen my father use violence once or twice in my life, but when he did, it became real ugly quick. But he and Cortez stayed away from each other.

Cortez was a musician that I met at a dance, and we seemed to be kindred spirits. We continued to see each other against my father's wishes. My mother covered for me because my father didn't want Cortez in the house or around me.

She would tell my father, "She's in love, and at least we will know where she is. If we stop him from coming here, we won't know where to find her."

My father would tell her, "I don't want him in my house! When I come home, he better not be here, or we will have a problem!"

She would get Cortez out of the house before my father got home. She never had to do it a lot because that was the agreement. So he didn't run into my dad, and my dad didn't run into him. I knew my father would never approve, so we decided to elope (December 13, 1973) and kept it a secret for seven months. Nobody wanted us to get married, his people or my people. We stayed married for sixteen years before I finally decided to divorce him.

My father was very disappointed when he found out I was married because he wanted to walk me down the aisle and give me away at my wedding. Ironically, I found out much later that he was going to elope with my mother. It seemed that his family didn't want him to marry her, but he decided to do it anyway. They felt that he should have married a nice West Indian girl and not someone who was the descendant of Southern slaves. It was Aunt Ollie (Johnson) who found out that he and Ruthe were going to elope and encouraged them to get married in her living room in Oxford.

Unsettling turbulent times at home took a turn for the worst when the marriage everybody thought was made in heaven between Charlie and Ruthe came to a disappointing conclusion. Being the wife of a Secret Service agent can be very tough and sometimes similar to being the wife of a military man, who is often called away from home on a tour of duty in some far-off land, or a doctor who is constantly called away at all hours of the day or night to work, or an actor, who is always in the public eye and spends months away from home making a movie. The main difference, however and especially in Charlie's case, is that Secret Service agents often get called to do undercover work or do things that they cannot share with their families. This often results in a void that develops between individuals as they grow in different directions.

"Traveling and being away from your family was tough," lamented Charlie as he recalled the difficulties of being a family man and married to the Secret Service at the same time. "If you've got a wife who doesn't like to travel a lot, you could have a problem. Some liked it and some didn't. Ruthe didn't mind the traveling because she was a traveler herself. She was always on a plane going to Europe, Canada, and different places. She worked for the internal revenue and traveled for her job. I was gone all of the time, but being gone all of the time to me was positive. Ruthe and Sharon had their friends, and they could go to parties and stuff like that. But all Secret Service men were like that, especially in those days. Most Secret Service men had big families. I was probably the only one who didn't have a big family. I just had Sharon, and when she grew up and left home, Ruthe didn't have anyone. I also couldn't share a lot with my family. It was hard coming home telling my wife and kid what I did during the day. How could I tell them about drug dealers, counterfeiters, killers, and stuff like that? Other kids would come home and hear from their fathers, 'Guess what happened at Sunday school today?' One kid's father is coming home with a duffle bag filled with guns that he took off of somebody while the other fathers talk about more average things. So I usually didn't talk about my day. I made sure that Sharon never saw my guns, and I always had a place around the house to hide them. I think this was a dilemma for all law enforcement personnel."

Some of the things that Charlie did, Ruthe did not want to know about. "I can remember coming out on a street in Puerto Rico and seeing the name on a building that said CIA Company," Sharon recalled. "One day my parents and I were sitting in the car eating my favorite pizza, and my dad was telling my mom, 'You see how that says CIA? In a lot of places it is a front, and if they are not doing what we need them to do, tomorrow it won't be there and it will look like it had never been there.' My mother looked at him, shook her head, and said, 'Honey, pass me a slice of pizza. I don't want to know what you do! Let's just go.' She didn't want to talk about it especially in front of me."

Charlie had some personal experience with the Central Intelligence Agency in various capacities. "I was fascinated with the spy business," Charlie once said. "All agents don't necessarily do the same thing. During the Cuban missile crisis, I was in a specialty school, a spy school. At that school they did special training in explosives and other things. Even though we might never have to do some of that stuff, we were trained, and people who knew I was in that school thought I did all of that stuff. The school used to be held in the CIA headquarters over there on the road near the airport. The building used to be really secret, but these days it is now a place where schoolchildren can visit and see what the CIA does. I never did any assignments with the CIA, but I would have liked to. In 1971, I was granted a special intelligence clearance by the Secret Service based on an investigation completed by the CIA. I worked with guys from the CIA, and I have loaned some of my agents to the CIA for certain assignments. They would call and ask to borrow our guys to work with them for a month or two. The army has a major spy-type agency as well. There are so many secret organizations doing covert things around here you would be surprised. Nobody knows where the CIA does all of their training today and where all of their facilities are located."

Charlie and Ruthe's marriage was able to survive the long period of absences, the many hours of loneliness, the growing in different directions, but the one thing that it could not tolerate was the episodes of infidelity. Charlie was a very gregarious person and came into contact with all kinds of people in his line of work. "He was bit of a flirt," according to his daughter Sharon. "I don't think my mother left him because he was with the Secret Service, or because he was gone all of the time. She left him because he was unfaithful. One day, after Martin Luther King Jr. had gotten assassinated, I came home and my mother was sitting in the dark crying. I turned on the light and asked her what was wrong, and she showed me a letter that a woman had written to him revealing an illicit relationship. We were living in Puerto Rico at the time, and after that, things began to change. She stayed with him for another ten years until she found evidence of another relationship, and that was the end. She had to take a trip to Atlanta for her job and was on her way to the airport when she suddenly remembered she left something at home. She turned around to go back and get it, and when she got home, another woman was in the house. She *went off*, and they got separated. They had been married for twenty-nine years when Ruthe made the decision to end the relationship. After a year of separation, she filed for and was granted a divorce in 1979."

Losing a wife and having a strained relationship with his daughter was devastating enough, but it seems like bad news always comes in threes. Charlie had always been the pillar of health, but the years of undercover work, the pressure of protecting the president, the pressures of running an important office, the pressures of being a black man who was a Secret Service agent, along with the drama produced by the dissolution of his happy home took a toll on his body. His health began to deteriorate, and he finally decided to go to the doctor to check it out. He was diagnosed with a severe case of hypertension. The doctor who examined him stated that his case was so severe that if he didn't take better care of himself, he wouldn't last much longer. A simple case of high blood pressure, however, was not enough to stop him or slow him down, and so Charlie continued to work, needing the job more than ever now. He was promoted to deputy assistant director of the Office of Inspection in July 1977, which made him responsible for overseeing Secret Service offices all over the world. He was given a temporary assignment as the special agent in charge of the Europe/Africa/Middle East field office located in Paris, France, in December 1978 and finally returned to his duties as the deputy assistant director of the Office of Inspection in 1979. He was able to physically continue working for twenty-four more years before his kidneys finally started to give out, and he had to go on dialysis in September of 2003. He got a kidney transplant in the fall of 2005 at the age of seventy-five.

Ruthe, on the other hand, was not as fortunate. Her years of smoking cigarettes led to a terminal case of lung cancer. Though she waged a valiant fight for her life, her battle ended on May 17, 1991. Charlie and Ruthe, though divorced, had an amicable relationship and remained friends. They continued to work on the same block and continued to use the same cleaners. When she got sick, he went to the hospital every day on his lunch hour and made sure she had her food and whatever she needed.

As the 1970s drew to a close, another chapter in Charlie's life came to a conclusion as well. After twenty-three years, Charlie decided that his tenure with the Secret Service had reached its conclusion, and on September 30, 1979, he ended his career. His departure was somewhat bitter-sweet. The service had been like a family to him and gave him the opportunity to travel, to earn a very comfortable living, to meet people from all walks of life, and to fulfill his childhood dreams. He worked hard and was very appreciative of the opportunity. He became a beacon of hope for other black men and women who saw him, always impeccably dressed, well-spoken, and in a position of power, which was not normally given to black men during this time. He had received numerous letters of commendation for the way the Secret Service was able to coordinate and handle the numerous activities of the 1976 bicentennial celebrations in Washington and was commended by foreign dignitaries for the professional way in which he made them and their families feel welcomed when they came to Washington, DC. He was well regarded by the workers whom he supervised while serving as special agent in charge of the Washington field office.

He was a little disappointed, however, by the fact that when he got promoted to deputy assistant director of the office of inspections, he did not receive the customary salary increase that went along with the senior executive service rate of pay. He was given extra responsibilities, which included scheduling special investigations for all of the Secret Service offices worldwide and running the office when the deputy director was traveling or not in the office and had the same grade (GS-15) and pay he received as the special agent in charge of the Washington office. More importantly, even though he was able to break into *the circle of thirteen* in the executive office of the Secret Service (i.e., six deputy assistant directors, six deputy directors, and the director), he felt that he should have gotten one of the deputy director's positions. He was the most senior of the twelve assistant directors and deputy directors, with the longest career record and impeccable credentials. In fact, he had his eye set on the director's position, but all indications seemed to point to the fact that that position was not within his reach.

Overcoming obstacles had been something Charlie had to deal with all of his adult life, but this hurdle came at a bad time for him (health and family issues), and he had grown weary of fighting and trying to justify why his excellent record was not good enough. He submitted his retirement papers and was given the customary send-off (i.e., retirement party, gifts, well wishes, etc.) and walked out of the door. He left the Secret Service on a Friday, and the next Monday he walked into a new office and a new position as the deputy director for operations, in the criminal division, office of special investigations for the Department of Justice—so much for retirement!

His next challenge was hunting down Nazi war criminals.

CHAPTER 13
The Hunt for Justice

As deputy director, Charlie brought instant law enforcement credibility to our fledgling program. He knew the ins and outs of the federal bureaucracy better than anyone on the staff, and he had better nationwide law enforcement contacts than any ten OSI staff members put together. Charlie made enormous contributions to the success of our program—contributions that were essential to OSI's becoming, by far, the most successful unit of its kind in the world. Thanks in significant part to Charlie's talent, industry, wise counsel, and well-honed leadership skills, OSI succeeded in obtaining a measure of justice on behalf of more than two million victims of Nazi inhumanity.

—Eli Rosenbaum, Director
Office of Special Investigation, Criminal Division,
US Department of Justice

The snow fell briskly on the tracks, and the temperature dipped below freezing as he stood patiently on the stoop waiting for the train to arrive. He was comforted by the ingenious idea he had the night before that would resolve his problem and was dying to try it out. To do so, he needed a set of identical twins and was hopeful today would be the day.

As the rickety train finally pulled into the station, he observed with a keen eye as the weary passengers exited the train in single file, silently worried about their fate. With a wave of his experienced hand, he divided the passengers into two groups as they filed by, sending each group in different directions. The fortunate ones were sent to the left where they entered their sleeping quarters before being assigned to a work detail. The unlucky ones were sent to the right where their journey took them to a huge shower facility that spewed the deadly gas before ending in the crematory.

Day after day the train arrived bringing more and more victims. As he scanned over thousands of faces before making his fatal decision, he finally found what he had been desperately searching for. There stood two little frightened Jewish girls clinging to their mother's coat sleeves, and he instructed his soldiers to take them to his office. The last thing the innocent little girls saw, before the searing pain arrived from the twenty-inch needle that was inserted into their unprotected eyes, was the name on the certificate hanging on the wall. To his colleagues, he was known as Josef Mengele, the resident medic; to the people trapped in the concentration camps of Auschwitz in 1944, he was known simply as the Angel of Death. He now began dividing the train passengers into three groups: one marked for immediate death; the second group would be overworked, ill-fed, and the victims of a slow death; and the last group would be used for live experimentation, usually without the use of anesthesia.

Josef Mengele was a German doctor, anthropologist, and SS officer whose mission was to create a master race fit for the German Third Reich under the leadership of Adolph Hitler. One of his tasks was to carry out experiments to discover by what method of genetic quirk twins were produced and then to artificially increase the Aryan birthrate for Hitler. Mengele used Auschwitz as an opportunity to continue his research on heredity, using inmates for human experimentation. He was particularly interested in identical twins; they would be selected and placed in special barracks. After an experiment was over, the twins were usually killed and their bodies dissected. Mengele's experiments also included various amputations of limbs, attempts to change eye color by injecting chemicals into children's eyes, and other surgeries. He was personally responsible for the horrible deaths of many Jews during the Holocaust, but when the war came to an end, he fled Germany. Mengele fled Europe for South America in the face of the Russian army advance in January 1945. Shuttling between Argentina, Paraguay, and Brazil, he managed to evade justice before his death in 1979.

In the book *Mengele: The Angel of Death in South America* the Argentine historian Jorge Camarasa, a specialist in the post-war Nazi flight to South America, has painstakingly pieced together the Nazi doctor's mysterious later years. He reveals how, after working with cattle farmers in Argentina to increase their stock, Mengele fled the country after fellow Nazi, Adolf Eichmann, was kidnapped by Israeli agents. Camarasa claims that Mengele found refuge in the German enclave of Colonias Unidas, Paraguay, and from there, in 1963, began to make regular trips to another predominantly German community just over the border in Brazil—the farming community of Candido Godoi. Not long after the arrival of Mengele, Camarasa claimed that the birthrate of twins began to spiral. There is testimony that Mengele attended women, followed their pregnancies, treated them with new types of drugs and preparations, that he talked of artificial insemination in human beings, and he continued working with animals, proclaiming he was capable of getting cows to produce male twins.[48]

Mengele lived in a small shack in this small rural community and was said to sleep with a loaded pistol by his bed for fear of being captured by the Israeli Secret Service (MOSSAD). His health had been deteriorating for years. He died on February 7, 1979, when he accidentally drowned, or possibly suffered a stroke, while swimming in the Atlantic.[49] He was buried under an assumed name.

At the conclusion of World War II, twenty-four major political and military leaders from Nazi Germany and more than one hundred additional defendants representing the political, economic, and military sections of German society were put on trial for aggressive war, war crimes, and crimes against humanity. The series of trials were conducted by a United States military tribunal held from November 1945 to October 1946 in Nuremberg, Germany, and were known as the Nuremberg Trials. At the conclusion of the trials, eleven of the war criminals were sentenced to death by hanging while most received long prison terms. It has been estimated, however, that hundreds of Nazi war criminals were able to escape persecution for their crimes following WWII, in some cases with the aid of the American CIA and in other cases with aid from high officials in the Catholic church. German scientists had been leading the race to develop nuclear technology during WWII before their efforts were sabotaged by Allied forces. The Germans had developed the V-1 and V-2 rockets that were launched against England and the first jet fighter planes used in combat. There was an intense effort to smuggle as many of the Nazi scientists, engineers, and doctors as possible into America and western Allied nations so their knowledge and experience could help develop American rocket technology. This ultimately led to development of the America's space program as well as helped discover cures for many diseases. American leaders also did not want those German scientists to fall into the hands of the Soviet Union. According to declassified CIA secret documents released by the national archives, Nazi war criminals were also used as spies and double agents in Europe and Russia in an attempt to win the Cold War.

The fact that many of the perpetrators of vicious and inhumane crimes which occurred during the Holocaust were allowed to live out their lives as citizens of the United States did not sit well with many Americans, and as a result, the Office of Special Investigations (OSI) in the criminal division of the United States Department of Justice was created in 1979. The goal of OSI was to investigate and prosecute cases against Nazi offenders who were complicit in the genocide that exterminated eleven million people (six million of them Jews) living in the United States. OSI conducted civil proceedings, because criminal prosecutions in the Nazi cases were, in effect, barred by the ex post facto clause of the United States Constitution. Sanctions imposed as a result of successful civil prosecution by OSI were denaturalization (revocation of United States citizenship) and deportation.

Despite initial predictions that its work would soon be finished, OSI was active for over twenty-five years. It opened hundreds of investigations and initiated proceedings leading to the denaturalization and/or removal of more than one hundred Nazi offenders from the United States. In addition, with the assistance of the Immigration and Naturalization Service (INS) and, since 2002, its successor, the Department of Homeland Security, OSI succeeded in blocking attempts made by more than two hundred individuals suspected of participating in Nazi crimes to gain entry to the United States. In December 2004, Congress expanded the jurisdiction of OSI to cover post-WWII offenders who obtained US citizenship after participating in genocide, torture, or extrajudicial killing abroad under cover of foreign law.[50]

According to Eli Rosenbaum, who started working for OSI as a summer intern and went on to become its fourth director in 1994, "the process by which OSI was created was so much like the development of any agency in Washington. An office is usually created when the media uncover a scandal, which usually leads to a congressional hearing and then finally the Executive Branch acts. In this instance there was a series of media exposure in the mid-1970's by a variety of newspapers (e.g. the *Philadelphia Inquirer*, the *New York Times* and both of the Chicago newspapers and television networks as well) focused on the fact that there were a number of fugitive Nazi criminals in this country from WWII and the Justice Department was doing nothing about it. Back then the Immigration and Naturalization Service was a part of the Justice Department. INS had the responsibility for these matters along with the US Attorney's office and wasn't doing anything. Finally that led Elizabeth Holtzman, a young congresswoman representing Brooklyn at that time, to press for hearings. Two days of hearings were held in the Immigration subcommittee of the House Judiciary Committee in 1976-77. That led the Justice Department to create a special unit in the Immigration Service to handle these cases. That unit had no real success and finally Holtzman and others in Congress pressed the Justice Department to give that unit, what we jokingly call now 'adult supervision' and move it from the Immigration Service to the Criminal Division, which had a better reputation than INS. That's when in 1979 Attorney General Benjamin Civiletti under President Carter, issued an executive order creating OSI in the Criminal Division. At first it meant taking all of those people in the special unit and moving them to the Criminal Division and then additional resources were given and we were able to hire more people."

The development of OSI came at a very opportune time in Charlie's life. His tenure with the Secret Service was coming to an end, but his desire to serve his country and his thirst to experience new challenges was far from extinguished. He was only fifty-one years old and had no desire to sit on the fence and watch life go by. Up until this point, he had a front-row seat while history was being made, was a voracious reader concerning world events, had an opinion about everything that was political in nature, and would talk about it and debate with anyone who would sit with him long enough to listen. When he heard about the creation of this new organization (OSI), it whetted his appetite, and he jumped at the opportunity to join. Coming in at the inception of the program gave him the opportunity to use his organization skills, knowledge, and contacts to help build a top-notch criminal investigative unit. More importantly, Charlie felt that the mission of OSI was a just one, and it gave him the opportunity to complete a mission that had motivated him to enter the military when he was a high school student back in Cambridge. He once said that if he had to die, he "wanted to die with one of Hitler's bullets in him" and eagerly joined the army to fight in WWII. Fortunately, that prophesy was not fulfilled, and he ended up in the Pacific theater shortly after the conclusion of WWII. He never got the chance to battle Hitler, but now had the chance to finish the job. His motivation to go after Hitler could have been stimulated by the stories he remembered from his childhood mentor, friend, and local store owner Hyman Rudolph, who was Jewish and who had to escape the hatred and bigotry of anti-Semitism in Europe long before the horrors of the Holocaust. Charlie had been fighting for justice all of his adult life, and ultimately his motivation were stimulated from the fact that what the Nazis did was a crime against humanity, and they had to be brought to justice.

"He went to the Department of Justice, and he started searching for war criminals," his old friend and colleague at the Secret Service Victor Gonzalez once said. "I used to tease him and say, 'Hey, Charlie, these guys are in their eighties! Come on, man, what kind of job is that?' He would say, 'Nah, it's important. These people are bad people.'"

To OSI, Charlie was a gold mine. His experience, knowledge of investigative procedures, ability to communicate—both orally and in writing—and gregarious nature was just what this brand-new organization needed not only to survive but to grow into an efficient machine that was able to piece together evidence from various foreign countries, including the Soviet Union.

"After I left the Secret Service, I became a member of the Department of Justice," Charlie reflected. "I spent a year in Russia helping to wrap things up and thanked them for helping us in the investigations of Nazi war criminals. It was more of a protocol thing. It was me and another guy named Alan Ryan (who became the OSI director 1980–83). We took a lot of pictures and made lots of speeches. I also had the opportunity to travel to Germany and went to Hitler's secure and most secret places."

Charlie was put in charge of handling the critical public relations campaign designed to thwart the many vicious attacks OSI received from private organizations and governmental opposition, claiming that OSI should not receive government funding. His ability to present a convincing argument in writing—with supporting evidence and documentation—was crucial in helping OSI obtain and maintain funding and support.

"Charlie was the deputy director of OSI from 1982 until he retired in 1999," stated Al Matney, who was an investigator hired by Charlie and who later became the director of the US Marshals Service's Witness Protection Program. "I traveled to the Soviet Union, to Latvia, which at that time was one of the fifteen republics of the Soviet Union. I was also in Moscow. The investigators and attorneys in that division would travel around the world taking depositions and interviewing people who had information against immigrants that came into the United States who were guilty of Nazi war crimes and who were living in the United States."

"Our program was without precedent in federal history, tasked with responsibility for proving crimes that had taken place decades earlier, thousands of miles outside the United States," exclaimed Eli Rosenbaum. "So there really wasn't any roadmap or playbook available for us to consult. Not to worry. Charlie knew how to get done what needed to be done. He traveled to Europe early in his OSI career to help cement the law enforcement partnerships that were crucial to our work. He shaped up the staff of investigators who had come to OSI from a variety of different federal agencies, from the INS to the US Fish and Wildlife Service. He had the respect and affection of his colleagues and made enormous contributions to the success of our program. Thanks in part to Charlie's talent, industry, wise counsel, and well-honed leadership skills, OSI succeeded in obtaining a measure of justice on behalf of more than two million victims of Nazi inhumanity. By capturing and bringing these criminals to justice, even if they were in their eighties, it sent a message to would-be war criminals that no matter how long it took, they would be found and brought to justice.

"Our program was frequently on the front pages of America's newspapers back then, and we were constantly under media and congressional microscopes. Former OSI Director Alan Ryan put Charlie in charge of congressional matters for OSI, and everything was soon running smoothly on that challenging front. Charlie had seen a lot in Washington and knew what was important and what was just static interference."

"We had a highly visible program," exclaimed Neal Sher, who was the director of OSI from 1983–94. "We were relatively new, and we were becoming quite successful. There was a lot of publicity surrounding our endeavor, and some of that publicity produced a lot of controversy. There were people who just didn't want us to do the Nazi prosecutions at all for all sorts of reasons. There were an enormous amount of public inquiries and congressional inquiries, and Charlie was masterful at dealing with that. That responsibility fell on his shoulders, and it was very important. He did it very effectively.

"Some of the public opposition came from rabid anti-Semites who would send vicious letters to us and made anti-Semitic statements about what we were doing and why we should not be funded by the federal government. There was also opposition from the Eastern European immigrant community who did not like the fact that a lot of our defendants and suspects came from Eastern Europe. They weren't necessarily German, but they had collaborated with and did the dirty work of the Germans. That community was adamantly opposed to our work. This public outcry lasted for many, many years. We would get challenged in court, and there was a public relations campaign against us that came from private organizations as well as from some members of Congress. Charlie was masterfully gifted in handling these challenges. He would respond to allegations from the public and Congress. He knew the cases and what the evidence showed, and he would prepare responses for the White House, Capitol Hill, and the general public. He was a consummate professional. He was older than virtually all of the lawyers and historians who came on board and he had been around. He was a veteran of Washington, he was sophisticated and sharp, and he always carried himself with dignity. He had a fascinating career, was always breaking new ground, and was a dedicated civil servant, a dedicated citizen, and a dedicated American."

Rosenbaum explained, "Most of the opposition was in the 1980s during the first decade of OSI's existence when we were still in the era of the Soviet Union—the Soviet Union collapsed in 1990–91. From then on we were in a post-Communists world, at least in Europe. Most of the crimes that we were able to prosecute occurred during WWII on territory that was, after the war, behind the iron curtain. That meant that the Red Army [i.e., the Soviet Army] had captured most of the documents that were relevant to our prosecutions. There were activists, primarily in the Baltic, Ukrainian communities, who used that as an excuse to criticize our office, and I think they had other problems with what we were doing. I actually had an opportunity to discuss this with some Ukrainian-American leaders in a very good meeting I had in Canada. In Canada, you could have a good conversation, but not in the United States. They were very aggressive, and they formed entire organizations that were solely devoted to closing us down.

"They lobbied the White House and found an ally in Pat Buchannan. He, I think is fair to say, was the only White House official in history who somehow had a license to attack other cabinet-level agencies. He was constantly attacking the justice department, not only in his columns when he was outside the government, but when he was communications director in the Reagan White House. It was pretty unpleasant. He referred to us in one of his syndicated newspaper columns as "those hairy-chested Nazi hunters at the Justice Department," which came, of course, as a surprise to some of our women prosecutors. He defended John Demjanjuk and defended Nazis who were not even in the United States, which included some really notorious people like Klaus Barbie. He too would focus on the fact that the evidence came from behind the Iron Curtain, but sometimes he would find other ways to criticize us. All of this evidence was tested forensically, some by experts from Charlie's old agency, the Secret Service, who had one of the finest forensic laboratories in the world. Stuff was tested by them and by the FBI and the immigration service lab. There was never any question about the authenticity of the documents. In fact, on many occasions the defendants themselves would admit that the stuff was correct.

"We also received hate mail from people who were anti-Semitic. There was an interesting overlap, and I know that Charlie saw it too. We got hate mail from people who hated Jews and Blacks. Even though I never saw the mail that Charlie got attacking him because of his race, it wouldn't surprise me that he received letters like that. It also wouldn't surprise me that Charlie never said anything about it. He would always take things in stride and never let it get to him. He probably would just file the letters or throw them away. He was incredibly modest. He never even mentioned that he was the first African American in the Secret Service, even though we all kind of knew it, or mentioned any of the accomplishments he made or accolades he received. When you went into his office, there was nothing on the walls or on the bookshelves about his career. He would just come to work and do his job."

"I know he got derogatory letters working with the justice department hunting down Nazi war criminals during the late 1980s and early '90s," his daughter Sharon said. "I think he was called the Nigger Nazi Chaser in some of those letters. He was responsible for writing the letters requesting that the United States go forward with a particular case or writing Congress to ensure they continued to receive appropriated money. A couple of times he brought home letters that would include things like, 'Have that little nigger write . . . ,' or 'Don't think that nigger's letters are going to cover everything' or something like that. In some of the letters there were references made about the KKK and that they would burn a cross on his lawn or burn him. He was the one whose name was on the letters composed to Congress for the things that were happening in the office. Some people didn't want OSI to remain funded because they felt it was a special interest office for Jews, or that Jews weren't the only people murdered in Nazi concentration camps, and American people shouldn't be funding it. They felt that no other special interest group was getting federal money.

"My father felt that one of the reasons he was recruited to come to OSI probably was because they wanted to have all types of Americans on the team to calm some of those accusations. He was second in command . . . he was an administrative officer. Under him were the lawyers, who were generally historians and maybe some anthropologists I don't know, but I know they had a lot of lawyers who were historians as part of the investigative team. Even though the majority of the team members were Jewish, about 12 percent of the team was black, and they had women."

While Charlie was hunting for Nazi war criminals during the day, he spent his off-duty hours hunting for something else. That something else was companionship. Reeling from the breakup of his marriage with Ruthe, Charlie resumed dating with the same passion that he employed in all of his other endeavors. That search concluded with a very attractive young woman he had met while traveling in the US Virgin Islands. Her name was Maureen Peterson Espersen.

Charlie had always been attracted to lovely ladies and as a world traveler had come into contact with some of the world's finest. Dr. Larry Hamme, one of Ruthe's close relatives, would often joke with Charlie and tell his friends a story making fun of Charlie's attraction to women. He would say, "Charlie loved football, or so I thought. One Sunday when I came to visit him when he lived in Maryland, the Dallas Cowboys were playing the Washington Redskins, and he overheard me saying that the game came on at 1:00 p.m. He got very excited. Now I've known Charlie all of my life, and I never saw him get excited about a football game. When the game came on, he was outside working in his garden. I told him that the game was coming on. He didn't come in until about an hour and a half later and said, 'Is it halftime yet?' I said, 'In about a minute.' He said, 'Good, because I want to see the Dallas Cowboy cheerleaders!' Charlie wasn't in love with the game—he was in love with halftime and the cheerleaders! That was Charlie."

Maureen was born and raised on the island of St. Thomas. When Charlie first met her, she was working as an administrative secretary for the Department of Public Safety in the commissioner's office on the beautiful island. She held this job for ten years before becoming an entrepreneur. In addition to her administrative duties for the commissioner, she served as the official hostess for the government of St. Thomas and would often meet and greet dignitaries coming to visit the island. Her father (Hans Christian Peterson) was a well-known meat merchant and businessman on the island. She was married to Raymond Jens Espersen, and they had two beautiful daughters, Cherri and Carolyn. Maureen became the owner and manager of a ten-room guesthouse known as Villa Fairview with her husband. When her husband passed away in July 1978, Maureen took over the running of the business. In 1979, she began working as a development assistant for the University of the Virgin Islands where she managed the office, worked as a supervisor for office staff, assisted the director of development with fund-raising for the university, and conducted tours of the campus and island. Her knowledge of the island and her long friendship with many people who lived on the island made her a valuable asset to the goals of the development program and the mission of the college. She was very affable, and her personality made her the perfect person to represent the college and the island in their public relations campaigns.

Charlie and Maureen got reacquainted after Maureen's husband passed, had a whirlwind romance, fell in love, and got married in a small church wedding in St. Thomas on January 9, 1982. He moved his new family into a luxurious home in Fort Washington, Maryland, and gave them the best of everything. He was a new man with a new family, and it invigorated him. It was always the stability of his home life that enabled him to handle the trials and tribulations of a stressful career. This union, however, only lasted ten years before Charlie and Maureen decided to go their separate ways.

Charlie's career in public service finally came to an end in 1999 when he retired for a second time. Ever since his seventeenth birthday, when he dropped out of high school to go fight in WWII, he had given his life in the service of his country. He served eight years in the United States Army (both active and reserve duty), twenty-three years in the United States Secret Service, and now twenty years in the United States Department of Justice. Even though he wasn't really ready to let it all go, he realized that the time had come. He was seventy-one years old and eligible for a second retirement. Financially, at that point in the old social security system, you wouldn't make any more working than you would in retirement, and he had two pensions. With two pensions, he would actually make more than anyone working in the office. In addition, by the time he left, OSI had done most of the work that could be done in the Nazi cases, which is what he came to the office to do. The mission was 85–90 percent completed and the process regularized. He had put in the system what was needed, and the unit operated like it was on autopilot. He had helped to create a well-oiled, smooth-running machine by then. He was a good investor, so he was financially secure. His children were launched into the world successfully. He had other things to do with his life. One of the few things he talked about in his private life was that he used to go to see people who were sick, elderly, or shut-in. He would visit the local hospices or nursing homes, and these visits brought meaning to his life. It probably reminded him of the days his mother made him visit his father in the mental institution, but it also helped him realize there were more important things in his life than just work. Whenever possible, he attended every graduation ceremony or wedding for members of his family and friends.

His health took a turn for the worse in 2001 when his kidneys, feeling the effects of years of stress and high blood pressure, began to give out and he had to go on dialysis. By the fall of 2004, his kidneys finally gave out, and he had to get a kidney transplant. His mental health began to deteriorate with the onset of dementia, and by December of 2010, his daughter was forced to put him in an assisted living facility. In July 2011, Sharon took him to the doctor for an examination. He had had a few episodes where he lost his balance, fell down, and hurt himself. It was revealed later that he had suffered a series of small strokes. After reading the MRI, the doctor said,

"You're not going to get your father back. He has had pretty bad high blood pressure, and he is a kidney recipient. I see that he was a federal agent."

Sharon quietly responded, "Yes, sir."

"The job must have been pretty stressful."

"Very stressful!"

"What branch?"

"The United States Secret Service. He was the first black Secret Service agent."

"Oh, did he come in under President Carter?"

"No, President Eisenhower."

The doctor stopped, took off his glasses, put his papers down, and, with an incredulous look on his face, said, "That was in the 1950s! Are you sure?"

"Yes, sir, I'm quite sure."

"Well, that would explain a lot of things. It was a very different America during the 1950s under President Eisenhower."

"He served every president from Eisenhower to Carter. He was also in charge of the Washington field office of the Secret Service, and he did a lot of undercover work when he was a young agent."

"Your father's case of hypertension was so bad that he should have died while he was in his forties or sixties. The fact that he got to his eighties is truly remarkable."

"That's my dad. He was always beating the odds."

Two days later, the man we affectionately knew as Charlie was gone.

CONCLUSION
A Legacy of Excellence

Mr. Gittens was a pioneer, a history maker, and an example setter for African Americans in the United States Secret Service. He had matriculated through the ranks and was well respected by all, whether it was white agents, black agents, Hispanic agents, administrative personnel, or technical employees. He was respected by all. He was the example of professionalism, and he was a presence in so far as his demeanor, decorum, and his dress were concerned. He would often say to young employees, "Hey, if you are going to be in this outfit you've got to look the part." He was a firm supervisor and held people accountable. He didn't make people feel bad when he had to admonish them for their performance. He got right to the point, made his point, and was willing to move on and give the individual an opportunity to redeem himself. It was easy for me to relate to him simply because he had an endearing personality.

—Keith Prewitt, Deputy Director,
United States Secret Service

Both my brother-in-law Theodore "Ted" Harvey and I are retired, and we had gotten into the habit of playing golf every Monday morning at East Potomac Golf course located in Washington, DC, but somehow this Monday seemed a little different. The golf course was unusually empty as we pulled our golf cart on to the tee at the third hole of the white course. It was a very cool brisk February morning, and the chill in the air probably prevented many of the usual patrons from attempting to get in a few holes before going to work. We were leisurely talking and joking around as we tried to shape the different shots that we hoped would make us golf legends or would at least help us from being embarrassed when the real golfers came out in the upcoming spring season, when suddenly a relatively well-built white gentleman appeared—it seemed like out of nowhere. He was very stocky, had a very close-cut haircut (almost military style), and wore sun glasses. We were in no rush, so we waved him on so he could pass in front of us, but he refused and acted like he didn't even see us. As we finished the hole and turned the corner to the fourth tee, I saw a man and woman sitting in a golf cart on the adjacent course. They were just sitting under a tree, not playing, not talking, not doing anything but just sitting there watching. As I suspiciously gazed at them, I noticed that they both had military haircuts, seemed physically fit, had sunglasses, and it seemed like golf was the furthest thing from their minds. We played a few more holes before I shared my thoughts with Ted.

I turned to Ted and said, "You see that guy behind us, I bet he is Secret Service! And look at those two over there. I bet they are too. Somebody must be here."

Ted turned to me and responded, "Why do you say that?"

A short time later, we saw a motorcade speeding away on Ohio Drive surrounded by screaming police escorts with sirens blazing and people getting out of the way. It turned out that Vice Pres. Joseph Biden had been on the range hitting a few golf balls and shaping his golf shots before going to work for the nation. When we turned around, the muscular young man who had been trailing us was mysteriously gone as well.

I began telling Ted the story I was writing about Mr. Gittens and how it introduced me into a world I had seen in the movies and on television, but I realized I knew very little about. We got into a conversation about counterfeiting, sharpshooters, listening devices, racism, and my journey to Cambridge and Oxford. I told him about all the people I had met on this journey and all of the stories they shared.

Ted had a thousand questions about Mr. Gittens and the Secret Service, but most of all he wanted to know how Mr. Gittens was able to handle the hate, discrimination, and bigotry a black man must have had to deal with during the early twentieth century in America. How did he internalize it, and where did he put all of the rage? More importantly how was he able to rise above it all. We both grew up in a segregated Washington, DC during a time when it was affectionately referred to as Chocolate City. We lived in an all-black community and went to all black schools. With the exception of my junior high school teacher constantly telling me, "Why do you want to go to college . . . all you are ever going to do is sweep the floors!" most of the racism we encountered was covert in nature—that is, until we became young adults and began venturing into a world outside of our segregated communities. Ted had gone to work for the *Washington Post,* and I had ventured off to Bowdoin College, which is located in Brunswick, Maine.

To answer his questions in a way that made some sense to the both of us, I had to reach back into my personal experiences and reactions to racism and bigotry that had to be somewhat similar, but in no way as serious as to what Mr. Gittens had to go through. Bowdoin College was a predominately white, all-male institution when I first got there in the fall of 1970. I cherished and enjoyed my four years there, got a top-notched education, and when I left I felt I was ready for whatever the world could throw at me, but it was by far one of the most difficult things I ever had to do in my young life. The college made an honest attempt to try and address some of the social dilemma's occurring in our country during the early 1970s and went into the urban centers to recruit outstanding black students who demonstrated not only academic excellence but leadership ability. The culture shock I encountered was not only staggering and stressful, but the lessons I learned, some hurtful, most educational, gave me a frame of reference that helped me to understand what Mr. Gittens went through. It was at Bowdoin where my racial and sociopolitical consciousness began to emerge, a direct result of my association with the other politically active and intellectually brilliant black students I met and, unfortunately, the many culturally insensitive and racially ignorant students, professors, and townspeople that challenged the childhood teachings of my parents (i.e., color was not important and that you should judge people by the content of their character as opposed to the color of their skin). Etched in my mind was the time when I was struggling with physics and went to my professor after class for help and him yelling at me, exclaiming, "How in the world did you get into this school?"

I will never forget my sophomore year when I was one of only two black players on the varsity football team and my roommate Al Session won the starting running back position. The decision to make him the starter over a popular white player was not received well, and I have to give credit to Coach Jim Lentz for standing by his opening statement that all positions were open and the best man would win the job. Al was black and Muslim, and I remember sitting in the locker room when some of his teammates exclaimed, "There's no way I'm blocking for a nigger!" I also remember the night before the game when Al dropped to his knees and prayed for the strength to get him through the game and told me that he was going to do whatever it took to rush for one hundred yards and make the coach proud of him. The next day, Al only got the ball three times the whole game. Every time he touched the ball, he was crushed in the backfield by two or three players. He was taken out of the game and sat on the bench for the remainder of the day. I guess those guys made good on their promise and didn't block for him. Al quit the team when we returned to school. I never gave quitting a single thought because I loved the game too much, and I had made a promise after quitting football in high school that I would never quit anything else in life. But that year was a very difficult year for me, and I was glad when it was over.

I will never forget my junior year when I got injured during a game and had to go to the locker room before the game was over to get dressed. When I came back to the sidelines, all of the black students who sat together in one section of the stands had walked out after I left the game. I later heard that when I went out, they all got up and walked out in single file as if it was some kind of protest. It was only then did I become aware of the expectation and importance placed on a black athlete and the impact it had on the minds and psyche of black students who seemed to be starving for any sense of belonging or something to cheer about. I was an average athlete, but this revelation forced me to work twice as hard in order to live up to that expectation.

More importantly, I'll never forget the indignity I felt by the little things that may seem like nothing individually, but when they are stacked up high on top of each other, they created a feeling that made you uncomfortable and would eat away at your self-confidence or self-esteem. Little things like people getting off the elevator when you got on and then wait for another one to come; or store clerks following you around the store and keeping a watchful eye as if you were trying to steal something; or when a mother clutched her toddler, shrieked in horror, and hustled her child away when her son came over to speak after recognizing me from the day care center where I did volunteer work; or when the airport taxi driver would pick up everyone's luggage and put it in the trunk but left mine sitting on the ground. The Afro-American center was the only place I could go where I didn't have to speak for all black people, or explain why my hair looked and felt the way it did, or defend the actions of Malcolm X or Martin Luther King or any other black political figure. I didn't have to be Superman or Shaft or Stepin Fetchit. I didn't have to always be on guard. I could just be me.

Even when I went to my brother's graduation in 1973 at one of America's finest institutions that claimed, according to my brother, to be void of racial discrimination, I couldn't escape the reach of racial discord. My brother (Major Ernest E. Butler Jr.) had gone to the United States Air Force Academy and became the first African American to make the varsity parachute team. He participated in competitions all over the country representing the academy. However, when it came time for the time-honored tradition of graduating cadets parachuting onto the parade ground during the graduating ceremony, he was not allowed to jump. I will never forget the look on the sergeant's face as he marched over to my mother after the ceremony and tried to explain to her why my brother was not allowed to jump. He had a look of shame and was extremely apologetic. I surmised that the decision not to let my brother jump was not his decision. It wasn't until much later did I find out that the black and white cadets were fighting like cats and dogs; white cadets were posting the confederate flag on their walls, and the black cadets had to join together and write a manifesto outlining the examples of racial discrimination and what should be done about it on the campus of the air force academy.

These experiences with racial discrimination occurred in the 1970s; however, they paled in comparison to what Mr. Gittens had to go through in the 1940s, '50s and '60s. I can't imagine going to a restaurant or hotel and being told that I could not receive service because of the color of my skin, being told to get in the back of public transportation, or being told that I was good enough to pay my money but not good enough to sit on the first floor of a movie theater. Worst yet, have terrorist groups burn crosses on my lawn, sending hate mail threatening my life or the lives of my family members, or being lynched and burned simply because of the color of my skin. Or then again maybe I can.

All of these images and memories flashed up as Mr. Gittens talked about his experiences in the military, working in the South, and working with the Secret Service. As Mr. Gittens relayed his story, the one thing that was a constant was his incessant love for the things and experiences he encountered. He would make statements like, "I loved the army!" or "I loved the South!" and I would say to him, "How could you!" He would look at me, smile, and say, "Son, when you are trying to accomplish something, you can't let anything stand in your way. What was I supposed to do, stop chasing my dream because someone didn't like me?" He talked about the way things were supposed to be and the way things were. He talked about the fact that he accomplished things because he was good at what he did and how he worked hard. He talked about the fact that he didn't want to be known as a black Secret Service agent, but a Secret Service agent, no better or no worse. He did not want to be viewed merely as a black man but a *man*. But he understood that being the first of his race could open doors for others, and those doors could have been closed even tighter if he did not live up to the standard. He knew that eyes were on him and he could not slip up. He was a very patient man, and he believed that unless you were in a position of power to effect immediate change, then you had to go about it gradually by planting seeds and helping those in power to see the wisdom of your opinion or point of view. More so, he believed that the key to growth and obtaining power was through education! He witnessed people in the South rise above their delegated position in society as a result of going through strenuous academic preparation and believed if it could happen there it could happen anywhere, if you were willing to accept the challenge.

His formula for success—which included vision, perseverance, academic preparation, fearlessness, and the heart and willingness to step out on faith—worked beyond his wildest imagination. His lists of impressive accomplishments included but are not limited to

- Administrative NCO of 289th Army Band in Yokohama, Japan
- Executive officer of Military Police Company at Fort Bragg, North Carolina
- First Lieutenant Military Intelligence Branch US Army Reserves
- Graduating with honors from North Carolina College with degree in English and Spanish
- First Black special agent of US Secret Service (Charlotte, North Carolina field office)

- Special agent (New York field office)
- Special agent in charge (San Juan field office)
- Special agent in charge (Washington field office)
- Deputy assistant director (Office of Inspection, US Secret Service) – First African American to hold this position
- Member, Department of Treasury Equal Employment Review Board
- Counselor, Equal Employment Opportunity
- United States representative at the INTERPOL Conference
- Deputy director of the Office of Special Investigations, Department of Justice, Criminal Division
- Keynote speaker at the 1996 Secret Service Academy Graduation Ceremony
- Founding member of NOBLE (National Organization of Black Law Enforcement Executives)
- Member, National Council of Teachers of English
- Member, American Association of Teachers of Spanish and Portuguese
- Alpha Kappa Mu National Honor Society
- Who's Who Among Students in American Colleges and Universities
- Lifetime member, North Carolina Central University Alumni Association
- Member, BASS (Black Agents in the Secret Service)
- Lifetime member, NAACP
- Presidential Protection Detail (Presidents Eisenhower, Kennedy, Johnson, Nixon, Ford, Carter and numerous foreign heads of state)

He did not, however, accomplish all of these feats on his own. There is an adage that says, "We are the products of our past," and his family, relatives, and friends played a major role in his development. When you look carefully at Mr. Gittens's makeup, you will find he carried within him the wisdom, political, and economic savvy of his mother Winifred; the fearlessness and spirit to travel and explore new worlds from his father Randolph; the humorous and gregarious nature of his brother George (Sonny); the internal strength, determination, communication ability, and intelligence of his brother John (Pepper); the mentoring nature of Hyman Rudolph; and the ability to become a passionate and caring person from his sister Ruth-Olga (Ollie) as well as his wife's Aunt Ollie Johnson. His friendships with guys like Victor Gonzalez, Enid Quinones, Hubert Bell, Art Lewis, Donald Tucker, and Andre Jordan (assistant chief of police, United States Park Police Department) helped to keep his head grounded in reality so that his fame and accomplishment did not cause his ego to get out of hand. The love and support of his wife Ruthe, both financial and emotional, was critical in his development during his years in the military and Secret Service, while the love and support of his second wife Maureen and her daughters Cherri and Carolyn helped him to navigate through his later years. The devotion and unconditional love of his daughter Sharon kept him alive and gave meaning to his existence.

Walking and talking with Mr. Gittens was a remarkable experience. Most of the conversations took place in his historically adorned apartment in the Collington Episcopal Life Care Community, the gated assisted living facility where he was relocated as a result of his failing health. On his walls were pictures of John F. and Jackie Kennedy with personal signatures, pictures of him with foreign dignitaries, heads of state, other political leaders, and awards that he received. Some of our conversations, however, took place as we walked around the facility or sat in one of the dining areas where residents gathered to chat, play cards, or just have a snack. His gregarious nature erupted throughout our discussions as he would stop our conversation to greet any and everyone who would pass by with a warm smile and a grandiose hello. As we walked through the halls, he would stop briefly to have a conversation, in fluent Spanish of course, with the workers who were toiling away to make sure things in the facility looked good and worked correctly. They would laugh, and I would look at him in amazement and then he would pick up our conversation at the precise spot where we left off.

Even though he talked freely, he was very guarded when it came to the subject of how he felt about the insults and discrimination he suffered or when the subject came up about the personalities of the presidents he served. When I asked questions like, "What was JFK really like or did you really like Nixon?" he would respond, "Oh, that will remain confidential." He stayed true to his oath not to talk about the people he guarded, and there was a concerted effort not to say anything bad about his beloved Secret Service. If he had a time machine and could go back in time to relive his life, I believe he would do it all over again. I could tell, however, that there was a hint of sadness in his voice and in his eye. He inferred that even though his current living arrangements were comfortable and nice, he would have preferred to be somewhere else. His thirst for traveling, exploring, venturing, and meeting challenges head-on and overcoming them had not been quenched. His need to be free and do as he pleased was still burning bright. He talked about being in Russia and remembering how extremely cold it was, or being in Hitler's bunker where so many ugly decisions were made, or returning to the warmth of Oxford and living out his days hunting and fishing, or returning to Ponce and watching that beautiful sunset over the quaint little fishing village, or just enjoying the comfort and independence of his fabulous home in Fort Washington, Maryland. He always talked fondly of Cambridge and constantly reminded me that he went to Cambridge High and Latin High School, something that he held dear to his heart. When I asked him about regrets that he may have had in his life, he said that he had a few, but that was none of my business. And so we moved on to another subject. Even when he was briefly confined to a hospital room after suffering a series of small strokes, his desire to explore and venture out could not be contained as he sometime stood in the doorway of his room to observe the constant activity that characterizes a busy hospital and spoke to the people as they went by. All of the nurses knew him by name and would take personal time to speak or tell him to go back to his room. Most of them did not have a clue as to his history or list of accomplishments. To them he was just a friendly old man who was very curious and always poking his head into things.

The strokes began taking their toll, and his condition began to deteriorate rapidly. The next time I went to visit him (Tuesday, July 26, 2011), I was shocked at the change in his condition. He was sitting in the lobby in front of the television, but it appeared that he was not paying much attention. We went to his room and I tried to strike up a conversation, but that effort was fruitless. Gone was that gleam in his eye and the enthusiasm in his voice. That omnipresent smile had also dissipated, and it seemed like his body was there, but his spirit had moved on. So we just sat for a while in silence when I decided to read a draft of the introduction that I had written for this book. He did not respond one way or the other, so after a short while, I decided to leave. He asked me why I was leaving so early, and I responded by saying that I thought he didn't feel like talking today and that he seemed tired. I sat for a little while longer thinking that he had something to say or that he just wanted some company. I finally got up and told him that I was leaving a copy of the introduction and that I would see him again next Tuesday. I picked up my belongings, gave him some *dap*, and walked out of the door. I got a call from his daughter Sharon the next day saying that her father passed away in his sleep. Even though I hadn't known him that long, a deep sadness began to tug at my heart.

His funeral was held at the Trinity Episcopal Church in Washington, DC and had all of the pomp and circumstance of a funeral of a dignitary of his stature. His coffin was draped with the traditional American flag, and members of the United States Secret Service Uniformed Division honor guard took turns standing guard over him. The overflowing crowd heard representative after representative pay homage to the individual who had accomplished so much and meant so much to so many people. Representatives from the United States Secret Service, the Justice Department, North Carolina Central University, the National Organization of Black Law Enforcement Executives, the Association of Former Agents of the United States Secret Service, the National Association for the Advancement of Colored People, friends, family members, and his daughter Sharon bellowed out accolades and humorous stories highlighting his life and career.

As I sat listening to these numerous reflections and historical references, I began to silently wonder why I hadn't read anything about this information in my history books or been able to do a Google search and have this information at my fingertips. Before his passing, one would have to conduct an intensive search to find any information about Mr. Gittens except for a few articles in the black press (e.g., *Ebony Magazine*, *The Afro-American News*, etc.) and the fact that a scholarship was offered in his name. But a conversation with Eli Rosenbaum, Donald Tucker, and Art Lewis kind of made things clear and confirmed something that I had suspected for a while. Mr. Rosenbaum shared a story with me that was told to him by Mr. Gittens. According to the story, when John F. Kennedy was elected president, he appointed his brother Robert to be attorney general. Supposedly, Robert wanted to know if there were any African American FBI agents because he had never seen one. He sent a memo to J. Edgar Hoover, the director of the FBI, asking how many Negro agents he had and he got no response. So he sent another inquiry and still did not get a response. Finally it was clear to Hoover that at some point he was going to have to respond that day, so he supposedly had his drivers, who were African Americans brought up to his office and had them sworn in as FBI agents. They had not been to the academy or had any training or anything. He just wanted to report to Kennedy that he did have some African American agents. Mr. Rosenbaum told me that I would have to do some research to verify that story, which of course I did.

What I discovered during my research was that there was a plethora of talented black FBI agents who honorably served their country during the roaring twenties and beyond, but you never saw them on popular television programs or in the movies when the tales of the FBI became folklore. There were men like James Wormley Jones, who was a captain of the famed African American army unit named the Buffalo Soldiers during World War I and was used in undercover work for J. Edgar Hoover when Hoover was the head of the General Intelligence Division (an antiterrorist unit) of the FBI in November 1919. There was James Amos, a former bodyguard of Pres. Theodore Roosevelt, who joined the FBI in August 1921 and had a thirty-two year career. Earl Titus (January 1922), Thomas Leon Jefferson (September 1922), and Arthur Lowell Brent (August 1923) were hired by the FBI and used as undercover agents to investigate Marcus Garvey. Jefferson received a commendation from Hoover for his work on a bankruptcy investigation. The father-and-son team of Jesse and Robert Strider worked in the Los Angeles office of the FBI from the 1940s through the 1970s. Aubrey Lewis and James Barrow became the first African American agents accepted in the FBI Academy in 1962.[51] Both Donald Tucker (Federal Bureau of Narcotics and US Secret Service) and Art Lewis (Federal Bureau of Narcotics) relayed stories to me of how black agents served faithfully but were relegated to roles as undercover agents and thus their stories, accomplishments, and places in history have remained *undercover* as well. As in the case of Mr. Gittens, I find that it is time to bring these guys out of the shadow of their undercover roles in history and into the glorious sunlight of discovery so that we can pay homage to their contributions to America just like every other American hero.

When it came time for Mr. Gittens to retire from public service for good, he did so reluctantly. If given the opportunity to work for free, he probably would have done so, but age and physical ailments would not let him. Retirement, however, did not bring to an end to Mr. Gittens's service to the public. He would often visit the sick and elderly who were institutionalized in order to sit and chat with them and bring a ray of sunshine into their lives. He treated all of the children of his relatives as if they were his own children, attending graduation and birthday celebrations and providing guidance and financial support.

When I think about the legacy that Mr. Gittens leaves behind, I think of the many friends and relatives who were inspired to follow in his footsteps by having dreams that far exceeded what people thought their position in this society should be, who prepared themselves academically so that they would have the credentials and training to accomplish things that may seem to have been beyond their grasp, and who had the fortitude to step out on faith and to *just do it*, to coin a phrase. I think of David Gittens, one of Charlie's nephews, who became a high school athlete whose records stood for decades and who became a decorated police officer even after his poor vision denied his entry into the Secret Service. I think of his niece Nicole Gittens whose foray into education inspired her to become a celebrated principal of the Urban Science Academy, a public high school in Boston. I think of his daughter Sharon, who had opportunities to teach anywhere in the world she wanted but decided to teach in an inner-city school in Washington, DC and to motivate young students to dream while arming them with the tools they would need to bring their dreams to fruition.

I think of Barry Wilkerson who was born and raised in Oxford, North Carolina, and married Debbie Tyler, his childhood sweetheart. Barry had a dream of one day owning his own home on a piece of land with a pond and owning his own business. He joined the United States Air Force in 1980 and started doing maintenance on airplanes and eventually learned to fly them. He became a pilot but left the air force after fourteen years of service. He was ostracized and criticized by family members and friends for leaving before gaining his military retirement pension, but he was not satisfied with the treatment he received from the military and had developed a plan that would help him achieve his dream of ownership. He met Charlie at family gatherings in Oxford (Barry's wife was related to Ruthe, Charlie's first wife), and it was Charlie who kept encouraging him to follow his dream.

"I've known Charlie ever since I was in the military," Barry recalled. "I used to tell him what my plans were and what I wanted to do. When everybody thought I was crazy or stupid for leaving the air force, it was Charlie who kept saying, 'Young man, you are different and you can do anything you want to do!' He would say, 'There are always those guys who have done things and those guys who will do things, and you are one of those guys who is going to do great things!' He was always encouraging me to follow my dream and not let anyone stand in my way.

"I left the air force and started flying for a company called Tower Airlines out of New York and then moved over to ATA (American Trans Air) as a copilot. I took a huge gamble and applied for a pilot's position at a Japanese airline. Charlie's words always stuck with me and gave me the confidence to reach out and take that chance. He would take me into a corner and tell me, 'You're different than most of the young men around here today, and you can reach any goal you set out for.' I went over to

Japan, interviewed, and got the pilot job as captain. I was selected over seventy-five other candidates for the position. When I came back and told Charlie what I had done, he was elated and reminded me that I was special and could do anything I set my mind to.

"His words and encouragement helped me to make another bold career decision, and I left the Japanese airline, after making a lot of money and started my own business. I am currently the owner of a business called Carolina Energy Heat and Air, Inc. which is based out of Stem, North Carolina. We also have an office in Durham, North Carolina. My business is doing exceptionally well, especially for being in business for only seven years. We just signed a contract with fifty-seven hotels and have approximately six hundred customers that we service. I have no regrets about any of the decisions that I made, and I have Charlie to thank for encouraging me to go after my dream. Oh, and by the way, I got that fabulous house that sits near a pond in North Carolina."

When I think about the legacy that Mr. Gittens leaves behind, I also think about Alexandria Berry, whom relatives refer to as the next Charlie Gittens in the family. Alexandria's mother (Jill) was adopted into the Gittens family by Yvonne Gittens, Charlie's niece by marriage, and Charlie treated her as one of the family. Alexandria was born in Berlin, Germany, to parents (Anthony and Jill Berry) who were members of the United States Army and met while serving in the Iraq War. They married when they got back to Berlin where they were stationed. Alexandria is already a world traveler by virtue of the fact that her parents move from station to station at the request of the United States Army. She has been forced to leave friends and move from school to school as her family moved from Berlin to California, then to South Carolina, back to Berlin, then to Massachusetts, and finally to North Carolina.

When she was young, Alexandria saw a *Scholastic Magazine* article that illustrated how liquid would form neat little symmetrical balls when squirted out of a bottle in zero gravity, and she thought that was cool. It was at that point she started dreaming about becoming an astronaut. Mr. Gittens found out about her dream, and on her sixth birthday he bought her a telescope.

"My Uncle Charlie sent me a telescope, and I fell in love with it," Alexandria exclaimed. "I would take it out on the balcony every night and look at the stars."

After finding out that the naval academy graduated more astronauts than any other institution, it became her dream to go there. She applied and was accepted. Her Uncle Charlie was elated when he found out the news. He told her that a neighbor who lived across the street from him had gone to the naval academy but didn't like it, so he quit. Uncle Charlie told her that he was glad that she got accepted, but she had better not quit, no matter how hard it got! He expected to see her commanding a starship one day as it explored new worlds, seeking out new life forms, and boldly going where no one has gone before.

Alexandria started her plebe year (June 2011) in the naval academy one month before Mr. Gittens passed away, and she made it through, exhausted but unscathed. She was pleased that her Uncle Charlie was able to witness one last obstacle being hurdled before he rode off into the sunset. I'm sure he is out there somewhere, looking down on her with a Cheshire cat grin on his face, guiding her through the dangerous pitfalls and having a sense of satisfaction in his heart for a job well done. Alexandria is more determined than ever not to quit and to do her part to fulfill her dream and the legacy of Charles Leroy Gittens.

REFLECTIONS
Remembering Charlie

Charlie and daughter Sharon

Charles Gittens passed away on July 27, 2011. He lived a full life and touched many lives. Too often people live and die and never find out how other people felt about them, but this was not the case in Charlie's life. He was loved by many and influenced countless others. He never really wanted to publicize his story and avoided attempts to popularize it, stating that he had not done anything special. When the word of his passing went out, however, it was printed and his life was celebrated across the nation and around the world. The announcement of his passing appeared in *Washington Post, Telegraph* (United Kingdom), *Boston Globe, Hinterland Gazette, National Public Radio, Tom Joyner Morning Show,* and many more. A Google search will now reveal information about him, and there is an effort to have his story placed in the new National Museum of African American History and Culture. On June 22, 2012, North Carolina Central University sponsored a room-naming ceremony for Charlie and Ruthe, both celebrated alumni. Many of his friends and relatives shared stories and anecdotes with me. I could not include all of them in the text, but some are listed below.

I actually saw Charlie as the black James Bond. He was the first of his kind. He was a very smooth, low-key, articulate, intelligent person who chose his words carefully. He was always an immaculate dresser. When he first came out to our farm in Oxford, he wore a suit and had wing-tipped shoes. I'll never forget him walking around the farm, among the chickens and pigs in those shoes. He truly loved his family, and he loved his career. He couldn't wait to get to work. He loved people. It didn't matter who you were. He loved politics. He would talk politics to anyone who would listen. In fact, he'd talk politics even if you weren't listening.

I never heard Charlie say bad things about anybody. Once we went down to North Carolina Central University for Charlie's fifty-year anniversary since he graduated in 1955. Charlie came down and asked if I was going (I graduated from NCCU in 1970). So we went down, and a lot of people knew Charlie. There was a chancellor there, I don't want to say his name, and some guy said, "Hey, Chancellor, this is Charles Gittens. He's the first black Secret Service agent!" To my surprise, the chancellor was very dismissive and just kept talking to someone else. This really pissed me off. I couldn't believe he disrespected Charlie like that, but Charlie just said, 'Oh, don't worry about it maybe he was just busy.' That was Charlie! Here you had the first black Secret Service agent, and he was supportive of the university, and this guy was so dismissive that it really made me upset. But Charlie never skipped a beat, he never got upset. Somehow Charlie could always rationalize a situation, and he saw the good in everybody!

Charlie was always pushing me to improve myself. I had to take a break from graduate school in order to get a job to help meet my financial obligations. I got what I thought was a good job teaching at the college level and decided that I really didn't need a PhD at this point in my life. On one of my visits with Charlie, he asked me when I was going back to school to complete my degree. I told him I was not sure and that I had a good job making good money. He sat for a few minutes, looked at me sternly, and said, "I know why you are not going back. You can't compete! It's too tough for you, and you're giving up!" As hard as I tried explaining to him that was not the reason, he wouldn't accept my explanation. His accusatory tone got me really upset. I decided to return to graduate school and finally got my degree. As I reflect on that situation, I realize that Charlie was just pushing me, in his own way, and was helping me reach my potential. For that I am forever grateful.

—Dr. Larry Hamme

Charlie was the greatest guy in the world. I am not surprised that he went as far as he did in life. He never got into trouble. The Gittens family, they were spic and span. Charlie would have been a good candidate for president.

Every time I read in the paper about him and his accomplishments, I was so proud. Charlie sent me two invitations: one when he became a second lieutenant and then when he became a first lieutenant. I remember when he had a choice, many years ago, of getting married or going to West Point. He fell in love with this young lady, but West Point did not take married cadets. The love thing was greater than anything else, so he gave up the honor of going to West Point and decided to get married.

The section of Cambridge where we lived, I would call a poor section of Cambridge. We were all just working people. When we were about fifteen years old, we used to keep about thirty chickens outside his house. He had an electrical cord coming out of the window down his three-story house during the winter months, and it was plugged into two toasters he put in the coup. This is what kept his chickens warm and laying eggs all winter long. We used to sell the eggs to the neighbors.

—Paul Snelgrove

Charlie and my husband (Enid Quinones) were great friends. My husband was a postal inspector, and his job was to apprehend criminals who stole the mail out of mailboxes. When government checks were stolen, the Secret Service would get involved, and that's how Charlie and Enid met. They would often work on cases together. They had a lot of camaraderie, but at the same time they were very competitive and wanted to show each other up. They would compete by comparing who made the most arrest.

They were always being harassed by the police in Brooklyn, probably because Charlie was black and my husband was Puerto Rican. There was one incident that comes to mind, when they were following a car driven by drug addicts. The drug addicts made an illegal left turn at the intersection of Tompkins Avenue, and when Charlie made the same turn, the cops went after Charlie and my husband. Charlie and my husband turned and looked at each other and said, "Oh, here we go again!" This had become a daily ritual because they got stopped by the cops so often. They both got out of the car and showed their badges and guns. After some checking, the cops let them go, but of course the drug addicts got away.

Another humorous incident that I remember occurred when they ordered tickets for a Mohammed Ali fight, and the tickets were stolen out of the mailbox. Charlie and my husband were furious and decided to go to the fight and arrest whoever was sitting in their seats. The only problem was this occurred when Ali was in his prime and knocked out his opponent in the first minute of the first round. By the time Charlie and Enid got there, the fight was over and the fans were leaving the arena.

—Josie Quinones

Uncle Charlie was like a second grandfather to me. He was always celebrating all of his younger relatives. He came to all of our graduations and showed up for many of our celebrations. He was a really important man but took time out of his busy schedule to make us feel important. I remember when he went to Moscow on an assignment. He seemed like he was a global traveler. He achieved many great things and went beyond the boundaries that people of color often set for themselves.

—Nicole Gittens

When I came on the job, Charlie was like my big brother and my trainer. He was a person I could always go to and depend on for answers. I had a great deal of respect for him because he earned his position. I felt bad for Charlie because I hate to hear people say that he got the job as a Secret Service agent or special agent in charge because he was black. He got the job, as far as I was concerned, because of his capabilities. The man could do it all, and he was a great leader. He could do whatever was needed to be done in order to achieve his goals or solve a case. He was very proud to be a Secret Service agent.

—Victor Gonzales

I met Mr. Gittens at a cookout in Fort Washington, Maryland, right across the creek from where he lived. He was quite the gentleman, a little flirtatious, but a very nice person. He was easy to talk to, and I enjoyed our many conversations.

I am a computer network engineer. I worked for the Department of Justice (DOJ) for two years before moving to the Drug Enforcement Administration (DEA). When I worked for the DEA, I ran into a lot of agents who knew Charlie and felt that he was a person of great character. Charlie was older than I, and he told me that when he was with DOJ, they made him retire because of his age. He loved his work and really didn't want to stop.

—Charl Jones

Charlie was a good-natured person and a great storyteller. He made us very proud, and we always looked forward when he visited. He was our uncle. We always knew he worked for the Secret Service, but what he did was a secret. We never knew what he actually did. He was a part of history, and he loved history.

When Yvonne (Gittens) finished her masters at Harvard, and Caroline Kennedy was finishing her bachelor's degree, Charlie came up for the graduation. That was the only time he ever talked about his job with the Secret Service because Jackie and John-John was there, and the Secret Service was there to protect them. We lost Uncle Charlie during the ceremony. When he caught up with us, we asked him where he had gone, and he said, "Oh, I was talking to Jackie, John, and another agent." We said, "Wow, he really knows them!" I remember saying to him in the crowd, "Did you really know them?" And he said, "Yeah, I was in protection." He talked about Cape Cod and coming up to the compound in Hyannis Port and being there. He talked about the time a bat got into Jackie Kennedy's bungalow, and she was screaming and waving her head and hands trying to get it out. He said she asked us to get it out, but not to kill it.

—Irma Sullivan

Charlie always carried himself as an executive but was always very friendly and approachable. He was full of energy and wanted to be involved in everything. His enthusiasm was contagious. He knew how and when to be serious and when to have fun. Moreover, he knew how to get things done.

—Ike Hendershot

The Cambridge Family
Back Row (L–R): Yvonne Gittens, Irma Sullivan
Middle Row (L–R): Nicole Gittens, Charlie Gittens, Sharon Gittens Quick
Front Row (L–R): Mark Pappas, David Gittens

Front Row (L–R): Isaiah Berry, Anthony Berry, Jill Berry, Sharon
Gittens Quick, Yvonne Gittens, David Gittens, Thelma Gittens.
Back Row (L–R): Charles "Kitt" Eccles, Edward "Ned" Eccles, Nicole Gittens

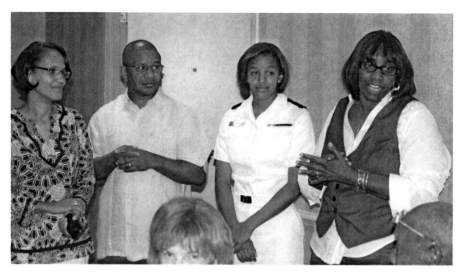

(L–R) Jill Berry, Anthony Berry, Alexandria Berry, Sharon Gittens Quick

The Oxford Family
Front Row (L–R): Marilyn Tyler Brown, Mildred Hamme, Sana
Hamme, Sharon Gittens Quick, Carolyn Hamme Allen, Bobby
Allen, Eshe Hamme Allen, Tokay Allen, Thomas Hamme Jr.
Back Row (L–R): Hugh Brown, Cornell Hamme, Larry Hamme

Marilyn Tyler Brown and Sharon Gittens Quick and family
members participate in a room-naming ceremony at North Carolina
Central University in honor of Charles and Ruthe Gittens

The Oxford Family
Back Row (L–R): Jonathan Harmon, Hugh Brown, and Barry Wilkerson
Front Row: (L–R): Brandi Wilkerson Harmon (with baby Mason),
Marilyn Tyler Brown, Sharon Gittens Quick, Debbie Tyler Wilkerson,
Shanna Wilkerson Flynn (with baby Brooklyn), Tommy Flynn

Gittens shares his story with staff and students at Theodore Roosevelt High in 2009
(L–R) Sharon Gittens Quick, Nigist Getaneh, David Parker,
Charlie Gittens, Michael Spikes, Yanelys Barrett, Diara Rowland

Mr. Gittens meets the staff at Theodore Roosevelt High School in Washington DC

FOOTNOTES

CHAPTER 1 (In the Shadow of M.I.T.)

1. Page 11 **Slavery and Economy in Barbados**
http://www.bbc.co.uk/history/british/empire_seapower/barbados_01.shtml
2. Page 15 **Cambridge History**
http://Wikitravel.org/en/Cambridge_(Massachusetts)-
2a. Page 15 Cambridge History
http//:en.wikipedia.org/wiki/Cambridge_Massachusetts
3. Page 16 **Pogroms** Http://grossmanpoject.net/pogroms.htm
4. Page 17 **Bernard Rudolph:** *Immigrant to American Patriot* http://friendsof
fortwashington.org/BernardRudolphimmigrantAmericanPatriot.aspx

CHAPTER 2 (We Love You Chocolate Soldier)

5. Page 35 **EBONY** *Pictorial History of Black America: Reconstruction to Supreme Court decision 1954* (p 259)
6. Page 36 **EBONY** (p 261)
7. Page 37 **EBONY** (p 277)
8. Page 39 **Yokohama History** http://en.wikipedia.org/wiki/Yokohama_Japan
9. Page 43 **The Art of Becoming a Jazz Musician:** *An Interview with Toshiko Akiyoshi* http://quod.lib.umich.edu/m/mqr/act2080.0043.307?rgn=main;view=fulltext

CHAPTER 3 (Destined to Lead)

10. Page 54 **Officer Candidate School (US Army)**
http://www.ocshistory.org/army_museum/ocshistory.html
11. Page 55 **EBONY** (p. 252)
12. Page 55 **EBONY** (p. 304)
13. Page 55 **Desegregation of the Armed Forces**
http://www.trumanlibrary.org/whistlestop/study_collections/desegregation/large/index.php?action=chronology

CHAPTER 4 (And Then She Walked In)

14. Page 66 **Pullman Porters**
    http://www.aphiliprandolphmuseum.com/evo_History.html
15. Page 71 **G.I. Bill** http://en.wikipedia.org/wiki/G.I._Bill

CHAPTER 5 (Oxford: An Oasis in the South)

16. Page 75 **City of Oxford** http://www.oxfordnc.org/history.htm
17. Page 82 **The Murder of Henry Marrow**
    http://blackhistorymonth.blackamericaweb.com/indexphp?option=com_
    content&view=article&id=422:the-murder-of-henry-marrow&Catid=112.
    general&Itemid=292
18. Page 83 **Slave Codes** http://ushistory.org/us/6f.asp
19. Page 83 **Black Codes**
    http://home.gwu.edu/~jjhawkin/BlackCodes/BlackCodes.htm
20. Page 84 **Jim Crow Laws**
    http://www.jimcrowhistory.org/history/creating2.htm
21. Page 87 **Historically Black Colleges and Universities**
    http://en.wikipedia.org/wiki/Historically_black_colleges_and_universities
22. Page 88 **National Alumni Coalition of Black Boarding and Private Schools**
    http://www.nacinc.org
23. Page 88 **Mary Potter Academy**
    http://ncmakers.com/print_marker.aspx?id=G119
24. Page 88 **George Clayton Shaw & Museum History**
    http://www.shawmuseum.com/about_dr_shaw.html

CHAPTER 6 (The Perfect Storm)

25. Page 111 **Looking back and seeing the future: the united states secret service 1865-1990,** (p. 2)
26. Page 112 **History of the Secret Service**
    http://www.secretservice.gov/History.shtml
27. Page 113 **Federal Bureau of Narcotics**
    http://en.wikipedia.org/wiki/Federal_Bureau_of_Narcotics
28. Page 114 **Harrison Tax Act**
    http://en.wikipedia.org/wiki/Harrison_Tax_Act
29. Page 116 **Looking back and seeing the future** (p. 49).
30. Page 117 **Secret Service Chief,** (pp. 75-76)
31. Page 118 **Looking back and seeing the future,** (p.56).

CHAPTER 7 (New York Undercover)

32. Page 130 **Secret Service Chief** (pp. 23-26)
33. Page 134 **Looking back and seeing the future** (p. 56)

CHAPTER 8 (Dark Clouds Rising)
34. Page 146 **Puerto Rico** http://en.wikipedia.org/wiki/Puerto_Rico

CHAPTER 9 (We Live in the Shadows)
35. Page 170 Assassination attempts
    http://americanhistory.about.com/od/uspresidents/a/assassinations.htm
36. Page 174 *Shake Up in White House Secret Service Detail* by Helen Thomas
    World Horizon News Release (Sunday, March 4, 1973)
37. Page 181 **Secret Service Chief** (pp. 4-5)
38. Page 182 **Secret Service Chief** (pp. 9-10)
39. Page 183 **Secret Service Chief** (pp. 1-3)

CHAPTER 10 (Changing Times)
40. Page 202 **The Civil Rights Act of 1964 and the Equal Employment Opportunity Commission** www.archives.gov/education/lessons/civil-rights-act
41. Page 202 **Transcripts from Treasury Department Employment Policy Review Board Meeting – January 19, 1965.**
42. Page 203 **Women in the Secret Service**
    www.wifle.org/conference1991/pdf/46-52.pdf
43. Page 206 **The Two-Edged Sword** p. 178
44. Page 206 **The Two-Edged Sword** p. 179

CHAPTER 11 (The Color of My Skin)
45. Page 227 **Plantation Economy**
    http://en.wikipedia.org/wiki/Plantation_economy
46. Page 229 **Let's Make a Slave**
    http://www.angelfire.com/ne/savedbygrace/lynch.html
47. Page 239 **NOBLE** www.noblenatl.org/index.php?option=com_content&view=section&id=48&Itemid=41

CHAPTER 13 (The Hunt for Justice)
48. Page 259 **Nazi angel of death Josef Mengele 'created twin town in Brazil'**
    www.telegraph.co.uk/news/worldnews/southamerica/brazil/4307262/Nazi
49. Page 259 **Josef Mengele** http://en.wikipedia.org/wiki/Josef_Mengele
50. Page 261 **OSI**
    http://www.ushmm.org/wlc/en/article.php?Moduled=10007105

EPILOGUE (A Legacy of Excellence)
51. Page 285 **The FBI**
    http://www.fbi.gov/news/stories/2011/february/history_021511

REFERENCES

1. Baughman, Urbanus Edmund (1961). *Secret service chief.* New York: Harper & Rowe, Publishers.
2. Black, Henry Campbell (1979). *Black's Law Dictionary.* St. Paul, MN: West Publishing Co.
3. Bolden, Abraham (2008). *The echo from Dealey Plaza.* New York: Three Rivers Press
4. Ebony (1971). *Pictorial history of Black America: Reconstruction to Supreme Court decision 1954.* Nashville, TN: Johnson Publishing Company
5. Kessler, Ronald (2009). *In the president's secret service.* New York: Three Rivers Press
6. Roberts, Marcia (1991). *Looking back and seeing the future: The United States secret service 1865-1990.* Dallas, Texas: The Association of Former Agents of the United States Secret Service, Inc.
7. Tucker, Donald (2010). *The two-edged sword.* Indianapolis, Indiana: Dog Ear Publishing

CPSIA information can be obtained at www.ICGtesting.com
Printed in the USA
LVOW062359270912

300569LV00002B/8/P